The Asbury Theological Seminary Series in Christian Revitalization Studies

This volume is published in collaboration with the Center for the Study of World Christian Revitalization Movements, a cooperative initiative of Asbury Theological Seminary faculty. Building on the work of the previous Wesleyan/Holiness Studies Center at the Seminary, the Center provides a focus for research in the Wesleyan Holiness and other related Christian renewal movements, including Pietism and Pentecostal movements, which have had a world impact. The research seeks to develop analytical models of these movements, including their biblical and theological assessment. Using an interdisciplinary approach, the Center bridges relevant discourses in several areas in order to gain insights for effective Christian mission globally. It recognizes the need for conducting research that combines insights from the history of evangelical renewal and revival movements with anthropological and religious studies literature on revitalization movements. It also networks with similar or related research and study centers around the world, in addition to sponsoring its own research projects.

In this study, Colleen Derr demonstrates John Wesley's readiness to resource the need for child catechesis and spiritual formation with a plethora of documents directed to that end, and she engages these resources in response to the dire situation which contemporary Protestant Christianity in the United States is facing as it watches the disappearance of a generation of its children and youth from its membership. She explores the cultural and theological reasons for this tragedy, which has received insufficient attention from American denominations in general, and United Methodism in particular. It is ironical that this development, which reflects the decline of the family, makes children the problem rather than the key to understanding the meaning of genuine Christian discipleship, as they are presented in the ministry of Jesus in the New Testament. The disjunction between these two realities is what renders urgency to the present series of studies in Christian Revitalization, in which it now appears.

J. Steven O'Malley
General Editor
The Asbury Theological Seminary Studies in World Christian Revitalization

John Wesley and the Faith Formation of Children

Lessons for the Church

Colleen R. Derr

EMETH PRESS
www.emethpress.com

*John Wesley and the Faith
Formation of Children:
Lessons for the Church*
Copyright © 2018

All rights reserved. No part of this book may be reproduced, or stored in a retrieval system or transmitted in any form or by any means, electronic, mechanical, photocopying, recording, scanning or otherwise, except as permitted by the 1976 United States Copyright Act, or with the prior written permission of Emeth Press. Requests for permission should be addressed to: Emeth Press, P. O. Box 23961, Lexington, KY 40523-3961.
http://www.emethpress.com.

Scripture taken from The Holy Bible, English Standard Version.
Copyright © 2000; 2001 by Crossway Bibles, a division of Good News Publishers. Used by permission.

Library of Congress Cataloging-in-Publication Data

Names: Derr, Colleen, author.
Title: John Wesley and the faith formation of children : lessons for the church / Colleen R. Derr.
Description: Lexington, Kentucky : Emeth Press, 2018. | Series: Asbury Theological Seminary series: the study of world Christian revitalization movements in Pietist/Wesleyan studies
Identifiers: LCCN 2017060929 | ISBN 9781609471217 (alk. paper)
Subjects: LCSH: Wesley, John, 1703-1791. | Christian education of children. | Faith development. | Spiritual formation.
Classification: LCC BX8495.W5 D47 2018 | DDC 268/.432092--dc23
LC record available at https://lccn.loc.gov/ 2017060929

Dedication

This book is dedicated to my parents, Earle and Sylvia Wilson, for their unfailing love, support, and faith and for giving me the gift of a love for learning.

Table of Contents

Acknowledgements / xv

Chapter One Introduction / 1

    Background / 3
    Problem Statement / 5
    Purpose / 6
    Organization / 6
    Key Assumptions and Limitations / 7

Chapter Two Literature Review / 9

    The Nature of Faith / 9
        Corporate Nature of Faith Formation / 10
        The Role of Christian Education in Faith Formation / 12
        The Inherent Nature of Faith / 12
            Inherent faith in Scripture / 13
            Inherent faith demonstrated through questions children ask / 14
            Inherent faith demonstrated in a child's Godly play / 15
            A theological perspective on inherent faith / 17
            Conclusions on inherent faith / 17
    Faith Development in Children / 18
        Faith Development Insights from Developmental Psychology / 19
            Fowler and faith development / 20
        Child Faith Dev. Insights from the Field of Christian Ed / 24
            Westerhoff's view of faith development / 24
            Richards and Stonehouse's views on child faith dev / 26
        Conclusion on Child Faith Development / 26
    A Biblical Perspective on Child Faith Development / 27
        God's Covenants and Child Faith Development / 28
        God's Commands and Child Faith Development / 29

                    Conclusion of God's covenants and commands / 31
               Jesus' Teaching and Child Faith Development / 31
                    Jesus' interactions with children in His cultural context / 32
                    Jesus' interaction demonstrates children's worth / 32
                    Parents and child faith development in Scripture / 33
                    Child faith development and the church / 34
               Conclusions on Child Faith Development / 35
          John Wesley's Theology of Childhood Faith and Education / 36
               Eighteenth Century England / 36
               Wesley's Childhood / 38
               Wesley's Influencers / 40
               John Wesley's Theology / 40
                    Wesley's view of humanity / 44
                    Wesley's view of sin / 46
                    Wesley's view of grace / 47
               Sanctifying grace / 52
                    The means of grace / 54
                    Wesleyan Quadrilateral / 56
                    Conclusion on Wesley's theology / 58
               Wesley's View of children / 59
               Wesley and the Religious Education of Children / 61
                    Family's role in religious education / 63
                    Pastor's role in religious education / 64
               Publications by Wesley for Children / 66
               Conclusion on John Wesley / 67

Chapter Three Methodology / 69

          Methodology / 71
          Type of Study / 71
               Source selection / 72
               Data collection and analysis / 73
               Coding / 74
               Record storage / 75
          Threats to credibility and transferability / 75
               Triangulation for validity / 76
          Summary / 77

Chapter Four Findings and Conclusions / 79

Wesley as Writer and Publisher / 79

Excluded Documents from Research / 80

Research Method / 81
    Coding Process / 82
    Reports of Findings / 85
    Engagement with the Coded Data / 86
    Annotations / 87

Findings by Document / 87
    Descriptive Summation of Sources / 87
    Chronological Comparison of Sources / 88
    Sermons / 89
        Context and audience for sermons / 90
        Sermon 94, "On Family Religion" / 90
        Sermon 95, "On the Education of Children" / 93
        Sermon 96, "On Obedience to Parents" / 95
    Susanna Wesley's Letter / 97
        Summation / 98
        Descriptive codes / 99
        Why teach / 99
        Who should teach / 99
        How to teach - when / 99
        How to teach - methodology / 100
        What to teach / 102
    Serious Thoughts Concerning Godfathers and Godmothers / 102
        Summation / 103
        Descriptive codes / 104
        Why teach / 104
        Who should teach / 104
        How to teach / 104
        What to teach / 104
    A Thought on the Manner of Educating Children / 105
        Summation / 105
        Descriptive codes / 105
        Why teach / 106
        Who should teach / 106
        How to teach - when / 106
        How to teach - methodology / 106
        What to teach / 107
    A "Short Account" and "A Plain Account" of Kingswood / 107
        Summation / 108

- Descriptive codes / 109
  - Why teach / 109
  - Who shall teach / 110
  - How to teach - when / 110
  - How to teach - methodology / 110
  - What to teach / 111
  - Concluding remarks of Kingswood school / 111
- Hymns for Children / 112
  - Contextual analysis / 112
  - Summation of Hymns (1747) / 114
  - Engagement with codes / 114
- A Lessons for Children / 116
  - Summation / 116
  - Descriptive codes / 118
  - Why teach / 118
  - Who should teach / 118
  - How to teach / 118
  - What to teach / 119
- Instructions for Children / 119
  - "Instructions" adapted from French work / 120
  - Format of "Instructions" / 120
  - Summation / 121
  - Descriptive codes / 122
  - Why teach / 122
  - Who should teach / 123
  - How to teach / 123
  - What to teach / 123
- Prayers for Children / 126
  - Summation / 127
  - Descriptive codes / 127
  - Why teach / 128
  - Who shall teach / 128
  - How to teach / 128
- Findings by Research Question / 131
  - Descriptive Codes / 131
  - Why Teach / 131
  - Who shall Teach / 131
    - Relationship to child (REL) / 131
    - Expected lifestyle of instructor (EXP) / 132
  - How to teach / 132
    - When instruction should occur (WHN) / 132
    - Where instruction should occur (WHR) / 133
    - Methodology of the instruction (MET) / 134
  - What to Teach / 135
    - God (GOD) / 136

    Grace (GRA) / 136
    Human nature (MAN) / 137
    Sin (SIN) / 139
    Jesus (JES) / 139
    Salvation (SAL) / 140
    Holy Spirit (HOL) / 141
    Eternity (HVN) / 142
    Christian lifestyle (LIFE) / 143
    Prayer (PRA) / 145
    Scripture/Bible (BIB) / 146
 Conclusion / 147
  Objectives of Religious Instruction / 147
  Responsibility of Religious Instruction / 147
  Methodology of Religious Instruction / 148
  Content of Religious Instruction / 148
  Outcomes of Religious Instruction / 149

Chapter Five Interpretations, Implications, and Recommendations / 151

 Findings / 152
  Who shall Teach / 152
   Who shall teach – relationship / 152
   Who shall teach – lifestyle / 152
  How to Teach / 153
   When instruction should occur / 153
   Where instruction should occur / 153
   Methodology of instruction / 154
  What to Teach / 155
   What to teach – who is God and what does He do / 155
   What to teach – who are we and what are we to do / 156
   What to teach – prayer and scripture / 156
  Wesley's Practices and Teachings in Light of Modern, Educational Theory / 156
   Wesley and 18th century ed. theory / 157
   Wesley and contemporary ed. theory / 158
  Surprising Insights about Wesley from Findings / 159
 Implications for Today / 160
  Implications for objectives of Christian education / 160
  Implications for the responsibility of Christian education / 160
  Implications on the methodology of Christian education / 161
  Implications on content in Christian education / 163
  Implications for outcomes of Christian education / 164

            Implications in light of Wesleyan quadrilateral / 165
      Threats to Validity and Research Limitations / 165
      Recommendations for Further Research / 167
            Engagement with research in light of other works / 167
            Deeper engagement with individual documents / 167
            Development of a conceptual framework / 168
            Impact of non-integrated instruction / 168
      Conclusion / 168

References / 171

Appendix A / 181

Appendix B / 183

Appendix C / 187

Appendix D / 189

Appendix E / 191

Appendix F / 193

Appendix G / 197

Appendix H / 201

Appendix I / 203

Appendix J / 213

Appendix K / 215

Appendix L / 217

Appendix M / 223

Appendix N / 225

Appendix O / 229

Appendix P / 231

Acknowledgments

It is with incredible gratitude that I offer thanks and acknowledgement to those who made the completion of this book possible. I am grateful to my family for their patience with my state of constant distraction and their unwavering belief that I could do this. My husband, Wayne, made me laugh and reminded me to not take myself too seriously; and our children, Jerica, Zachary, Tyler, and Anna, were my inspiration and source of incredible joy. Thank you to my Regent family: Maggie and Tania for walking beside me through this journey, Dr. Cox and my committee for your words of advice and guided instruction that pushed me to pursue excellence, and my professors who exemplified Christian scholarship. I offer sincere thanks to my colleagues and friends at Wesley Seminary and Indiana Wesleyan University for their support, prayers, insights, and gracious welcome into the world of academia . Finally, I want to thank the Lord for His guided providence, His sustaining grace, His all consuming love, and the gifts from His hand too numerous to count. I am blessed beyond measure and truly thankful.

Chapter One

Introduction

"When the son of man comes, will he find faith on earth?" (Luke 18:8, NIV).

Jesus asked this question during one of His final, formal teaching moments. On Jesus' way to Jerusalem for the beginning of Holy Week, He offered a series of parables on the Kingdom of God. When He addressed the coming Kingdom, Jesus made the point that His return will come unannounced (Luke 17:20-37) and the people are to wait in persistent prayer (Luke 18:1-8). He concluded the second teaching with the question: "When the son of man comes, will he find faith on earth?" (v. 8). These verses seem to indicate that humanity's faith is not inevitable. In examination of these verses in light of today, Groome (2011) cautioned that contemporary, cultural conditions are not favorable for continued religious faith, and he called for a "whole new vision and approach to religious education if Christian faith is to flourish in our time and culture" (p. 4).

The Greek word for faith used in verse eight is *pistis* (Strong's G4102), which means: "A conviction or belief respecting man's relationship to God and divine things, generally with the included idea of trust and holy fervour born of faith and joined with it" (Blue Letter Bible, *pistis*, 2012, para. 1). Kittel and Friedrich (as cited in Bromiley, 1985) suggested it means faith, trust and "has the sense of a 'confidence,' 'certainty,' 'trust,' then 'trustworthiness,' and 'guarantee' or 'assurance' in the sense of a pledge or oath with the two nuances of 'trustworthiness' and 'proof'" (p. 849). Gingrich and Danker (1979) noted that in Luke 18:8, *pistis*, refers to "true piety, genuine religion" (p. 663). The word faith, *pistis*, denotes Christian belief that is identified as trust with a holy commitment or passion. It is a noun in the Greek language that brings with it the expectation of an action. It occurs 244 times in 227 New Testament verses (Blue Letter Bible, *pistis*, 2012, para. 1). One example is the story of the friends who brought their paralytic friend to Jesus. "When Jesus saw their faith [*pistis*], he said to the paralytic, 'Take heart, son; your sins are forgiven'" (Matthew 9:2, NIV). The paralytic and his friends' belief in Christ that spurred them to action resulted in the paralytic's salvation and physical healing. Gingrich and Danker (1979) noted that in this verse faith refers to the "belief and trust in the Lord's help in physical and spiritual distress" (p. 663).

If the son of Man returned today, would he find faith? The National Study of Youth and Religion (NSYR, 2011) survey revealed that mainline Christian denominations are losing their youth and young adults, and the Pew Forum's report (2012) on religion in America reported that 28% of emerging adults (age 18-29) say they have abandoned the faith that they were raised with. The NSYR concluded that churches today are "failing rather badly in religiously engaging and educating youth" (Smith & Denton, 2005, p. 262). Dean (2010) suggested, "churches seem to have offered teenagers a kind of 'dinner theology': a bargain religion, cheap but satisfying, whose gods require little in the way of fidelity or sacrifice" (p. 10). This religious "training" has resulted in what Smith and Denton (2005) "call Moralistic Therapeutic Deism", which they suggested is "supplanting Christianity as the dominant religion in American churches" (p. 171) and is the faith most teenagers in America practice. Smith (2010) identified five descriptors of Moralistic Therapeutic Deism:

A God exists who created and orders the word and watches over human life on earth;

God wants people to be good, nice, and fair to each other, as taught in the Bible and by most world religions;

The central goal of life is to be happy and to feel good about one-self;

God does not need to be particularly involved in one's life except when he is needed to resolve a problem;

Good people go to heaven when they die (pp. 46-47).

Smith (2010) noted that today's adolescents are not rebellious to their parents' and church's religion, but rather "our religiously conventional adolescents seem to be merely absorbing and reflecting religiously what the adult world is routinely modeling for and inculcating in its youth" (p. 51). While religious practices such as church attendance, scripture reading, and prayer were engaged by a greater percentage of conservative protestant teens, of whom The Wesleyan Church and most denominations within the Wesleyan movement would be a part, than most of the other categories the statistics were still significantly lower than expected (Dean, 2010). In addition, of the religious concepts linked to Wesleyan beliefs and practices such as grace of God, holiness, loving one's neighbor, God is holy, self-discipline, social justice, justification, sanctification, and honoring God with one's life, relatively few if any teens made reference to these terms and phrases in their interviews (Smith, 2010, pp. 52-53). In contrast teens were much more likely to talk about happiness and feeling good (Smith, 2010). Smith (2010) concluded based on these outcomes that "either Christianity is at least degenerating into a pathetic version of itself or, more significantly, Christianity is actively being colonized and displaced by a quite different religious faith" (p. 57).

Westerhoff (2000) saw this trend and asked the question: *Will Our Children Have Faith?* He concluded that our current Christian education systems are ineffective in nurturing faith. Westerhoff (2000) studied the practices in Christian education and suggested that current practice in Christian education reflects the "schooling-instructional paradigm" (p. 5), with school as the context and instruction as the means. He suggested that this schooling-instruction paradigm "leads us to focus on religion rather than faith" (p. 19). Westerhoff (2000) offered a suggestion for a different paradigm, "a community of faith-enculturation paradigm", that included specific elements such as community, ritual, interactive experiences, and biblical context with the desired outcome to nurture faith in the lives of children within the community of believers (p. 45).

If it is true, as Westerhoff (2000) suggested, that the Christian education system within our churches is broken and is no longer nurturing the faith of our children, then what is the solution? How can the church respond and change our Christian education approach so that the resounding answer to Jesus' question in Luke 18:8 is "Yes!"?

Background

Wesleyan-Armenian theology, or Methodism, is based on the teachings and writings of John Wesley (Harper, 2003; Stonehouse, 2004; Willhauck, 1992). There are a variety of protestant denominations that trace their theological roots to John Wesley's Methodism and are considered to be part of the "Wesleyan tradition" or "Wesleyan movement" (Coleson, n.d.; Maddix, 2001; Willhauck, 1992). These include Methodist and holiness churches. Holiness churches have a concern with continued faith formation in the life of believer sometimes referred to as Christian perfection or entire sanctification (Dayton, 1975).

John Wesley, eighteenth century Anglican pastor and theologian, discussed his view of faith in his sermon, *On Faith*, (Rotz & Lyon, 1999, Sermon #106). He first suggested the "most comprehensive definition of faith" as being "a divine evidence and conviction of God, and of the things of God" (Rotz & Lyon, 1999, Sermon #106, para. 1). Wesley further defined faith "which is properly saving; which brings eternal salvation to all those that keep it to the end" as "a divine conviction of God, and the things of God, as, even in its infant state, enables every one that possesses it to 'fear God and work righteousness'" (Rotz & Lyon, 1999, Sermon #106, para. 13). The conclusion of Wesley's sermon provides the most refined statement of faith that fears God and works righteousness:

> Walk in all the good works whereunto ye are created in Christ Jesus....Yea, and when ye have attained a measure of perfect love, when God has circumcised your hearts and enabled you to love him with all your heart and with all your soul, think not of resting there. That is impossible. You cannot stand still; you must either rise or fall; rise higher or fall lower. Therefore the voice of God to the children of Israel, to the children of God, is, 'Go forward!'. (Rotz & Lyon, 1999, Sermon #106, para. 20)

Wesley's definition of faith, like that of Jesus' in Luke 18:8, is a belief that is identified as trust with a holy commitment or passion that requires action.

Because of his strong conviction that it is not possible to rest on your salvation, but the believer must continue to actively pursue righteousness, Wesley developed Christian education practices that would nurture faith formation in the lives of believers (Blevins & Maddix, 2010; Maddix, 2001; Matthaei 2000; Willhauck, 1992). Faith formation was a critical issue for the early Methodists (Matthaei, 2000). "It was so important that the first Methodist Conference in 1744 discussed 'what to teach' and 'how to teach' in order to shape the Methodists' life together" (Matthaei, 2000, p. 73). Also evidenced in the conference minutes was attention to the additional question: "who shall teach?" (Matthaei, 2000; Wesley, 1744).

Because of the importance Wesley placed on the role of educational practice in faith formation, it is reasonable to expect that educational practice or Christian education within Wesleyan churches today would reflect Wesley's teachings. In an attempt to examine if this expectation was being met, Maddix (2001) asked: "To what extent are John Wesley's theology and educational perspectives being applied to educational practices today" (p. 6). He used a convenience sample to survey pastors, professors of Christian education, and Christian educators serving in fulltime ministry within the Nazarene denomination, a denomination within the Wesleyan tradition. His research revealed that educational practice did not reflect theological beliefs, including what they believed to be true about faith formation. Although the pastors and educators could articulate Wesley's theological views and supported those viewpoints, their Christian education practices did not reflect Wesley's educational practices. Maddix (2001) concluded that this disconnect between what the pastors, professors, and Christian educators believed to be true about faith formation and their educational practices, is due in part to a lack of literature on a Wesleyan approach to Christian education. He suggested further research was needed on Wesley's practices and the development of Wesleyan distinct educational practices (Maddix, 2001, pp. 236-237).

Similarly, Willhauck (1992) suggested that there is a need to recover Wesley's view of child faith formation as reflected in Christian education practices. Her book addressed Wesley's view of the faith of children and offered elements to be considered in contemporary Christian education. She concluded that the effectiveness of Christian education in child faith formation is an issue of concern in Methodism today. In addition to overall ineffectiveness, Willhauck (1992) cited the decline of Sunday school and the Search Institute's report that Christian education is "a tired enterprise in need of reform" as motivation for this recovery of Wesleyan theology and educational practice (as cited in Willhauck, 1992, p. 258). Willhauck (1992) posited: "An appeal to Wesley's understanding of the child would make a difference in the modern theory and practice of Christian education, focusing on the importance of children and the possibility of childhood faith" (p. 274).

Heitzenrater (2001) concurred with Willhauck (1992) and Maddix's (2001) assessment that Wesley's theological and educational viewpoints would be beneficial to educational practice and specifically the Christian education of children today. In an earlier work he posited, "the problem for the last two centuries in Wesley studies has been that no adequate base of primary research has been present" (Heitzenrater, 1989, p. 207). In a response to this need, Heitzenrater (2001) researched the culture of Wesley's era, Wesley's personal experiences as a child, and his methodology of Christian education. He noted Wesley's high view of a child's potential for faith development and concluded that churches today would do well to embrace Wesley's perspective of educational instruction.

There appears, however, to be little research that defines Wesley's educational practices regarding child faith formation (Benzie, 2010). Willhauck (1992) and Benzie (2010) focused on Wesley's view of faith formation in children, but neither spoke to the impact of that view on local church educational practice beyond suggesting further research was needed. Maddix (2001) surveyed pastors and Christian educators to discover that although they had a good grasp on Wesley's theology, their educational practice in general was not directly formed by Wesley's theological views. He concluded that much of our practice in Wesleyan churches lacks a distinctly unique Wesleyan influence. Maddix (2001) called for Wesleyan churches to recapture the distinctive elements of Wesleyan theology and instructional practice. Blevins and Maddix (2010) also concluded that there is a lack of "a comprehensive approach to Wesleyan Christian education" and fear that a lack of this type of approach will threaten Wesleyan identity (p. 20). The Wesleyan identity is described by John Wesley as "holiness of heart and life" and defined as having the mind of Christ and "walking as Christ walked" (as cited in Benzie, 2010, p. 41). The Wesleyan movement is a holiness movement that believes in the possibility that we can live holy lives demonstrating a love for God and others. However, the Wesleyan movement has abandoned its own terminology of holiness and adopted the more generic identity of evangelicalism (Drury, 1995). Evangelicalism implies a broader group of Christians who do not all ascribe to Wesley's teachings on holiness (Blevins & Maddix, 2010). Blevins and Maddix (2010) concluded:

> The need for a Wesleyan approach to Christian discipleship is evidenced by the lack of literature in the field of Christian education, the concern about a loss of theological identity within the Wesleyan tradition, and the significant role theology plays in informing Christian discipleship. (p. 25)

Matthaei (2000) studied the faith formation practices of the early Methodists in order to seek insights for today and proposed the need for a "Wesleyan ecology of faith formation" (p. 33) that she described as interconnected "relationships, structures, and practices to nurture faith for churches in the Wesleyan tradition" (p. 33). She also suggested the need to answer the questions of what to teach, how to teach, and who shall teach – questions addressed by John Wesley and the early Methodists. Matthaei (2000) concluded that Wesley's theology and Christian education principles offer a frame of reference for current practice. Matthaei's (2000) work focused on faith formation of adults, however, her methodology bears merit for a Wesleyan approach to faith formation of children as well.

Problem Statement

Christian education in the Wesleyan movement demonstrates a lack of congruency between Wesley's view on faith formation and current Christian education practice (Blevins & Maddix, 2010; Maddix, 2001, Willhauck, 1992). There is a lack of literature on Wesley's educational practice to help inform current practice (Heitzenrater, 1989; Maddix, 2001; Willhauck, 1992) and limited curriculum and materials written from a Wesleyan perspective that would encourage faith formation as described by Wesley (Blevins & Maddix, 2010). Wesleyan Christian education is in need of a rediscovery of Wesley's faith formation practices in order to recapture his message on how faith formation occurs specifically in the life of a child with application for Christian education practice in today's church.

Purpose

There is a need in Wesleyan Christian education to reclaim an understanding of Wesley's Christian education practices that encourage faith formation in children (Maddix, 2001; Willhauck, 1992). This book will look at the writings and practices of John Wesley, identify biblical texts and themes he addressed, note the Christian education practices he employed in the church, home, and school settings, and make application of those practices for today's church based on what we now know from modern educational theory. This will be done to shed light on Wesley's teachings and practices in regard to child faith formation and identify valuable insights for Wesleyan Christian education for children today.

> He [Wesley] instructed his hearers to start young, to teach children early and to continue this education throughout their lives. For Wesley knew, without benefit of a scientifically conducted survey, that a lifetime of exposure to Christian education was the most effective means to come to faith and experience the new birth. (Willhauck, 1992, p. 260)

Organization

How can Wesley's Christian education practices as they specifically relate to child faith formation define what we teach, how we teach, and who shall teach in the local Wesleyan church children's Christian education context today? This will be determined through a systematic study of child faith, faith development, Wesleyan theology, and Wesley's educational practices and teachings. Chapter two will address the inherent faith of a child, the potential for faith development in childhood, the biblical view of child faith formation, the cultural context for Wesley's ministry and writings, Wesley's personal background and influencers, and Wesley's engagement with children, theology, educational practices, and writings. Chapter three will define the methodology that will be employed and suggest the major themes drawn from the literature review. The methodology is adapted from the field of qualitative research theory and the work of Matthaei (2000). Chapter four will follow the prescribed methodology, recapture Wesley's teachings and educational practices that relate to child faith formation, and seek to answer the questions: What to teach; How to teach; and Who shall teach – questions addressed by Wesley at the first conference of Methodist ministers in 1744 and noted by Matthaei (2000). Chapter five will summarize and synthesize the findings and make suggestions for application and further research.

Key Assumptions and Limitations

There is a need for continuity in theological perspective and educational practice within Wesleyan churches grounded in the teachings and practices of John Wesley. Based on the research, there appears to be a need for a greater understanding of Wesley's educational practices that encouraged faith formation (Blevins & Maddix, 2010; Heitzenrater, 2001; Maddix, 2001; Matthaei, 2000; Willhauck, 1992) with specific attention to Wesley's teachings and practices regarding the faith formation of children (Benzie, 2010; Blevins & Maddix, 2010; Maddix, 2001; Matthaei, 2000; Willhauck, 1992). Due to a lack of literature on Wesley's teachings and practices regarding the faith formation in children, this book seeks to rediscover Wesley's teachings that address child faith formation and his educational practices that impacted child faith formation.

This book will focus on archival qualitative research of the teachings and practices of John Wesley. Although there will be common themes and instructional principles that may be transferable to adolescents or adults, child faith formation will be the focus. The themes and principles that emerge will be drawn from John Wesley's teachings and thus specific for Christian education in the Wesleyan movement, although there may be generalities that can be applied beyond the Wesleyan movement. In addition, while it is understood that Christian education occurs in other settings such as the home and school, the primary emphasis for this research will be on Christian education in the local church setting. Finally, John Wesley wrote and practiced in the eighteenth century and although considered progressive in thought by some, he was a product of his culture and time. The teachings and practices gleaned from his work are placed in that cultural timeframe and consideration must be given to reading his work in light of contemporary educational theory and culture in order for it to be beneficial to today's culture.

Chapter Two

Literature Review

The following literature review addresses child faith formation with attention to the inherent quality of faith, how faith is formed in children, and what the Bible says about faith formation in children. It also examines John Wesley and his teachings. In order to reclaim Wesley's understanding of child faith formation and his Christian education practices that encouraged faith formation in children, it is important to understand the cultural context for Wesley's ministry and writings, Wesley's personal background and influencers, and Wesley's engagement with children, theology, educational practices, and writings.

The Nature of Faith

Faith is "that firm belief of God's testimony, and of the truth of the gospel, which influences the will, and leads to an entire reliance on Christ for salvation" (Webster, 1828, para. 6). Martin Luther (1483-1546) defined faith as "the response of the total person in trust to the graciousness of God as it was revealed in Jesus Christ" (Harvey, 1997, p. 96). Migliore (2004) suggested faith could be described as: "The personal response of trust and confidence in the gracious God made known in Jesus Christ" (p. 410). He goes on to suggest that it is not "blind submission" and it incorporates the "whole person, including mind, will, and affections" (p. 410). These definitions suggest that faith includes trust in God that engages a persons mind, affections, and behaviors.

In the New Testament, Jesus used the word faith, *pistis* to signify a belief or trust in God as creator and author of eternal salvation and in Jesus as Messiah and Savior that results in a holy commitment (Blue Letter Bible, 2012; Bromiley, 1985; Gingrich and Danker, 1979). *Pistis* is a noun (a belief) that includes the expectation of action (commitment). This reference to faith, *pistis,* can be seen in Jesus' encounters with individuals who demonstrated faith: the woman with the flow of blood in Matthew 9:22, the blind men in Matthew 9:29, the mother of the demon possessed daughter in Matthew 15:28, the paralytic man in Mark 2:5, the disciples in Mark 11:22, the centurion with the ill servant in Luke 7:9, and the lame man healed by Peter and John in Acts 3:16. The writer of Hebrews in chapter 11 also uses the word *pistis*. In the first three verses the author describes the nature of faith as "the substance of things hoped for" and the "evidence of things to come" (v. 1). Matthew Henry (1996) suggested in his commentary on these verses that faith is a "firm persuasion and expectation that God will perform all that he has promised to us in Christ" (para. 2); it is belief or trust. It is also "a full approbation of all that God has revealed as holy, just, and good; it helps the soul to make application of all to itself with suitable affections and endeavours" (Henry, 1996, para. 2); it is an action of commitment that engages the whole person. "Faith in Hebrews is holding on and enduring, continuing in our journey toward the promised rest and the heavenly homeland. The essence of faith in Hebrews is enduring in faithfulness because we trust in what God has promised, even though we do not visibly see any evidence that it is going to come true" (Schenck, 2003, p. 66). There is this essence of faith in Hebrews that includes both trusting belief and the associated action or works.

Eisenbaum (1997) suggested that the objective of the writer was not to provide a formal definition of the word faith but rather to provide a description of the characteristics associated with faith. The author of Hebrews "describes his audience as 'those who have faith and so are saved'" in doing connects the audience to the list of heroes of the faith (Eisenbaum, 1997, p. 137). The writer provides a "heroes catalog" of the faithful beginning in Hebrews 10:35 and continuing through chapter 11 (Eisenbaum, 1997, p. 137). The heroes' catalog does not reference that "the heroes have faith, but rather they act *by* or *through* faith" (p. 146).

Wesley identified faith as the conviction in the things of God that leads to the work of righteousness. He further elaborated the work of righteousness was attaining perfect love for God with your heart, soul, mind and strength and pressing on to your "high calling in Christ Jesus" (Rotz & Lyon, 1999, Sermon # 106, para. 20). Wesley emphasized the forward movement of faith enthusiastically calling for believers to: "Go Forward!" (Rotz & Lyon, 1999, Sermon #106, para. 20).

Corporate Nature of Faith Formation

Although there is a personal nature to faith, in that every individual has the independent responsibility to respond to the work of the Holy Spirit extending God's grace through faith (Harvey, 1997; Migliore, 2004) faith also has a corporate nature. In the book of Ephesians Paul is writing to the church in Ephesus whom he calls "the faithful in Christ Jesus" (1:1). In chapter four, Paul calls the church in Ephesus to "unity of faith" (Eph. 4:1-6, 12-13) with an inference that "faith changes as people learn and grow in the faith community" (Stonehouse, 1998, p. 146). The word Paul uses for faith here is the same word used in Hebrews 11 and by Christ in Luke 18; it is the Greek word pistis. In these verses Paul acknowledges that there are different gifts of service within the body (vs. 11-12) and suggests that there are three aims: For the perfecting of the saints" (vs. 12), which Wesley (1981) posited means: "The completing them both in number and their various gifts and graces" (Ephesians 4:12 notes); "to the work of the ministry" (vs. 12) defined as Wesley (1981) as: "the serving God and his church in their various ministrations" (Ephesians 4:12, notes); and "to the edifying the body of Christ" (vs. 13) or the building of the body "in faith, love, holiness"

(Wesley, 1981, Ephesians 4:13, notes). Paul suggests that within the body of believers there is diversity of gifts, and he challenges the believers to use their gifts corporately in humility and with love for one anther (vs. 3) in part to obtain unity in faith. Unity of faith is accomplished when the body of believers exercises his or her individual gifts corporately. "Unity of faith" (vs. 13) defined by Wesley (1981) as "an experiential knowledge of Christ as the Son of God" (Ephesians, 4:13, notes).

The author in Hebrews 10 also addresses the means by which faith, *pistis,* is possible and the way in which faith is developed. Hebrews 10:1-18 suggests that it is through Christ's final and ultimate sacrifice of death on the cross, His resurrection, and ascension (v. 14) and through the witness of the Holy Spirit (vs. 15) that faith is possible. "Our 'Great Priest' over God's house has provided access into the very presence of God" (Cockerill, 2012, p. 472). The writer of Hebrews also suggests the way in which faith, *pistis*, is developed and perseveres. The writer instructs believers to draw near to God (vs. 22) and to hold fast to the profession of their faith (vs. 23). "Their present continuous drawing near is the means of perseverance until they enter his presence finally and forever" (Cockerill, 2012, p. 473). Cockerill (2012) suggested that "a true heart in full assurance of faith" (v. 22, NKJ) suggests "obedient confidence and singleness of purpose" (p. 473). The means to perseverance of faith is through encouragement, love, and good works shown to other believers (vs. 24) and through meeting together and exhorting one another (vs. 25). "Encouragement to persevere follows the invitation to 'draw near'. The two are intimately related....Perseverance in faithful living is dependent on an adequate grasp of Christ and his sufficiency" (Cockerill, 2012, p. 476). Cockerill (2012) posited: "the pastor brings these exhortations to a climax with 'Let us give attention to one another for the provoking of love and good works'. Such mutual concern, in turn, creates and sustains a community conducive to perseverance in a hostile world" (p. 478). Faith is possible through the work of Jesus Christ made known through the witness of the Holy Spirit and faith is preserved through drawing near to God and holding fast. Holding fast to faith is possible when believers love one another and come together in community.

If faith is a personal belief in God the creator and in Jesus the Savior as well as the active response of trust that includes a forward motion of growth developed and persevered in part through engagement in the community of believers known as the church, then faith should be a primary focus of our Christian education efforts (Westerhoff, 2000). Westerhoff (2000) suggested that our current practices in Christian education result in religion rather than faith. Faith, he posited, requires nurturing in a community with a shared story, authority, rituals, and culture (pp. 74-75). "Shared experience, story telling, celebration, action, and reflection between and among equal 'faithing' selves within a community of faith best help us understand how faith is transmitted, expanded, and sustained" (Westerhoff, 2000, p. 87).

The Role of Christian Education in Faith Formation

If as Scripture suggests the development and perseverance of faith occurs in the context of the community of believers (Ephesians 4 and Hebrews 11), Christian education in the local church context plays a critical role in faith formation. Christian education is Christocentric instruction that encompasses intentional and unintentional experiences (Drury, 2011) that leads to cognitive, affective, and behavioral outcomes (Aukerman, 2011). Blevins and Maddix (2010) asserted that Christian education includes "acts" that "shape and form people as they grow in grace" (p.17). Christian education, according to these definitions, is all of the "acts" or experiences both intentional and unintentional that serve to transform people holistically "as they grow in grace". Westerhoff (2000) suggested that Christian education that aids in faith formation "is dependent upon the theological underpinnings which judge and inspire its efforts" (p. 25). Blevins & Maddix (2010) affirmed the connection of theological belief and Christian education when they suggested, "theology is the foundation for Christian educational practices" (p. 53).

However, research has revealed that Christian education practices in the local Wesleyan church are not consistent with a Wesleyan theological perspective (Blevins, 2001; Blevins & Maddix, 2010; Willhauck, 1992). A Wesleyan perspective is one that is founded on the writings and teachings of John Wesley, an eighteenth century Anglican pastor and theologian (Harper, 2003). Willhauck (1992), in her book on Wesley's view of children and its impact on Christian education, suggested further research is needed in this field as we work to provide Christian education from the Wesleyan perspective. Blevins and Maddix (2010) concurred with Willhauck and suggested a need for a uniquely Wesleyan approach to Christian education that embraces the Wesleyan theological identity and tradition - an identity and tradition whose hallmark is "holiness of heart and life" (Matthaei, 2000, p. 35).

The Inherent Nature of Faith

For you created my inmost being;

You knit me together in my mother's womb.

I praise you because I am fearfully and wonderfully made;

Your works are wonderful, I know that full well.

My frame was not hidden from you when I was made in the secret place,

When I was woven together in the depths of the earth.

Your eyes saw my unformed body;

All the days ordained for me were written in your book

before one of them came to be.

(Psalm 139:13-16, NIV)

The psalmist writes of an omniscient or all knowing God (139:1-6) who is also omnipresent (139:7-12) from the heavens to the depths of the seas. It is suggested in verses 13-16 that this all knowing and always present God is also a personal creator and "custodian" of His creation (Lennox, 1999). The creator God is present in the life of the unborn child (Maslen, 2003). Are the words of the Psalmist those of a dreamer or is there evidence that the awareness of God is present at birth?

Inherent faith in Scripture

In Luke 1:41-44 we are provided the story of the unborn babe, John the Baptist's, response to Mary's presence. Mary had just received the news that she would be the mother of God's Son, Jesus the Messiah. She left immediately to tell her cousin Elisabeth and upon entering Elisabeth's home, before Mary had an opportunity to tell her good news, the unborn John the Baptist leapt in his mother's womb. The Matthew Henry Commentary (1996) suggested that John's in utero leap served as a signal to Elisabeth, his mother, that something miraculous was about to be known. It also demonstrated the confirmation of the Angel's words to Zechariah in Luke 1:15: "He will also be filled with the Holy Spirit, even from his mother's womb" (NKJV). The unborn babe, filled with the Holy Spirit, responded to Mary's voice and provided confirmation to his mother Elisabeth that the insight given to her by the Holy Spirit was true – Mary was to be the mother of the Lord. The pre-birth John the Baptist demonstrated a super natural awareness.

Likewise Paul makes reference to Timothy's spiritual awareness from infancy in 2 Timothy 3:14-15:

> But as for you, continue in what you have learned and have become convinced of, because you know those from whom you learned it, and how from infancy you have known the Holy Scriptures, which are able to make you wise for salvation through faith in Christ Jesus. (NIV)

The Greek word for "infancy" used here is *bréphos* which according to Kittel and Friedrich (as cited in Bromily, 1985) means " 'embryo,' 'young,' 'infant,' or 'small child'" (p. 759); and the Greek word for "to know" or "understand" is *oída* (Kittel and Friedrich, as cited in Bromily, 1985, p. 673). The word Paul uses conveys an understanding of Scripture that Timothy incurred as an infant.

In the Psalm there is an indication that we are known to God and know of God prior to birth, while in utero. The example of John the Baptist's response while in utero to the presence of Mary and the Holy Spirit's prompt provides evidence that the Psalmist's words are not just poetic. Additionally the reference by Paul in 2

Timothy of Timothy's understanding of Scripture in infancy or *bréphos* signifies the awareness of God and things of God in infancy.

Inherent faith demonstrated through questions children ask

Is there evidence in research that children are spiritual beings born with a propensity toward faith, as suggested in Scripture? There is awareness within everyone that there is something other, greater, than us. Even young children ask the questions: "Where did we come from?" and "What are we here for?" (Cavalletti, 2002; Coles, 1990). When faced with difficult situations or dilemmas where there is no apparent answer, children look for answers in a greater being, in a spiritual being outside their physical state of reality (Coles, 1990). Coles (1990), a clinician, pediatrician, child psychiatrist, and psychoanalyst, documented children who pondered "the great questions of human existence" (Meehan, 2002, p. 67). He engaged children who were going through traumatic physical illnesses, experiencing severe social stress, or undergoing educational trauma. He engaged children from the rural south, suburban Boston, Spanish-speaking Arizona, Eskimo children in Alaska, Native American children in New Mexico, and Appalachian children. He also interviewed children in South Africa, South America, Northern Ireland, Poland, Nicaragua, Brazil, and Canada (Coles, 1990; Meehan, 2002). Through his interviews and conversations with children from various cultural, socio-economic, and religious backgrounds, he discovered a universal curiosity about faith and an understanding of spirituality.

Children from non-religious, atheistic, or agnostic backgrounds seemed to have a desire for the answers to the questions too. And although their parents offered answers outside of a spiritual awareness of God, the children exhibited that something inside of them knew there was more – an inherent spirituality that led them to faith in something greater and something more (Coles, 1990). Sylvia, who was angry that her little brother had a horrible illness and was going to die, suggested at first that there couldn't be a God but, after she had paused and reflected, suggested that perhaps there was a God and some day He would give them the answers to why (Coles, 1990, p. 299). An eight-year-old Jewish girl who lived near Boston told Coles that she knew God was here and that she could "feel him nearby a lot of times" (Coles, 1990, p. 37). Likewise, Mark suggested about God: "If you ignore Him, that's the worst thing you can do. He'll be sad, and you'd see it on His face. He doesn't want us to praise Him just be nice, though. He wants us to praise Him because we've realized who He is – He's the creator of all the people" (p. 52).

Coles (1990) asked Mark and other children to draw a picture of God. He collected 293 pictures of God with over 250 of those just of God's face (p. 40). He suggested that children demonstrated in the faces of God they drew that what they understood about God was complex (Meehan, 2002). Lindner (2004), in reflecting on Coles' methods and interactions with children, posited: "His preservation and careful interpretation of children's drawings and his clinical methodology demonstrate children's profound capacity for voice and agency in moral, theological, and spiritual thinking" (p. 64). Children with an awareness of a spiritual being demonstrated the ability to engage in conversations about God, even draw a picture of what God looks like, regardless of their religious affiliation or lack of affiliation. Coles (1990) commented about his research into child spirituality: "It is a project that, finally, helped me see children as seekers, as young pilgrims well aware that life is a finite journey and as anxious to make sense of it as those of us who are father along" (p. xvi). He was amazed at how young they are when they begin to ask questions about the nature of the journey and "the final destination" (p. 335).

Coles identified spirituality in children, as did Morgenthaler (2003), Ratcliff (2004), and Cavalletti (2002). While the term spirituality can have various meanings, Morgenthaler (2003), Ratcliff (2004), and Cavalletti (2002) spoke of spirituality or the spiritual nature of children in meaning something that is beyond the natural or physical self and in reference to Christian faith. Morgenthaler (2003) addressed the question if children were capable of faith development and suggested that "young children are spiritual beings, having been so created by God" and this innate spirituality provides a propensity for faith, which is present at birth in everyone (p. 69). Ratcliff (2004) concurred with Morgenthaler and posited that "spiritual aliveness knows no age barriers; the young child and the aged philosopher stand on level ground" (Ratcliff, 2004, p. 8). Ratcliff (2004) additionally suggested that children appear to posses an "unusual level of consciousness and perceptiveness" in matters relating to faith (p. 9). This "spiritual aliveness", argued Ratcliff (2004) could be seen in the historical and biblical accounts of children, such as the accounts of John the Baptist and Timothy.

Inherent faith demonstrated in a child's Godly play

Children not only ask questions that demonstrate an awareness of a being other than themselves, Sofia Cavalletti, a theologian and scholar, witnessed young children's ability to know God and to describe their relationship with Him through questions specifically asked about God: "Who is God? Who was God with in the beginning of Creation? Was God by himself?" (Cavalletti, 2002, p. 1). Cavalletti (2002) developed an approach to child faith education called the "Catechesis of the Good Shepherd" (Cavalletti, 2002; Garrido, 2008). In the catechesis, children engaged biblical concepts and stories through tactile, "Godly play" (Berryman, 2009). The "Catechesis of the Good Shepherd", according to Garrido (2008), perceives "the child as someone who already has a deep relationship with God" (p. 11). The presumption behind the catechesis is that children are born not only aware of God, but in a relationship with God. Cavalletti's forty-five years of observation of children engaged in Godly play confirmed this presumption.

Children demonstrated the ability to discern the meaning of Jesus' parables without prompting. And although they didn't have the verbal skills to say what the parables meant, they were able to depict the meaning through drawings (Cavalletti, 2002). One example is that of a Mexican boy, who when presented with the parable of the mustard seed, drew the mustard seed, a tree, and a figure he designated as God standing beside the tree. At the very top of the picture he drew a present tied up with a bow and the sun spreading light on the entire scene (Cavalletti, 2002, p. 3). Cavalletti (2002) noted the child's drawing demonstrated an awareness that the gift is with us but comes from God and that in the process of the seed becoming the tree, there is great power. Another child, a four and a half year old girl, after presented the parable of the grain of wheat (John 12:24) drew a flower. When asked where the seed was, the little girl replied, "You can't see it because it's dead. It has given its life to the plant" (Cavalletti, 2002, p. 6). The little girl paused, reflected, and concluded by saying that the plant couldn't grow without the seed and that the seed's life had gone up into the stem and leaves of the plant. Cavalletti (2002) posited that the "depth and strength of the child's responses convince us that these parables offer a form of nourishment that corresponds to a child's particular needs" – needs fueled by a desire to be in relationship with God.

Cavalletti (2002) also discovered that young children referenced their faith in a way that indicated a close relationship with God while older children seemed to express their faith in terms of doctrinal statements and traditional church expressions. She suggested this demonstrated a loss of the personal connection with God they once enjoyed in the early years of life. She also discovered that young children (2 ½ to 3 years of age) enjoy an "intense, all-engaging experience of enjoyment" in their relationship with God (p. ix). In her observations of the very young, Cavalletti (2002) posited that their response to Godly play is joy, "a joy which renders the child at peace" (p. 1). She went on to reference Maria Montessori's words (as cited in Cavalletti, 2002) "joy is the indicator of interior growth, just as an increase in weight is the indication of bodily growth" (p. 1) suggesting that the child's response of joy indicated the internal growth of faith taking place. In Romans 14:17, Paul suggested that life lived in relationship with God is characterized by righteousness, peace, and joy; "joy that comes from responding as the Holy Spirit guides our conduct" (Harper, 1990, p. 1706).

Cavalletti (2002) and Coles (1990) both had opportunity to study children engaged in different activities from a variety of socio-economic classes, cultures, and experiences. Cavalletti was primarily interested in seeing how children engaged and responded to the Christian message, and she developed an approach of presentation of biblical concepts and stories that incorporated minimal storytelling with prolonged interactive play and drawing (Berryman, 2009; Cavalletti, 2002). Coles' purpose, on the other hand, was to offer therapeutic relief to children who were suffering, and he desired to gain insights into how those children responded (Coles, 1990, Meehan, 2002). Both discovered that children, even the youngest who had not developed a language to define their insights and beliefs, demonstrated an inherent spiritual discernment and capacity for faith; faith that came through thoughtful reflection and engagement with both the physical and spiritual world. These insights were demonstrated by the questions the children asked and the drawings they created.

A theological perspective on inherent faith

Karl Rahner was a contemporary Catholic theologian "regarded by many as the most important Catholic theologian of the twentieth century" and whose theological anthropology "has had an enormous influence on contemporary Catholic approaches to the religious education of children" (Hinsdale, 2001, p. 406). In his paper, "Ideas for a Theology of Childhood" Rahner suggested that "children are fundamentally oriented toward God" and "for Rahner a person's relationship with God is operative at every stage of human growth and development, childhood being no exception" (as cited in Hinsdale, 2001, p. 421). Rahner's theology "implies an absolute immediacy to God, the child his intended to be, right from the start, a partner of God" (Hinsdale, 2001, p. 423).

Rahner demonstrated a great respect for childhood suggesting that there are unique opportunities for relating to God that are only available in childhood. Hinsdale (2001) suggested that Rahner offered two important views of childhood. The first is his expression of childhood in terms of its "infinite openness to the infinite" and the second view that childhood "makes us receptive to Jesus' vision of the realm of God" (Hinsdale, 2001, p. 443). Children do not represent merely the potential relationship with God but are able to enjoy an actual and present relationship with God.

Conclusion on inherent faith

Scripture tells us that Christ is the Light, "which lighteth every man that cometh into the world" (John 1:9, KJV). Helen Keller, when writing of her religious experience, posited: "I know that life is given us so that we may grow in love. And I believe that God is in me as the sun is in the color and fragrance of the flower, the Light in my darkness, the Voice in my silence" (as cited in Silverman, 2000, p. xvii). Keller suggested that she had always sensed the Light but didn't have a name for it, until someone told her about Jesus. Like Helen, who in her blindness sensed the Light, the research, through observation and interviews with children, revealed that each child regardless of their culture, religious background, or personal status possessed an awareness of the Light (Cavalletti, 2002; Coles, 1990; Ratcliff, 2001). Children who were suffering incredible physical and emotional pain, sought to define their spiritual awareness and answer eternal questions (Coles, 1990). Likewise, children exposed to biblical teaching demonstrated an incredible ability to discern spiritual insights and displayed a deep understanding of faith and biblical themes (Cavalletti, 2002). The spiritual awareness and capacity for faith was consistently evident in children, and researchers and theologians alike concluded that the awareness of a realm outside the physical realm (spirituality) and the desire to be in relationship with God (faith) is inherent in all children (Cavalletti, 2002; Coles, 1990; Hinsdale, 2001; Morgenthaler, 2003; Ratcliff, 2001).

Cavalletti (2002) suggested that all the children she engaged over the forty-five years of observation posed similar questions: "Who is God? Where was I in the very beginning (before I was born)? How did I get here? Who was God with in the beginning of Creation? Was God by himself? Where is my grandmother who has died? What is life?" (p. 1). Robert Coles also discovered a similar pattern of questions asked by children through his over thirty years of engagement and dialogue with over 500 children (Coles, 1990; Meehan, 2002). "He [Coles] is convinced that children no less than the great minds of literature, philosophy, and theology ponder the great questions of human existence" (Meehan, 2002, p. 67).

When asked what they thought about God, children paused for reflection, unafraid of the silence, before responding to a question (Coles, 1990). "Again and again children have thought long and hard about who God is, about what God might be like, only to find refuge in the stillness of a room, the stillness of their own minds or souls, as they struggled to express what might well be for them the inexpressible" (Coles, 1990, pp. 168-169). Children are far more complex than most of us realize. What is intriguing is that in light of their diverse backgrounds, culture, economic situation, religious affiliation, or physical, social, and emotional experiences they all exhibited a profoundly spiritual component (Cavalletti, 2002). Something in them that yearned for answers as they were compelled by the inherent belief that there is something more, something greater than the obvious. These hurting children, like Sylvia, demonstrated a deep awareness of God, and in the midst of their struggle that awareness gave them peace and hope (Coles, 1990).

Depending on our perspective, we look at a child's cognitive ability, physical maturity, social skills, or emotional well-being, but there is far more to discover:

> The child's house has many mansions (quoting scripture) – including a spiritual life that grows, changes, responds, constantly to other lives that, in their sum, make up the individual we call by a name and know by a story that is all his, all hers. (Coles, 1990, p. 308)

Faith Development in Children

If children are born with an awareness of God and a desire to be in relationship with Him providing the potential for children to possess faith or the belief in God that results in hope and trust, how can that faith be nurtured and developed? Morgenthaler (2003) stated emphatically "all children develop concepts of God" (p. 69-71) and posited that children are capable of growing in their understanding of God and possess an ability to explore their relationship with God. This faith must be fostered and nurtured in a relationship with a caring, sensitive adult. An adult who is sensitive to the ways the child perceives and comprehends. She further contended that the strength of the relationship between the child and the adult has a significant impact on the child faith development and their understanding of their relationship with God (Morgenthaler, 2003). Cavalletti (2002) understood, as did Morgenthaler, that what is missing for children is not the ability to engage spiritual things or develop faith, but rather the environment to enable the relationship to develop and grow.

Leah, a girl dying of cancer, demonstrated that children could develop faith. Coles (1990) reported:

> I saw in Leah a child intensely attached to a family's religious and spiritual life, its prayers and food and ceremonies, its spoken acknowledgement of the Lord, its remembrance of His words, of what He and is people had experienced together in the past and were still, in that hospital room, in our time, undergoing together. (p. 276)

Leah told her dad before slipping into her final coma; "I'd like to go to that high rock". Coles (1990) suggested that for Leah the "rock" was a faith that stood firm even in the face of death. Leah demonstrated the ability of a child to have profound and deep faith, developed in the close relationship of her family.

Faith Development Insights from Developmental Psychology

Developmental theories "serve as frames of reference for examining changes in behavior over time" (Miller, 2002, p. 5). They are useful in helping to explain the processes of development and serve as a stimulus for further research (Seifert & Hoffnung, 2000). Miller (2002) posited that there are three tasks of a developmental theory:

> To describe changes within one or several areas of behavior;
>
> To describe changes in the relations among several areas of behavior; and
>
> To explain the course of development that has been described. (p. 8)

In addition theories of developmental psychology address the nature of humans, if development is quantitative or qualitative, if nature or nurture contribute to a greater extent in development, and what develops (Miller, 2002, p. 14). Developmental theories can also be looked at in terms of their emphasis on maturation or experience, continuous or stage development, and active or passive participation (Seifert & Hoffnung, 2000, p. 59). Developmental psychology theorist Fowler, who looked at the development of faith, built upon the work of Piaget, a cognitive-structural theorist who is considered "the most important figure in developmental psychology" (Miller, 2002, p. 26). Piaget's extensive recorded observations of young children led him to believe that children were highly active and self-regulating as they engaged with their environment and even infants demonstrated the ability to construct meaning through perception and action (Miller, 2002). He suggested that a child develops a new way of thinking through assimilation, the process of fitting a new idea with a pre-existing scheme, and through accommodation, changing an existing way of thinking based on new experiences (Miller, 2002; Seifert & Hoffnung, 2000). The stages of development build upon each other, with the child taking forward with them what they have previously learned (Miller, 2002; Seifert & Hoffnung, 2000). Piaget, while focused on the mental growth or mental development of the child, understood the interplay of physical, mental, and emotional development (Miller, 2002; Piaget & Inhelder, 2000). He also recognized pre-birth development that takes place suggesting: "in order to understand mental growth it is not enough to start with birth" (Piaget & Inhelder, 2000, p. xvii). Although Piaget did not focus on faith development or the spiritual aptitude of children, his influence can be seen in the work of Fowler.

Fowler and faith development

Faith is universal, "we are endowed at birth with nascent capacities for faith" (Fowler, 1981, p. xiii) and "we all begin the pilgrimage of faith as infants" (Fowler, 1981, p. 119). Fowler, a developmental psychologist and a premiere pioneer in the field of study of faith development, studied the common characteristics of individuals in the faith formation process across religions that include Christianity, Judaism, Islam, and secular humanism (Capehart, 2005, p. 80). Fowler (1981) suggested faith is a complex, universal "human phenomenon" (p. 33), that is more than just religion, which focuses on acquisition of knowledge, but rather faith engages the entire person. He acknowledged that faith is relational in nature and triadic in form in that our trust and loyalty to our community is enhanced by our shared faith in a transcendent other, for Christians that is God. Fowler also suggested that faith is imaginative. "In faith, imagination composes comprehensive images of the ultimate conditions of existence" (Fowler, 1981, p. 30). Finally, Fowler (1981) contended that faith was not static but dynamic and changing (p. 34). Faith, for Fowler, is universal and inherent, relational and triadic, holistic, imaginative, and dynamic.

While Fowler (1981) acknowledged that each infant begins the faith journey at birth, the different experiences and encounters they face serve as either stimulation and an incubator for positive faith development or a catalyst for mistrust and despair. He posited that our development and maturation have a great deal to do with the people in our environment who engage and interact with us, an assessment mirrored by Cavalletti (2002) and Morgenthaler (2003). Faith, he suggested, is "interactive and social" (p. xiii) and is shaped ultimately by "initiatives from beyond us and other people, initiatives of the spirit or grace" (p. xiii).

Fowler's work based on Erikson's Life Stages

Building on the work of Erikson, Fowler suggested that faith formed as individuals successfully navigated the crises described by Erikson. Erikson (1997) developed a theory on the stages of human development referred to as "The Life Cycle" which graphs human development through eight primary age-linked stages. Erikson saw the process of development occurring as the child responds to changes they encounter in their environment through relationships and subsequently manages those challenges, successfully or unsuccessfully. The labels attached to each stage represent outcomes, positive and negative, that must be resolved in order to move onto the next stage (Seifert & Hoffnung, 2000; Stonehouse, 1998). Erikson (1997) suggested that life includes both the positive and negative in which "conflict and tension are sources of growth, strength, and commitment" (p. 106). Successful mastery of a stage results in the acquisition of a virtue that will help the child meet future developmental challenges (Seifert & Hoffnung, 2000). The stages and corresponding virtues include "Trust vs. Mistrust" with hope, "Autonomy vs. Shame and Doubt" with will, "Initiative vs. Guilt" with purpose, "Industry vs. Inferiority" with competence, "Identity vs. Identity Confusion" with fidelity, "Intimacy vs. Isolation" with love, "Generativity vs. Stagnation" with care, and "Integrity vs. Despair" with wisdom (Erikson, 1997, pp. 56-57). As the crises or challenges change, faith changes as well becoming more complex and providing the individual with more profound relational opportunities with others and with God (Stonehouse, 1998).

Fowler's faith development stages

Fowler (1981) suggested that the earliest stage of faith development is really a pre-stage because it is not open for measured inquiry due to the infant's inability to communicate via formal language. However, he denoted significant faith accomplishments that occur within these first few months of life. "In the pre-stage called Undifferentiated Faith the seeds of trust, courage, hope and love are fused in an undifferentiated way and contend with sensed threats of abandonment, inconsistencies and deprivations in an infant's environment" (p. 121). Fowler (1981) suggested "the emergent strength of faith in this stage is the fund of basic trust and the relational experience of mutuality with the one(s) providing primary love and care" (p. 121). This early stage aligns with Erikson's who also saw trust as critical in the initial phase of development and saw trust as dependent on the caregiver's response (Erikson, 1997).

"Primal Faith" is the first phase that comes from Erikson's first crisis of trust versus mistrust. "Primal faith is a basic disposition to trust," relates Stonehouse (1998, p. 151). The responsive care of parents and caregivers to an infant develop within that child a feeling or disposition to trust. Fowler put forth that this trust is "the embryo of faith which can come to maturity in a relationship with God" (Stonehouse, 1998, p. 151). Families who speak of faith, sing songs of God, pray with small children and make faith real and present in everyday life help the young child engage in memory-building activities. Fowler (1981) suggested that these activities are the beginning of imagination that leads to children forming their image of God. This primal faith is the foundation upon which all other faith development is built.

The faith development stages beyond the earliest primal faith, pre-stage include: "Intuitive-Projective", "Mythic-Literal", "Synthetic-Conventional", "Individuative-Reflective", "Conjunctive", and "Universalizing" (Fowler, 1981, p. 113). The Intuitive-Projective faith stage generally occurs in the early preschool years and is characterized by imagination. It is the first step of self-awareness (Conn, 1986; Fowler, 1981). Long lasting faith images are established in these early years as imagination is employed through story telling and symbols. Intuitive-Projective Faith develops when children are beginning to use language to communicate and label experiences. Children in this developmental stage project their ideas and meanings onto events; therefore, images of God during this stage can be projected. Church memories, stories, symbolism, and ceremonies all form images that relate to a child's imagination. "They picture the event or the story as they imaginatively perceive it and combine with that picture the strong feelings stimulated by the story of the event to form an image that has a long-lasting influence on their faith" (Stonehouse, 1998, p. 153). This intuitive phase of faith development, according to Fowler (1981), occurs during early childhood.

Mythic-Literal Faith is the second stage, and it is here that symbol and ritual begin to be integrated by the child. This stage begins to form during the elementary and into the middle school years (Fowler, 1981; Stonehouse, 1998, p. 159). Control of the imagination, the differentiation between fantasy and real, and the beginning of linear thinking characterize this stage. It is in this stage that children form a strong belief in justice and a child's identity is formed along the lines of acceptance or shame (Conn, 1986, Fowler, 1981). Fowler (1981) highlights the role of myths or stories combined with literal thinking at this faith stage. Children at this developmental stage want to know what is real and are moving from predominantly using their imaginations to separating fantasy and reality. The child's view of God begins to change as he or she tries to form a more concrete image. This image includes power, fairness, and compassion. This stage of faith is built best with stories (Stonehouse, 1998).

The third stage is the Synthetic-Conventional Faith and typically occurs in adolescence, although it can occur earlier. Fowler (1981) also noted that there are people who spend their entire life in this phase of faith development. This stage includes the ability to reflect on past experiences in order to draw meaning. It also includes a concern for personal future and the importance of friendships. In this stage there is a desire to seek a personal relationship with God and experience His love (Conn, 1986; Fowler, 1981). At this stage of development, children have established the ability to process abstract thought and deep reflection. They are also expanding their social relationships, which bring differing belief conflicts (Stonehouse, 1998). Children at this stage of faith will use their reflective thought process to examine their stories of faith, which leads to the beginning of synthetic-conventional faith. This is "a faith constructed by synthesizing meanings, beliefs, and values received from various sectors of their world" (Stonehouse, 1998, p. 164). These "various sectors" come from parents and church but also peers, school, and cultural influences. At this stage of development, relationships become highly important; faith development highlights the child's relationship with God. God offers companionship, acceptance, guidance, and love. "Their [the children's] lives are powerfully influenced by what they understand as God's expectations – the values, beliefs, and commitments to which God calls them" (Stonehouse, 1998, p. 165).

Fowler's view of faith formation suggested that it is a dynamic pattern of personal trust in and loyalty to a center of value and involves trust in and loyalty to a shared metanarrative. Capehart (2005) in speaking of Fowler's view of faith, suggested: "Trust and loyalty are the foundation – the threads woven through all dimensions of faith" (p. 80).

Criticism of Fowler's stages of faith development

One criticism that has surfaced of Fowler's work is his dependence on the earlier work of Piaget and the structural approach, which suggested that faith develops in stages in a hierarchical fashion. A new stage cannot be entered until the previous is mastered, and one generally does not move backward through the stages only forward. Heywood (2008) takes exception with Fowler's theory in its adoption of the structuralism from Piaget and Kohlberg. Heywood (2008) suggested that "The idea that human meaning-making can be described as going through a series of stages which are invariant, hierarchal, sequential and consist of structural wholes may be seen to derive from Piaget's flawed theory of cognitive development and must for that reason be held as extremely doubtful" (p. 11). While Heywood (2008) does not take issue with the content of the stages or that people do develop faith, which includes the presence of trust, employs the imagination, and is added through relationship and ritual; he does find, however, the concept that people must pass through these sequentially and that there are identifiable ages associated with each stage not plausible or supported with research. Heywood (2008) noted instead an observation from his personal experience that demonstrated children experiencing the stages of faith out of sequential order:

> Children supposedly in the unordered or ordering stages of faith development were using sophisticated educational skills to bring reason to bear on some of the stories they were told. A 7-year-old hearing the story of Noah's Ark from a version of the bible neglected to mention the wives of Shem, Ham and Japheth used the questioning skills encouraged by current mainstream educational methods, together with a basic knowledge of biology, to wonder how we could be descended from three men. (p. 14)

Heywood (2008) suggested that this example demonstrates a child's ability to think for him or herself and employ questioning skills beyond what Fowler's stages of faith allows. Heywood (2008) went on to posit: "Children could easily exhibit features of unordered, ordered and conforming faith stages in quick succession" (p. 15) suggesting that the sequence and the age specification for each stage may not be accurate. Heywood (2008) points to Westerhoff's (2000) different styles and pathways to faith as a positive step forward from Fowler in further refining the identification of the faith formation process. While there is value in the study of faith formation and understanding how people make meaning in their lives, Heywood (2008) posited that Fowler's theory stops short of encompassing the variety of nuances at play and holds captive the child from advancing along the faith formation cycle in a way that has been observed. Children, it appears, are capable of deeper faith formation than Fowler originally expected.

Conclusion on Fowler's stages of faith development

James Fowler began his research in light of Erikson and Piaget's findings on development. "He found that as individuals coped constructively with the challenges and crises of life described by Erikson, the needed faith formed to allow for constructive coping." (Stonehouse, 1998, p. 150) Each developmental stage opened the door for a new faith stage and a deeper relationship with God.

Based on her reflection of Fowler's work, Stonehouse (1998) posited: "God created human beings with the capacity and the deep need to have faith…Children are born with readiness for faith" (p. 150). She suggested that Fowler highlighted that the development of faith is not automatic but requires a nurturing environment where trust and loyalty are nurtured.

Child Faith Development Insights from the Field of Christian Education

The field of developmental psychology has offered insight into how children develop cognitively, morally, and in their faith. Piaget, Erikson, and Fowler acknowledged that children begin the process of development early and along predictable paths. They also recognized that a child's development is impacted by their experiences and relationships. Fowler identified the universality, predictability and immediacy of faith development and suggested that as children move from one stage to another they have opportunity for a deeper relationship with God.

There are others who have also studied child faith development looking for common stages that could be predicted and supported and environments that were more conducive in creating positive faith development. These individuals' context is the field of Christian education.

Westerhoff's view of faith development

Westerhoff (2000), a student of Fowler, developed stages of faith formation that are similar to Fowler's but not tied to age and more fluid in that people move between the stages and a clear progression from one stage to another is sometimes difficult to define. Westerhoff's stages of development also specifically reflect Christian faith development, as opposed to Fowler's attention to a more general faith development. Westerhoff predicted the demise of faith formation if radical change in our Christian education paradigm did not occur. He proposed that the church had adopted the cultural educational paradigm for Christian education, and was now facing the same, if not greater, lack of success as the public educational system. Westerhoff (2000) called for a move from "schooling instructional paradigm" (p. 5) to the "community of faith-formation paradigm" (p. 21). Westerhoff (2000) defined the "schooling instruction paradigm" as one that sees the context as a school and the means as the form of instruction (p. 5). He posited that Christian educators have mimicked culture in our approach to education in which education is synonymous with school and instruction. The result was that Christian education in our local churches became classroom, instruction centered, moving away from the holistic approach that embraces the home and church that Horace Bushnell (1861) described in his text, *Christian Nurture* and had been previously practiced. In contrast, Westerhoff (2000) defined the "community of faith-formation paradigm" as one that embraces the entire faith community, acknowledges the role relationship plays in faith formation, and sees the critical role that home, church, and Christian school play together in faith formation. Westerhoff (2000) called for the church to be a "witnessing community" and suggested it "has a story to tell, a vision to share, good news to proclaim; and that story, vision, and news are communicated best through its life" (p. 43).

The move to a community of faith-formation paradigm embraces four "styles" of faith formation, that somewhat align with Fowler's stages of faith development yet are more fluid and not as tied to age. Westerhoff (2000) purposefully used the word "style" or path rather than stage and suggested that each style is a generalization and people "expand" through the styles as opposed to being contained in a stage, as contained in a box (p. 88). The styles of faith include "experienced faith", "affiliative faith", "searching faith", and "owned faith" (Westerhoff, 2000, p. 88).

Experienced faith is at the core of our faith formation and is present in very early childhood (Westerhoff, 2000). The beginning of faith formation occurs when children experience the faith of their caretakers. The impact of faith on adult lives makes a faith impression on young children. Westerhoff (2000) suggested that in the experienced faith style, children interact actively with faith, mimicking and responding to another's actions creating a "mirror and a test" (p. 90) for experiencing faith. This is an affective experience and is foundational for a lifetime of faith formation; it is primary and required (Westerhoff, 2000). Like Fowler and Erikson, Westerhoff (2000) included experiences of "trust, love, and acceptance" (p. 90) as critical for the establishment of faith formation and acknowledged that even the youngest of children are in the process of developing faith.

Children never outgrow the need to experience faith but this style, if fully grasped, eventually gives way to affiliative faith (Westerhoff, 2000). It is during this style of faith formation that children "seek to act with others in an accepting community with a clear sense of identity" (Westerhoff, 2000, p. 91). This is the belonging phase that aligns with Fowler's Synthetic-Conventional stage. It is during this phase, Westerhoff (2000) posited, that faith actions relate to affective responses such as "experiencing, awe, wonder, and mystery" (p. 92). Actions that generate affective responses include participation in the arts through singing, dance, drama, and art. Rituals, such as baptism, play a key role in this phase. The other characteristic in affiliative faith is the development of a sense of authority, which Westerhoff (2000) connected to the biblical metanarrative as children learn to internalize the story.

When a child has had the needs of affiliative faith met they move into the style of faith called "searching" characterized by doubts, critical judgment, and questions (Westerhoff, 2000). There is a parallel with Fowler's Individuative-Connective phase and Westerhoff's searching style. It is during this time of searching that students explore alternatives and question their held beliefs. Westerhoff (2000) suggested that it is during this phase that commitment is made.

The final style of faith is owned faith, which is acquired after the successful engagement with searching faith. Westerhoff (2000) concluded that this is the point when conversion is recognized and is characterized by the individual's desire to be a witness to their faith through their words and actions (p. 95). This is when the individual realizes their true identity of who they are in Christ. Although it appears to happen primarily in late adolescence or early adulthood, Westerhoff (2000) acknowledged that none of the styles of faith are completely age defined.

Richards and Stonehouse's views on child faith development

Lawrence Richards is considered one of the most influential writers in the field of Christian education theory in the twentieth century (Benson, 1984; Sell, n.d.). Richards (1983) referenced the work of Piaget in his text, *A Theology of Children's Ministry*, noting his agreement with Piaget's conclusions that children are "active and constructivist in their relationship with environment" (p. 170). He concurred with the developmental nature of children - the early age in which it begins and the impact of the environment on development. However, Richards (1983) separated himself from the theorists by suggesting that there is a structure to faith that is objective, as opposed to the belief that religious ideas originate within culture and are a construct of humanity. He argued that there is a spiritual world, like there is a material world, which is structured by God and revealed in Scripture. He further suggested that children could "know by experience" these spiritual realities and develop faith (p. 171).

Richards (1983) suggested that there were five processes or influences of faith development in children that contribute to the nurturing of faith. The five processes or constructs that contribute to child faith development include active participation and engagement by the child. The processes also included the importance of the adult's role in clearly communicating a sense of belonging, modeling faith for the child, and interpreting happenstances of life through the lens of faith (Beckwith, 2004; Richards, 1983). Like Westerhoff, Richards posited that early faith formation is possible and accentuated through relationships at home and within the faith community (Beckwith, 2004).

Likewise, Stonehouse (1998) concurred with Westerhoff (2000) and Richards (1983) in the belief that children are capable of faith development. Like Richards she suggested that this faith development occurs through a child's engagement in the biblical narrative, hearing contemporary stories of God's work in lives today, and personal relationships in the home and church. Stonehouse (1998) suggested "Children are born with readiness for faith but need an environment of mutual love, care, and interaction for the faith potential to become a reality" (p. 150). This faith develops, Stonehouse (1998) posited, in the normal flow of life, with parents as primary teachers, as the children see and experience faith in action, engage in ritual, and hear God's story (p. 25).

Conclusion on Child Faith Development

The potential to develop faith is inherent in all of us. Fowler (1981) spoke of the universality of faith, and in Scripture we can see that even the unborn have an awareness of the Divine presence and can respond to that awareness. If faith is inherent as research and Scripture suggest, then do children possess the ability to develop it? Can it be nurtured in a way that it grows and deepens even in young childhood and if it can, what are the conditions or the environment best suited for faith development to occur? Developmental psychologists Piaget and Erikson recognized that even the youngest child possessed a capacity for development and that experiential learning and engagement began very early. Piaget (2000) even noted the impact of pre-birth development.

Following in their work, Fowler (1981) recognized not just the cognitive and moral development but the faith development of children as well, with the capacity for faith development beginning in infancy. His research revealed identifiable and universal stages of faith. Although the sequential nature of his theory and the specific age-stage relationship has been questioned, his research identified that regardless of religious affiliation, or lack of it, children develop faith and in a somewhat predictable manner. Although there is a predictability to the sequence in which faith develops, Fowler (1981) recognized that the child's experiences impact the rate of development and whether the faith development is positive or negative, moving the child toward trust and hope or mistrust and despair. Like Cavalletti (2002) and Morgenthaler (2003), Fowler (1981) suggested the people in our environment impact our development because he recognized the social and interactive nature of faith.

Building on the work of Fowler, Westerhoff (2000) suggested that children even very young children – have the capacity for Christian faith development. He suggested that faith is a path where the child moves from experienced faith to affiliative faith then onto searching faith and finally arrives at owned faith. In the community of faith, there are individuals at every style or place on the path but going in the same direction. It is through engagement in this community that faith develops and grows.

Child faith development is possible and is possible in children when they are very young, even infants. The potential for faith development is universal and somewhat predictable in sequence. It is not dependent on a child's religious affiliations. The experiences of the child and the interactions with the individuals whom they have contact impact the development, either providing an environment where faith is nurtured in a positive way where they develop a sense of trust and hope or hampered, creating a sense of mistrust or despair. Developmental theorists from the fields of developmental psychology and Christian education concur that children develop faith, the development begins early, and it is influenced by the child's experiences and relationships.

A Biblical Perspective on Child Faith Development

"Sons are a heritage from the Lord, children a reward from him" (Psalm 127:3). Throughout Scripture, children are seen as blessings, rewards, signs of promise, a future hope, and representatives of the Kingdom of God (Barna, 2003). Scripture also addresses the potential children have for faith development and the means of that development, signified in the instructions given to parents and the body of believers in regard to child faith development and through the references to children in regard to their place in the Kingdom of God and their example to others.

God's Covenants and Child Faith Development

The Old Testament begins with the story of creation, which culminates with the creation of man and woman:

> So God created mankind in his own image, in the image of God he created them; male and female he created them. God blessed them and said to them, "Be fruitful and increase in number; fill the earth and subdue it". (Gen. 1:27-28, NIV)

God blessed Adam and Eve through the gift of children. "God blessed them Marked them as being under his especial protection, and gave them power to propagate and multiply their own kind on the earth" (Clarke, 1832, para. 61). Wesley (1765) in his commentary on Genesis 1:26-28 speaks of this blessing when he posited:

> Man was to be a creature different from all that had been hitherto made. Flesh and spirit, heaven and earth must be put together in him, and he must be allied to both worlds. And therefore God himself not only undertakes to make, but is pleased so to express himself, as if he called a council to consider of the making of him; Let us make man - The three persons of the Trinity, Father, Son, and Holy Ghost, consult about it, and concur in it; because man, when he was made, was to be dedicated and devoted to Father, Son, and Holy Ghost. That man was made in God's image, and after his likeness; two words to express the same thing. God's image upon man consists, in his nature, not that of his body, for God has not a body, but that of his soul.... That man was made male and female, and blessed with fruitfulness.... God having made them capable of transmitting the nature they had received, said to them, be fruitful, and multiply, and replenish the earth. Here he gave them, a large inheritance...a numerous lasting family to enjoy this inheritance; pronouncing a blessing upon them, in the virtue of which, their posterity should extend to the utmost corners of the earth, and continue to the utmost period of time. (Wesley, 1765, p. 5)

Wesley noted that the ability to multiply is a blessing of God attributed to Adam and Eve. Adam and Eve, who were created in the image of God, were given the ability to reproduce others who like Adam and Eve were "capable of transmitting the nature they had received" (Wesley, 1765, p. 5), which was the image of God, *Imago Dei*.

The first covenant God established with His people was the "Edenic Covenant" of Genesis one (Scofield, 1917, p. 3). God's covenant with Abraham in Genesis 15-17 was the second covenant God established with His people and also included the promise of future generations of children beginning with the miraculous birth of Abraham's son, Isaac (Scofield, 1917). Abraham and his wife were beyond the child-bearing years, but God promised Abraham: "Look up at the sky and count the stars—if indeed you can count them." Then he said to him, "So shall your offspring be" (Gen. 15:5, NIV). The promise of children was part of the blessing bestowed on Abraham, a sign of the fulfillment of the covenant.

Throughout the Old Testament and in the Jewish culture of the New Testament, children were valued as signs of the continuation of the covenant and the future promise they represented (Weber, 1979).

God's Commands and Child Faith Development

The reminder of the covenant fulfillment and the Israelites' role in that fulfillment is provided in Deuteronomy. Moses presents God's instructions on how the Israelites are to live, worship, and interact as a family in order to serve Him. Chapter six includes specific instructions on how the Israelites were to raise their children. The fulfillment of the covenant is connected to the Israelites' faithfulness in handing down their beliefs to their children and helping their children develop faith. Parents were to raise their children as active participants in the faith community (Richards, 1983). Deuteronomy six highlights the vital role parents and the entire faith community plays in the child's faith development:

> Love the Lord your God with all your heart and with all your soul and with all your strength. These commandments that I give you today are to be upon your hearts. Impress them on your children. Talk about them when you sit at home and when you walk along the road, when you lie down and when you get up. Tie them as symbols on your hands and bind them on your foreheads. Write them on the door-frames of your houses and on your gates. (Deut. 6:5-9, NIV)

These verses comprise the first portion of what is known in Hebrew as the *Shema* ("hear" in Hebrew) (Guzik, 2006). It is the Hebrew confession of faith that declares who God is and their duty to Him (Guzik, 2006). In the Jewish tradition, it was expected that these verses, along with the others that comprise the *Shema* (Deut. 6:4-9), would be recited in the morning and at night accentuating the priority of this command in their lives.

The verses provide a look at how God expected the Israelite families to function and how He anticipated their faith to be handed down. The first three verses in Deuteronomy six contain a command and a promise. The command is that the Israelites are to observe the "commands, decrees, and laws the Lord" (vs. 1-3) has given them through Moses. If they observe this command, then their children will also fear the Lord, they will enjoy long life, things will go well for them, and they will increase greatly (v. 3). The Israelites' faithfulness to the law would result in their children also being faithful to the law and enjoying the benefits or promises of the covenant.

The next section of verses outlines the exact command to follow - the command to love God with all your heart, soul, and strength. Jesus called this "the greatest commandment" (Matt. 22:37-38) which stands as a culmination of the law. Guzik (2006) in his commentary on Deuteronomy six posited:

> This great command must first be in our heart; then it must be communicated to our children, the topic of our conversation, and should always be in front of us - as near as our hand or our forehead, as ever before us as our door posts and gates. (para. 19)

The word for heart used in Deuteronomy 6:6 is *lebab* (Strong's #3824) and means the "inner part" or the "mind, soul, will, heart, understanding" (Blue Letter Bible, 1996-2012). It incorporates the heart but reaches broader than our English understanding to incorporate the mind with knowledge, thinking, and reflection. It also includes the conscience and the "seat of appetites" (Blue Letter Bible, 1996-2012). Koehler & Baumgartner (2001) suggested the understanding of *lebab* includes: "the organ; seat of vital force; one's inner self, seat of feeling and emotions; inclination, disposition; determination, courage; will, intention, attention, consideration, reason; mind in general and as a whole; conscience; inside, middle; the organized strength of life" (pp. 514-515). This robust definition identifies that broad perspective of the word heart referenced in Deuteronomy that goes far beyond our English understanding of "the organ". Because the heart was considered the center of the Israelites' being, this command suggested that their love for God was to be at the very center of who they were, the point from which everything else flowed – their thoughts, words, and actions. The suggestion here is that children are capable of more than just receiving instruction; their minds, hearts, and behaviors can be transformed through God's Word.

Not only was love for God to be at the center of what they are, they are to "impress" it on their children (Deut. 6:7). "Impress means to mark, brand, mold, impact, influence, teach, love, lead, and disciple our children. The mark that is made lasts for a lifetime and beyond" (Murphy, 2000, p. 36). Adam Clarke (1832), in his commentary on Deuteronomy 6, suggested:

> God's testimonies must be taught to our children, and the utmost diligence must be used to make them understand them. This is a most difficult task; and it requires much patience, much prudence, much judgment, and much piety in the parents, to enable them to do this good, this most important work, in the best and most effectual manner. (para. 11)

The Scripture suggests the diligence necessary to make an impression should occur when the families are sitting at home, walking outside, rising in the morning, going to bed at night, and when they are sitting down to eat a meal. Deuteronomy 6: 8-9 proposes the Lord's commands should be by tied to their hands, bound to their foreheads, and written over the doorframes and gates. In other words, the children should be impressed with the command to love God every moment of the day, hearing it as they go throughout their day, seeing it written everywhere they look, and having it lived out for them in their parents' lives (Joiner, 2009). Stonehouse (1998) posited: "The commands of God are taught best in the normal flow of life" (p. 25). The covenant requirements are to be internalized in such a way that they become integral to their every day life, conversations, and activities so that faith development in children occurs daily through common yet sacred experiences and godly relationships (Harper, 1990).

Later in Deuteronomy, we see that children are to be part of the community of faith: "Assemble the people – men, women and children, the foreigners residing in your land – so they can listen and learn to fear the Lord your God and follow carefully all the commands of this law" (Deut. 31:12). Worship of God and discipleship in His ways was provided for all ages with specific mention to children, giving a clear indication that children were a natural part of the church body and included in the assembling of believers. Richards (1983) posited this verse suggests: "Children are intended to be brought up as participants in a loving, holy community" (p. 18).

The idea of passing on a spiritual legacy is seen elsewhere in the Old Testament through festivals and rituals such as Passover and the Feast of Booths in which children played a role in both experiencing and remembering God's faithfulness (Pazmino, 2008). In Joshua chapter 4, the adults are instructed to build an altar of twelve stones to stand as a reminder to their children "to serve as a sign among you" (Joshua 4:6-7). The writer submitted that in the future children would ask the meaning of the stones and parents would have an opportunity to share the stories of God's faithfulness (Pazmino, 2008).

Conclusion of God's covenants and commands and child faith formation

Child faith formation in the Old Testament was seen as critical to the fulfillment of the covenant, children were a promise of God's covenant with Adam and Abraham but the fulfillment of the covenant relied on the Israelites passing faith in God onto their children. God provided instructions, through Moses, on the way the Israelite parents and faith community should life in order for their children to have faith. Deuteronomy six commands parents to be faithful to God's commands in their own lives and to impress God's commands on their children's hearts. This impression is to be made in the ebb and flow of daily living, talking about God, His commands, love and faithfulness when they rose in the morning, ate at their tables, walked along the roads, and laid down to bed at night. The children were to hear and see God's Word throughout their entire day. In addition, the community of faith was to include children in their festivals and commemorative celebrations and build monuments as reminds of God's faithfulness, using every opportunity to tell the children about God so they would also have faith.

Jesus' Teachings and Child Faith Development

Although the New Testament does not provide specific instructions on how to disciple or nurture faith development in children, similar to what is found in Deuteronomy six, the life and teachings of Jesus offer helpful insights (Stonehouse, 1998). Stonehouse (1998) suggested the incarnation is an example of the importance of children and Jesus' birth is a profound declaration of the importance of children and their role in the kingdom of God - "The Word became flesh and lived among us" (John 1:14). God chose to intersect humanity not as an adult, which was the expectation of many, but as a baby. As a child, Jesus grew and matured as all children do, experiencing the same things children experience - understanding perfectly all that childhood represents (Luke 2:52).

Jesus' interactions with children in light of His cultural context

The children mentioned in Jesus' interactions in the New Testament are not just metaphors; Jesus had genuine relationships with actual children (Weber, 1979). These relationships must be understood in light of the cultural context of Jesus' day in order to be fully appreciated. In the Greco-Roman culture of Jesus' day children were held in low esteem and had little or no worth (Gundry-Volf, 2001; Weber, 1979). Children were considered worthless and disposable. They were treated as slaves and pets or went unnoticed (Weber, 1979). In the Greco-Roman culture of Jesus' day, "people considered children fundamentally deficient and not yet human in the full sense" (Gundry-Volf. 2001,p. 32).

Jesus was also a Jew and lived not just in the Greco-Roman culture but in the Jewish culture as well. In the Jewish culture of Jesus' day children were more highly valued than in the Greco-Roman culture but primarily for their future potential and their representation of the fulfillment of God's covenant with Abraham (Weber, 1979). Although Jewish children were loved and cared for, they were still not seen in an entirely favorable light. Gundry-Volf (2001) posited that rabbinical literature contains references to children that address them as "deaf and dumb, weak-minded" (p. 35). In this perspective, they were seen more as "blank slates" in need of being written upon rather than having something to offer and being of value as children.

Jesus' interaction demonstrates children's worth

In the Greco-Roman Jewish culture Jesus engaged children in a way that suggests they are valuable, worthwhile, and deserving of time and attention. The first narrative of Jesus and children is found in three of the four gospels: Matthew 13:25, Mark 5:41-42, and Luke 8:54-55. It is the story of Jairus's daughter. Jesus lands on shore and is met by a large crowd of people. Within the crowd is Jairus, a leader in the Synagogue, with a request for Jesus to heal his daughter. Because of the crowd and the many others wanting Jesus' healing touch, Jesus is delayed. During the delay, Jairus is notified that his daughter has died. In spite of this news, Jesus went onto the home, took the girl by the hand, and called for her to get up (Mark 5:41). In this action, Jesus demonstrated that He considered the child worthy of His time and worthy of physical healing (Berryman, 2009, p. 12). Unlike Greco-Roman culture that would have seen the child as disposable or even Jewish culture that would have seen her potential value but not current value, Jesus demonstrated that even as a child she was worthy of His time, attention, and healing touch.

In another text, Jesus demonstrated a child's worth by offering them as an example of Kingdom living. During a conversation on the Kingdom of God, Jesus put a child in the middle of the disciples (Matthew 18:1-5, Mark 9:33-37, and Luke 9:46-48). In the Roman world children were called *erudire*, which meant "raw material" but in this text Jesus demonstrated their current value (Weber, 1979, p. 34). The disciples were having significant conversations about the Kingdom of God. In their Greco-Roman context it is conversation that would have been considered "adult" conversation in which children would have had nothing of significance to offer. However, in that moment Jesus refocused their attention on a child and suggests that the child has something worthwhile to teach them. The child represented the example of behavior – humility – the adult disciples were to emulate.

Parents and child faith development in Scripture

Matthew 19:13-15, Mark 10:13-16, and Luke 18:15-17 provide a glimpse into a parent or caregiver's role in their child's faith development. All three gospel accounts note that young children were being brought to Jesus and Luke's account specifically refers to "babies" (v. 15). The indication in all three accounts is that the children were too young to come on their own to Jesus and so they were brought to Him presumably either by a parent or a caregiver.

The parents brought their children to Jesus for Him to place His hands on them and bless them (Matthew 19:13, Mark 10:13, and Luke 18:15). Matthew Henry (1996) in his commentary on Matthew 19 suggested that those who brought the children demonstrated their own faith. There are other incidents in Scripture of people who brought their children to Jesus for healing, but these parents recognized the value of Jesus' blessing on the life of their children (Henry, 1996). The request for Jesus to lay hands on their children "intimates something of love and familiarity mixed with power and authority, and bespeaks an efficacy in the blessing" (Henry, 1996, p. 5). Gundry-Volf (2001) in speaking of Jesus' blessing of the children suggested:

> Children's vulnerability and powerlessness seem to lie at the heart of Jesus' extension of the reign of God to them. Children *qua children* in this sense – referring presumably to children within the covenant community are the *intended* recipients of the reign of God. It has come for them. (p. 38)

The narrative also includes the disciple's reaction to these young children being brought to Jesus and Jesus' reaction to that response. Jesus rebukes the disciples for their interference (Matthew 19:14). We cannot know if the disciples' reaction was an attempt to provide Jesus a rest from the crowds or if they doubted the priority of blessing children. What we do know is that Jesus called for the disciples to stop their interference and to "suffer" or allow the parents to bring their children to Him suggesting that in spite of the many people seeking His attention, his fatigue, or hurried schedule He found the children valuable enough to take the time to engage and bless them; children who were young enough to be held in the arms, even babies. Berryman (2009) suggested that children are bearers of God's presence and as demonstrated in this narrative Jesus is "violently clear about adults not distracting children from their true nature" (p. 18). Jesus not only rebukes the disciples for their interference, He tells them that Kingdom of God belongs to children (Mark 10:14).

The narrative of parents bringing their children to Jesus for a blessing found in Matthew 19:13-15, Mark 10:13-16, and Luke 18:15-17 provides an example of a parent's role in their child's faith formation; parents are to bring their children to Jesus. Jesus also demonstrates the value He placed on the children when he suspended His other ministry engagements and took the time to bless them and their value as Kingdom citizens. In addition, these verses highlight the severity of Jesus' reaction when well-intentioned adults interfere with children coming to Him (Stonehouse, 1998).

Child faith development and the church

Not only do Jesus' interactions with children offer insight into a parent's role in child faith development, but also His engagements with the disciples and other believers regarding children offer insight into the church, or body of believers', role in child faith development. In Mark 9:33-37 (also found in Matthew 18 and Luke 9) the disciples are disputing who will be the greatest in the Kingdom of God (vs. 34), and Jesus responds by offering a child as an example of Kingdom greatness (vs. 36-37). Jesus continued to instruct the disciples to not only look at the child as an example of Kingdom greatness but to welcome little children or show them hospitality. The Greek word used in verse 37 translated as receive or welcome is *déchomai* (Strong's 1209) and refers to the "hospitality to guests, which implies serving" (p. 43, Gundry-Volf, 2001). Kittel and Friedrich (as cited in Bromiley, 1985) suggested that "the first sense is 'to accept' and the second is 'to receive" in the sense 'to welcome, ' to extend hospitality'" (p. 146). They further suggested in receiving the child, because Christ came as a child, it is like receiving Him. Kittel and Friedrich (as cited in Bromiley, 1985) also noted that *déchomai* in a sense is the "equivalent to faith" in that "it brings out the fact that in relation to God we can only receive" (p. 147). Jesus is making a connection that greatness in the Kingdom is not only demonstrated in children, but it is linked to serving and loving children.

In this same narrative, Jesus offers a warning also related to children:

> If anyone causes one of these little ones—those who believe in me—to stumble, it would be better for them to have a large millstone hung around their neck and to be drowned in the depths of the sea. (Matthew 18:6, NIV)

People who would like to be considered great in the Kingdom, according to Mark 9, Matthew 18, and Luke 9, are to look to children as their example, welcome children through extending hospitality, and not cause any child to loose his or her faith.

An additional text that highlighted Jesus' interaction with children is in Matthew 21:14-16 where the children are in the temple and shouting "Hosanna to the Son of David". Gundry-Volf (2001) suggested, "Ignorant children can speak truly about Jesus because God has given them this insight and opened their mouths" (p. 47). The children had spiritual insight beyond that of the priests and scribes in this setting who could not see Jesus for who He truly was. "In the periscope on the children in the temple, literal children speak divinely revealed knowledge about Jesus" (Gundry-Volf, 2001, p. 47). This incident suggests that children can comprehend Jesus' true identity, they are able to offer praise to Him, and they demonstrate a Divine knowledge (Gundry-Volf, 2001). The church leaders were blind to the spiritual truths revealed in Jesus but the children in the temple were able to comprehend and respond.

Conclusion on Child Faith Development

A look at the biblical perspective on child faith development suggests that children are critical to the covenant between God and man, children are valuable to the community of faith, and parents and the faith community play a vital role in a child's faith development. Children represent the promise of the covenant from God (Gen. 1, 15-17), and the passing on of faith to the children is required for the covenant to be fulfilled (Deut. 6). God demonstrated a child's ability to receive spiritual instruction that results in faith development through His commands in Deuteronomy to parents and the community of faith. When parents and the faith community lived lives of faith as personal examples to the children and when they intentionally shared God's Word and His faithfulness with the children, the children would come to faith and grow in their knowledge and love of God.

Through His engagements with children, Jesus demonstrated that they have worth and they can serve as an example of faith. Jesus took the time to engage, heal, and bless children in spite of the adults who were demanding His attention (Matthew 19, Mark 10, and Luke 18). Jesus also suggested children are an example of Kingdom greatness (Matthew 18, Mark 9, and Luke 9) and children possess the Kingdom of God (Mark 10:14). The disciples attempted to define Kingdom greatness but Jesus suggested that greatness in the Kingdom of God could be found in a child. Jesus also called for the disciples and other believers to serve children (Matthew 18, Mark 9, and Luke 9) and submitted that when they welcome children, they were welcoming Him. In these narratives, Jesus also warned the disciples and other believers to be careful to not cause a child to stumble or falter in his or her faith (Matthew 18, Mark 9, and Luke 9). Life in the Kingdom required service to children and commitment to their faith development.

The New Testament narratives also provide a glimpse into a parent's role in their child's faith development; parents are to bring their children to Jesus (Matthew 19, Mark 10, and Luke 18). The parent's faith is exercised when they acknowledge the blessing Jesus can provide and when they bring their child to Jesus to receive that blessing. Not only are parents to bring their children to Jesus but also other adult believers are not to interfere.

> Children are not only subordinate but also sharers with adults in the life of faith; they are not only to be formed but also to be imitated; they are not only ignorant but also capable of receiving spiritual insight; they are not "just" children but representatives of Christ.... He invited the children to come to him not so that he might initiate them into the adult realm but so that they might receive what is properly theirs – the reign of God (Gundry-Volf, 2001, p. 60)

Jesus' interactions with children and His engagement with parents and believers in regard to children suggested that children are valuable to the Kingdom of

God, and it is the adult believer's responsibility to aid and support a child in their faith development, not hinder.

John Wesley's Theology of Childhood Faith and Education

John Wesley (1703-1791) is considered the founder of Methodism and an important theologian of his time whose educational and theological influence continues today (Heitzenrater, 2001). "Wesley must be credited with substantial contributions to English education in general and with helping to foster the later development of universal education in the nation" (Felton, 1997, para. 3). Towns (1970) suggested that Wesley was the only leader in eighteenth century England who demonstrated any real and practical interest in the education of children from all classes (p. 316). Heitzenrater (2001) posited of Wesley: "His views were very much in keeping with the prevailing English perspectives of the day, however, his interactions with and concerns for children indicate a much more compassionate view than one might expect" given the era in which he lived (p. 279).

18th Century England

In the early 1700's through the late 1700's England's population primary resided in the countryside with only about 15% living in towns and cities (Rack, 2002). While England in this era was predominantly a land of villages and agriculture, the pre-industrial rise of the textile industry and merchant-manufacturers introduced new employment opportunities and a new labor force, which included children. The shift away from village and rural life and the increase in urban populations was beginning. Rack (2002) in reference to Defoe's (1724-6), *Tour through the Whole Island of Great Britain,* suggested that this era "gloried in the thought of their [the children's] busy fingers being kept out of mischief" (p. 4). Children as young as four and five years old spent six days a week working in the mines and factories (Maddix, 2001). Infant mortality rates were extremely high, the number of children born out of wedlock was greater than those born in marriage, and alcoholism was rampant even with children (Maddix, 2001). McKenna (1999) in speaking of the English culture in the eighteenth century suggested:

> Broken homes, child abuse, alcohol addictions, lewd theaters, disenfranchised minorities, and impoverished lower classes. These were the symptoms of a society in which government was corrupt, law was biased, churches were irrelevant, and commerce was greedy. (As cited in Maddix, 2001, p. 57)

The class system was active, but the "people were more inclined to use the term 'rank' and associate with people of like trade, region, family, political party, or religion" (Rack, 2002, p. 5). A social hierarchy was in place but there was some room for movement up and down, which created a climate where people used any means to move up the economic ladder. In an effort to maintain power, the ruling class achieved consensus through "influence, persuasion and religion, though ultimately by force if necessary" (Porter as cited in Rack, 2002, p. 7). In summary of the era, Rack (2002) posited:

> The century was punctuated by riots against: high corn prices; low wages in the textile industry; turnpike roads; Papists, Methodists and Dissenters; and sometimes against political violations of the 'rights of freeborn Englishmen'. (p. 6)

This period was also marked by a shift in the way people thought about children. Up until the eighteen century, children were seen as "little adults", but according to Philippe Aries (as cited in Willhauck, 1992), the eighteenth century was a period of discovery of childhood, unfortunately this discovery did not have positive results for children. Instead it resulted in "hierarchical, tyrannical concept of the family that deprived and repressed children and led to their mistreatment and abuse" (Willhauck, 1992, p. 67). Sandford Fleming (1993) as cited in Willhauck (1992), criticized the Puritans for their attitude toward children and concluded that during this period of history prior to Horace Bushnell's (1861) work there was no place in the church for children, suggesting that Puritanism saw children as totally depraved "evil and dirty as opposed to converted adults who were washed cleaned" (p. 74). Bushnell's work, in contrast, urged parents to nurture the grace of God that he suggested was already present in their children from birth. The theological idea of "total depravity" resulted in a very negative viewpoint of children and opened them up for repression and abuse. The concept of "total depravity" was the theological notion that children were born evil at birth with a tendency to corruption. The thought was that this "bent" could only be corrected through stern and rigorous discipline (Willhauck, 1992).

Into this context, Jean-Jacques Rousseau (1712-1778) offered an alternative perspective and changed the way people thought about the nature of the child (Willhauck, 1992). Rousseau suggested that children are born with an innate goodness, which stood in stark contrast to the theological perspective that children are "born in sin". "Rousseau proposed that human beings are not born in a state of depravity but are contaminated as a result of living in a morally corrupt society" (May, Posterski, Stonehouse, & Cannell, 2005, p. 100).

John Locke (1632-1704) was also a philosopher of this era who offered yet another perspective on the nature of children that had a significant impact (Willhauck, 1992). His view of education was presented in *An Essay Concerning Human Understanding* (1690). In it he suggested that the mind was a "tabula rasa" or "blank slate" that acquired ideas through the use of senses (Willhauck, 1992). In this philosophy, children were born neither totally corrupt nor were they born innately good. Children were blank slates to be written on, impressed, and molded. He stressed experience and suggested that humans had a great capacity for knowledge. Because of a child's ability and need to acquire knowledge, Locke emphasized that training should begin early. He also stressed positive enforcement and proposed that children should be shielded from negative experiences and influences (Willhauck, 1992).

Through the introduction of these various philosophies on children, people began to pay attention to children and their education. May et al. (2005) suggested that during this time Christian leaders recognized the predicament of the disadvantaged poor children who worked in the factories six days a week. In response to this situation and the problems that arose from it, Robert Raikes (1736-1811) began the Sunday school. It was designed for poor children who had no opportunity for education and who were provided no structure on their only non-working day (May et al., 2005). The children were free on Sundays and Raikes used this opportunity to offer a time of structure and taught them to read using the scriptures. In the eighteenth century, the idea of Sunday school spread throughout England (May et al., 2005).

Wesley's Childhood

In a study on the religious and educational methods of John Wesley in the spiritual formation of children, it is critical to not only understand the culture in England in the eighteenth century, but it is also important to acknowledge Wesley's personal childhood, as it had significant impact on his philosophy and practice. Wesley was born June 17, 1703 in North Lincolnshire England at the Epworth rectory. He was the fifteenth of nineteen children born to Samuel and Susannah Wesley, of which only ten survived infancy (Fitzgerald, 1925; Tyerman, 1872; Willhauck, 1992). His father, Samuel, was an Anglican clergyman and considered a biblical scholar who also had an interest in poetry (Maddix, 2009; Rack, 2002). Samuel made sure his children received a liberal arts education that included instruction in the classical languages (Maddix, 2009). Unfortunately, he was a poor manager of the family's finances and landed himself in debtor's prison (Fitzgerald, 1925; Maddix, 2009; Tyerman, 1872). He was also considered a dissenter who took issue on several matters with the Church of England and the government. This was not well received by his parishioners in the rural village of Epworth and was the cause of great tension within the rectory (Rack, 2002).

Wesley's mother, Susanna, is the one who demonstrated the greatest influence on John and the one whom he fashioned his educational practices after. This was due in part because of Wesley's father's absence while in debtor's prison and his work both at the rectory and in politics. Prince (1926) suggested: "He [John Wesley] derived more of his convictions concerning the education of children from his cultured and pious mother, Mrs. Susanna Wesley, than from any other source" (p. 104). Southey, as cited in Fitzgerald (1925) suggested of her: "She was an admirable woman of highly improved mind, and of a strong and masculine understanding, an obedient wife, an exemplary mother, a fervent Christian" (p. 8).

Susanna saw education as incorporating discipline and reading. The discipline was used to break the will of the child, which she termed "curing the diseases of nature" (Maddix, 2009, p. 3). In addition to the strong discipline, she held Bible classes for her children and led them daily in singing the Psalms. Susanna was noted as saying: "Scripture, reason, and experience jointly testify that, in as much as the corruption of nature is earlier than our instructions can be, we should take all pains and care to counteract this corruption as early as possible" (Maddix, 2009, p. 3). To this end, her children were taught to read at age five and learned the alphabet in a day. The next day they were taught to spell and read one line of a verse, practicing it until it was perfect (Fitzgerald, 1925). Susanna taught even her daughters to read, which was not common in her day. She insisted that they learn to read before they learned to do work, and she required that they spend at least equal amounts of time each day reading as they spent doing chores (Prince, 1926).

Tyerman (1872) suggested that Susanna's methods were based on unique principles that included to "fear the rod" by age one and only cry in soft tones, eat only three meals a day, recite the Lord's Prayer morning and night, and spend six hours a day on school work. She wrote books to meet the spiritual needs of her children because she found none available that met her "severe requirements" (Towns, 1970, p. 319).

Susanna detailed her methods of child rearing and education in a letter she wrote to John, which appeared in his writing, *The Way of Education* (1872) (Maddix, 2009). She articulated the following principles in the letter:

Cowardice and fear of punishment often leads a child to lying. Therefore, if a child confesses their guilt, they would not be beaten;

No sinful action should ever go unpunished;

No child should ever be beaten twice for the same fault;

Every single act of obedience should always be commended and rewarded;

Show respect for personal property;

Promises are to be strictly observed;

No girl will be taught to work until she can read very well. (Towns, 1970, p. 319)

Fitchett (1908) shared the story of a fire that destroyed the Epworth home, when John was six. "No child of six could ever forget an incident like that. It burned itself upon the boy's imagination" (Fitchett, 1908, p. 33). The whole house was lost, but all eight children that were at home and the parents were miraculously saved. John was the last to be rescued. He was thought lost in the fire, when he was seen looking out his third floor bedroom window as the flames engulfed the entire home. Neighbors stood on each other's shoulders in order to reach the boy and rescue him. Wesley later referred to himself as a "brand plucked from the burning" (Fitchett, 1908; Willhauck, 1992). Wesley's mother, Susanna, was impacted by the fire and realized that she needed to spend more intentional time with each of her children. She made a habit of conversing one evening a week with each child; Thursdays were devoted to John (Towns, 1970). "She looked upon all of her children as talents committed to her in trust by God, it was her principle intention to save their souls" (Towns, 1970, p. 318).

In addition to his father's sentence to debtor prison, the unrest in the rectory due to his parent's penchant for dissenting opinions, and his near-death experience during the rectory fire at age six, Wesley survived small pox at age eight and was sent away to school by age eleven (Fitchett, 1908; Willhauck, 1992). Charterhouse School's culture was very different from that of his home. It lacked any form of significant discipline. Students were allowed to be disrespectful to each other and their instructors. Bullying was rampant and a young John Wesley found himself the object of much ridicule (Fitzgerald, 1925). Southey suggested Wesley ate nothing but bread during his stay because the other students robbed him daily of his meat (Fitzgerald, 1925). At Charterhouse, he became a favorite of the master because of "his quietness, regularity, and application" (Fitzgerald, 1925, p. 21).

From Charterhouse School Wesley attended Christ Church in 1720 and studied to take holy orders and become an Anglican priest. In 1725 he was ordained a priest in the Church of England and in 1726 became a fellow and tutor at Oxford. It was during his time at Oxford that Wesley began to keep a journal and continued that practice throughout his life (Willhauck, 1992). Many of his personal notes listed in these journals give us insights into Wesley's teachings, methods, and beliefs.

All of the experiences young Wesley encountered impacted his perspective on childhood and his methods in religious education of children.

> The peculiar care which was thus taken of his religious education, the habitual and fervent piety of both his parents, and his own surprising preservation, at an age when he was perfectly capable of remembering all the circumstances, combined to foster in the child that disposition, which afterwards developed itself with such force, and produced such important effects. (Fitzgerald, 1925, pp. 14-15)

Wesley's Influencers

Although Wesley had a tremendous influence on the educational perspectives and ultimately the educational system in England and beyond, he is not credited for developing any new theories of education (Prince, 1926). Some of his views would have been called eccentric in his era, perhaps even today. However, he did hold to some enlightened views about the capacity of children and saw that there was potential for faith development beyond what their ability and age would suggest, a rather radical belief in his day (Maddix, 2001; Prince, 1926; Willhauck, 1992). Prince (1926) posited that ultimately, however, Wesley was a "child of the eighteenth century and shared its blindness to the meaning of childhood" (p. 103). He read Rousseau's *Emile* but wrote in his journal that it was "a most empty, silly, injudicious thing" (as cited in Prince, 1926, p. 103). He was, however, powerfully influenced by Locke's *Essay on the Human Understanding*, and included it as a required text at Kingswood school (Maddix, 2001). While Wesley did not fully hold to the concept that children are born "blank", he did appreciate Locke's perspective on the ways children learn and the amount of learning they do in a short period of time. "Wesley, like Locke, believed in a spiritual 'sixth sense' within individuals to discern the spiritual world" (Maddix, 2001, p. 62).

Prince (1926) also suggested that Wesley's journal revealed that he had read and admired Milton's (1644) *Tractate on Education*,[1] noting his "indebtedness to it" (p. 103). Wesley read Rousseau, Locke, Milton and others as a student of education. While there were elements of some he accepted and much he discounted, their influence should be noted. Stonehouse (2004) suggested that Wesley was a student of the philosophers of his day and studied what they said about children and education.

In addition to his readings of these contemporary philosophers, the Moravians, whom he encountered on his voyage to the state of Georgia in America in 1735, also influenced Wesley. He was impressed with the "piety, simplicity, and the equanimity" of the Moravian shipmates (Fitzgerald, 1925, p. 55). In the midst of severe storms at sea, Wesley saw the calm assurance of his Moravian shipmates. When they were asked how they remained calm, they replied that they did not fear death (Collins, 1999). Collins (1999) suggested that Wesley saw the connection between "the powers of nature and the state of one's soul, between earthly tempests and spiritual distress" (p. 41). He was intrigued with their belief in immediate salvation and the assurance of their faith. He was amazed at the way they could sing in the midst of the storms (Maddix, 2001). Spangenberg, one of the Moravian leaders in America, asked Wesley if he knew that he was saved. Wesley noted later in a journal that while he responded "I do" he was not confident (as cited in Collins, 1999, p. 42). This conversation revealed to Wesley that he lacked the witness of the Holy Spirit that the Moravians possessed. The intrigue into the Moravian confidence and assurance of their salvation prompted Wesley to study the German language and the Moravians in particular (Collins, 1999). Wesley became friends with several of the Moravian leaders who introduced him to the writings of John Amos Comenius (1592-1670). Comenius is considered a Moravian pioneer in education during the seventeenth century. He wrote, *Didactica Magna*, which is translated to *The Great Didactic* or *The Great Art of Teaching*. In it Comenius took what was then a radical perspective that children were born with an innate desire for knowledge and goodness (Sadler, n.d.). Comenius taught that instruction should move beyond just rote memorization, children were capable of moral and spiritual development, and education should include understanding (Maddix, 2001). Some of Comenius' influence can be seen in Wesley's writings (Prince, 1926).

At Oxford, Wesley read Thomas a' Kempis' *The Imitation of Christ* and Jeremy Taylor's *Rules of Holy Living and Dying*. From these books he wrestled with two doctrines that distinguished his ministry: "God's love to *all*, and the privilege of living in a state of conscious salvation" or assurance (Tyerman, 1872, p. 35). He also noted in his Journals reading William Law's (1729) *A Serious Call to a Devout and Holy Life*. In his book, Law (1729) calls a person to live a life of complete devotion and surrender to God. Willhauck (1992) cited Tuttle (1961) when she suggested that Wesley learned the importance of holiness and humility

---

[1]Milton, English poet and author of *Paradise Lost,* wrote a letter to Puritan educator, Samuel Hartlib that outlined his personal view of education.

from these readings. In his journals, Wesley noted that he discussed these works with his mother who was also impressed by the authors' "pursuit of perfection and holiness" (as cited in Willhauck, 1992, p. 31).

While at Oxford, his brother, Charles, asked him to be the leader of a group of individuals who met for the purpose of prayer, Bible study, and theological reflection called the "Holy Club" (Willhauck, 1992). The group members were called, "Methodists", by those outside of the society because of their strict discipline and methods of study (Willhauck, 1992). Although it was not a name Wesley chose for himself or his group, "Methodist" is the name that continued with him throughout his ministry and to today.

Of all the influences on Wesley's perspective of religious education, however, his mother, Susannah, was the strongest. "He derived more of his convictions concerning the education of children from his cultured and pious mother, Mrs. Susanna Wesley, than from any other source" (Prince, 1926, p. 104). The importance of starting religious education early, her rigorous methods, strict discipline, personalized approach, appreciation for the uniqueness of childhood, and ultimately her true appreciation for her children can all be seen in Wesley's approach (Prince, 1926, p. 105). Susannah believed in strong discipline and home education. She held Bible classes for her children and led them in singing the Psalms. Although a strong disciplinarian and a belief in a strict schedule, she was not unreasonable but sought to avoid the brutal punishment that was typical of that day (Willhauck, 1992). She demonstrated practices suggested in writings by Locke and Milton (Heitzenrater, 2001). Her emphasis on breaking a child's will, for example, is found in Locke's writings. Willhauck (1992) suggested, "Susannah appeared more liberal and enlightened" than most in her era (p. 54). She educated her daughters alongside her sons, which was a rather progressive concept, understood the importance of physical activity, did not practice severe punishment, and awarded obedience (Heitzenrater, 2001; Willhauck, 1992).

Not only did Susannah influence Wesley through her consistent and purposeful religious education of John and his siblings, but she and John also maintained a close relationship throughout his adult years, as evidenced by the numerous letters exchanged and his journal references. Wesley sought her council on numerous topics and pursued her advice when he was establishing the methods for children's spiritual formation in the Methodist movement (Heitzenrater, 2001). He asked specifically for her to write of her child-rearing and educational principles. She responded with a lengthy and detailed letter in 1732, which he included in his published *Journal* and numerous excerpts of the letter appeared in his sermons (Prince, 1926).

John Wesley's Theology

"Theology is a discipline whose business is to help us reflect on our Christian faith in ways that makes a difference in our lives" (Grider, 1994, p. 19). According to this definition, John Wesley would be considered a theologian. The goal of his preaching, teaching, and writing was to help people discover the Christian faith and embrace it in such a way that they experienced the power of faith in their lives. However, John Wesley is not considered a systematic theologian but rather a "practical theologian" (Outler, 1964; Harper, 2003). A systematic theologian addresses biblical topics one at a time while a practical theologian seeks to apply biblical truth to every day life (Outler, 1964, 1985). Osmer (2008) suggested that practical theology answers four key questions: What is going on? Why is this going on? What ought to be going on? How might we respond? (p. 4). According to Osmer's (2008) definition, Wesley would be considered a practical theologian. He sought to discover why humanity behaved the way it did, what was possible for humanity, and how we could achieve that possibility.

In looking at Wesley's theology, Harper (2003) suggested that he was "primarily concerned about developing a faith that worked in every day living" (p. 14). Outler (1964) called Wesley's theology "folk theology" because it was what Wesley described as: "Plain words for plain people" (p. vii). It was a theology to be lived. Although he was incredibly well read and was a student of other theologians and church history (Maddox & Vickers, 2010) Wesley's theology flowed from his personal experiences (Heitzenrater, 1995).

It is a theology from personal experience and intended for practical living that was communicated through preaching (Hynson, 1985). Through looking at the sum total of his message, provided through sermons, journals, and other writings, a clearer image of Wesley's theological framework emerges, rather than through a precise, systematic, single writing (Outler, 1985). Thorsen (2005) suggested: "In writing about practical ministry, he [Wesley] wrote a great deal about theology" (p. 33). Hynson (1985) posited that the Methodist movement throughout its history has been dominated by preaching rather than systematic theology, beginning with Wesley himself. "The preaching would build squarely upon biblical grounds, developing an experiential accent" (Hynson, 1985, p. 20). Wesley practiced biblical preaching that communicated a practical theology for living a life of faith. Harper (2003) concluded: "The fact that his theology is biblical gives it a timelessness; the fact that it is confirmed by experience gives it an authenticity that theology in the ivory tower sometimes lacks" (p. 14).

Wesley did not set out to start a new denomination or to write a new theology. Heitzenrater (1995) suggested Wesley's goal was not "to develop a band of faithful 'Wesleyans,' but of faithful Christians" (p. 322). Wesley was an Anglican priest until his death and saw the Methodist movement as a "renewal movement" within the greater Anglican Church rather than a break from the Anglican Church. He encouraged the Methodists to continue participation in the Anglican Church in order to hear the Word preached and to partake in the sacraments (Jackson, 1872, 8:280). Wesley's issue was not with the institution of the Anglican Church but with some of the ways they interpreted Scripture. "He felt that the eighteenth-century Anglicanism had drifted from important scriptural norms, and he viewed the Methodist movement as simply describing 'the plain, old religion of the Church of England'" (Harper, 2003, p. 15). Methodism was an attempt to bring a biblical focus and centrality back to the Anglican movement rather than divide it.

Ultimately, Wesley's desire was to discover "the way to heaven". In the preface to his "Standard Sermons" Wesley wrote:

> I want to know one thing, the way to heaven: how to land safe on that happy shore. God Himself has condescended to teach the way; for this very end He came from heaven. He hath written it down in a book! Oh give me that book! (Burwash, 1988, p. XX).

His theology provides the roadmap to a powerful relationship with God. Harper (2003) suggested:

> Wesley was a man of intense discipline and engaged daily in devotional living. But his discipline was never an end to itself but was a means to a 'vital relationship with God and the resulting power that comes from that relationship'. (p. 14)

Wesley's theology developed out of his own context, through his personal experience with God and his own spiritual struggles and growth (Thorsen, 2005). It is a theology of a pilgrimage – Wesley's own pilgrimage and one that we can all relate to "interpreted in relation to the story of God's grace and in relation to our experience of this grace as we move through the days of our lives" (Harper, 2003, p. 11).

Wesley's view of humanity

John Wesley's theology is called a theology of love, God's love for us and our love in response for Him. "Wesley believed that God loved man as the supreme object of his creation. …Wesley believed in the original righteousness of man" (Harper, 2003, p. 22). Collins (2007) posited that for Wesley "the *imago Dei* must be understood in a relational way as the very emblem of holy love" (p. 51). "God is love, accordingly man at his creation was full of love" (Wesley as cited in Collins, 2007, p. 51).

Wesley provided a glimpse into his view of human nature in his sermons, "The Image of God" (Sermon #141 as cited in Outler, 2010) and "Free Grace" (Sermon #110, as cited in Outler, 2010). He spoke of this "original righteousness" in both of those sermons and cited Genesis 1:26, 27 in suggesting that man was made in the "image and likeness of God". Wesley described the image of God as being moral, political, and natural (Collins, 2007; Maddix, 2001). The political image is man's call for dominion over creation. The natural image was the ability to understand and choose, and the moral image was the "original righteousness" or holiness. "Adam resembled God in that he was just, perceived truth, his soul was filled with love, and he had a perfect will and unerring understanding" (Willhauck, 1992, p. 104).

> 'And God', the three-one God, 'said, Let us make man in our image, after our likeness. So God created man in His own image, in the image of God created He him' (Gen. 1, 26-27): not barely in his natural image, a picture of His own immortality; a spiritual being, endued with understanding, freedom of will, and various affections; nor merely in his political image, the governor of this lower world, having 'dominion over the fishes of the sea, and over all the earth': but chiefly is his moral

image; which, according to the Apostle, is 'righteousness and true holiness'. (Wesley as cited in Jackson, 1872, Vol. 6, p. 66)

In keeping with his inclination toward practical theology, Wesley asked that if man was created with original righteousness then what was the source of the imperfections or flaws that we all experience in ourselves and see evident in others. Wesley suggested in the sermon "Image of God" and the text above that part of the *Imago Dei* or Image of God was the natural image that included the ability to choose, or free will. Collins (2007) suggested that the elements of the natural image include understanding, will, and liberty: "In Wesley's view, however, it is the gift of understanding or reason that plays such an ordering role" (p. 53). "Wesley explained that freedom is an essential part of that image of God" and the fall is man's exercise of his free will (Willhauck, 1992, p. 104). Maddox and Vickers (2010) posited:

> Although Wesley believed that humans were created in the moral image of God, so that holiness, justice, and goodness reigned in their hearts, he also taught that humans were made in the natural image of God. By this he meant that God created individuals with a liberty to choose whether they would go on obeying the moral law within or whether they would reject it. (p. 194)

In his sermon, "The General Deliverance", Wesley posited:

> Now 'man was made in the image of God'…He was, after the likeness of his Creator, endued with understanding, a capacity of apprehending whatever objects were brought before it, and of judging concerning them. He was endued with a will, exerting itself in various affections and passions; and lastly, with liberty, or freedom of choice, without which all the rest would have been in vain, and he would have been no more capable of serving his Creator than a piece of earth or marble. He would have been as incapable of vice or virtue as any part of the inanimate creation. In these…the natural image of God consisted. (Jackson, 1872, Vol. 2, pp. 438-439)

In answer to his own question, Wesley concluded that the original righteousness was lost when Adam exercised his free will and disobeyed God's law, when humanity chose to reject the moral law within. Collins (2007) asserted that Wesley attributed the source of original sin to Satan: "for Adam and Eve, external temptation resulted in unbelief, a lack of trust in God, a break in the relations of holy love" (p. 58). Maddox and Vickers (2010) asserted that Adam's decision to reject God's moral law was a rejection of "the tie that bound him to God, namely, a heart characterized by love and holiness" (p. 195). Wesley wrote:

> It was not long before man rebelled against God, and by breaking this glorious law well nigh effaced it out of his heart; 'the eyes of his understanding' being darkened in the same measure as his soul was 'alienated from the life of God'. (Jackson, 1872, Vol. 2, p. 7)

This resulting inability to grasp the presence of God, Maddox and Vickers (2010) suggested also resulted in the loss of freedom to know, obey, and to love God (p. 195). The result was bondage and the mark of original sin on all of humanity (Maddox & Vickers, 2010; Willhauck, 1992). Collins (2007) suggested that there were both physical and spiritual effects to Adam and Eve's sin. Physically, death became a reality and the body became "corruptible and mortal" (p. 59). Wesley asserted that likewise, spiritual death was experienced: "For the moment he [Adam] tasted that fruit he died. His soul died, was separated from God" (Wesley as cited in Collins, 2007, p. 60). Wesley taught that when Adam and Eve sinned, original righteousness – defined as "title to God's favour and communion with God" (as cited in Collins, 2007, p. 60) - was lost.

It is critical to understand in Wesleyan theology that original righteousness must come first or precede original sin. Humanity had to begin with the unblemished image of God otherwise, as Harper (2003) suggested, "salvation makes no sense" (p. 22). The word redemption is defined in the 1828 Webster dictionary as: "to repurchase, deliverance, liberation" (definition #1, 2, 4) and "In theology, the purchase of God's favor by the death and sufferings of Christ; the ransom or deliverance of sinners from the bondage of sin and the penalties of God's violated law by the atonement of Christ" (definition #6). What is incredible is that God's response to humanity's rejection of Him was not to despise humanity but to love humanity and seek a way to redeem it, deliver it, repurchase it (Maddox & Vickers, 2010). A love described by songwriter George Matheson (1842-1906) as a "love that wilt not let me go" (Fettke, 1978, #606).

Wesley's view of sin

To understand Wesley's theology, you have to realize his view of sin. For Wesley, sin had a "twofold nature" that included our sinful actions and our sinful nature (Wilson, 2000, p. 75). Our sinful nature is the original sin that we inherited because of the Fall. Sinful actions are what Wesley described as "every voluntary breach of the law of love" (Telford, 1931, 6:327). Harper (2003) suggested that Wesley went on to suggest that "sin is not something that sneaks up on you; it arises out of you" (p. 23). Wesley submitted that we are not sinners because we commit acts of sin, but rather we commit acts of sin because we are sinners (Harper, 2003; Wilson, 2000). Original sin or the sin inherited from the Fall creates in humanity an inclination or pull toward intentional sin, the voluntary breach of God's law.

Original sin is described in Genesis 6:5: "The Lord saw how great the wickedness of the human race had become on the earth, and that every inclination of the thoughts of the human heart was only evil all the time" (NIV). Charles Wesley, John's brother, in his hymn "Love Divine, All Loves Excelling" called it a "bent to sinning" (Fettke, 1978, #648). Wesley saw sin as a disease and the result was sickness. "Wesley saw the effect of Adam's disobedience as disease of body and soul. And saw that all children inherit Adam's sin" (Willhauck, 1992, p. 109). Harper (2003) posited that sin hits all the way to the root or depth of humanity. He went on to suggest: "If sin were a thing, we might find some way to rid ourselves of it or cut it off, but because it is an infection of our humanity, the only option is transformation" (pp. 25-26). We sin because we are sinners. We are sinners because of the Fall, our moral nature has been damaged and we have lost fellowship with the Father. Because we are sinners, we fall into sin or willful acts of disobedience. We posses a sinful nature, which leads to acts of sin. It is a twofold view of sin that requires a twofold work of grace (Wilson, 2000).

Because of the Fall, original righteousness was replaced by original sin, original sin that creates within humanity a "bent to sin". It is important to understand Wesley's view of the depth of human sin, in order to fully grasp the presence of God's love. "The whole shape of Wesley's theology is an 'order of salvation' – the story of how grace operates to overcome sin and to restore original righteousness" (Harper, 2003, p. 23). Collins (2007) suggested that for Wesley "the effects of the fall are so devastating that respons-ability along the way of salvation is not a possibility at all unless God first of all sovereignly restores humanity through prevenient grace to some measure of the relation previously enjoyed" (p. 73). Stonehouse (2004) reminded: "Even though sin infects everyone from birth, Wesley believed in the power of grace that was also at work from the beginning of life" (p. 135).

Wesley view of grace

"Here is a trustworthy saying that deserves full acceptance: Christ Jesus came into the world to save sinners—of whom I am the worst" (I Timothy 1:15, NIV). Paul's letter to Timothy simply states God's loving response to the sin of humanity, Jesus Christ. "God took the initiative. He sought us. He provided the healing medicine" (Harper, 2003, p. 28). Jesus is our atonement. He made possible our reconciliation to God. "The final word for Wesley was salvation not damnation" (Willhauck, 1992, p. 113). Wesley's view of human nature was pessimistic but his view of grace was incredibly optimistic (Don Dayton, personal correspondence, February 28, 2012). Willhauck (1992) posited: "All are impacted by original sin, but grace has more effect" (p. 123). Wesley never described sin and its impact on humanity without speaking of the cure (Harper, 2003). Wesley saw sin as a disease at the root of humanity, but Jesus Christ was the source of deliverance and healing.

"The way to heaven is a journey in which we respond to grace all along the way" (Harper, 2003, p. 33). Grace is present at the moment of conception and continues to be active and present throughout our lifetime (Stonehouse, 2004; Willhauck, 1992). Not only is grace present throughout our entire life, it is available to all. For Wesley, grace was universal (Benzie, 2003; Harper, 2003; Outler, 1964) and free. "Simply put, the grace of the Most High is free; it is an utter gift of a God of holy love" (Collins, 2007, p. 160). May et al. (2005) suggested grace is defined as "an undeserved blessing bestowed by God, God's activity that flows from his nature" (p. 53). In speaking of grace, Wesley wrote:

> All the blessings which God hath bestowed upon man are of His mere grace, bounty, or favor; His free, undeserved favor; favor altogether undeserved; man having no claim to the least of His mercies. It was free grace that 'formed man of the dust of the ground, and breathed into him a living soul,' and stamped on that soul the

image of God, and 'put all things under his feet.' The same free grace continues to us, at this day, life, and breath, and all things. Or there is nothing we are, or have, or do, which can deserve the least thing at God's hand. (As cited in Telford, 1995, p. 81)

"God does not leave humanity at the mercy of sin, for in the heart of every person God plants prevenient (or as Wesley called it, preventing) grace" (Stonehouse, 2004, p. 135). Prevenient grace is the beginning of God's work in our lives to redeem us, and it is the first step in Wesley's order of salvation (*ordus salutis*).

Salvation begins with what is usually termed (and very properly) *preventing grace*; including the first wish to please God, the first dawn of light concerning his will, and the first slight transient conviction of having sinned against him. All these imply some tendency toward life; some degree of salvation; the beginning of a deliverance from a blind, unfeeling heart, quite insensible of God and the things of God. Salvation is carried on by *convincing grace*, usually in Scripture termed *repentance;* which brings a larger measure of self-knowledge, and a farther deliverance from the heart of stone. Afterwards we experience the proper Christian salvation; whereby, "through grace," we "are saved by faith;" consisting of those two grand branches, justification and sanctification. By justification we are saved from the guilt of sin, and restored to the favour of God; by sanctification we are saved from the power and root of sin, and restored to the image of God. All experience, as well as Scripture, shows this salvation to be both instantaneous and gradual. It begins the moment we are justified, in the holy, humble, gentle, patient love of God and man. It gradually increases from that moment, as "a grain of mustard-seed, which, at first, is the least of all seeds," but afterwards puts forth large branches, and becomes a great tree; till, in another instant, the heart is cleansed, from all sin, and filled with pure love to God and man. But even that love increases more and more, till we "grow up in all things into him that is our Head;" till we attain "the measure of the stature of the fullness of Christ." (Wesley, as cited in Jackson, 1872, *Vol.* 8, p. 509)

Prevenient grace

Prevenient grace is "the first faint desire for Him" (Grider, 1994, p. 351). It is what Robert Coles (1990) described as that questioning in every child for meaning, purpose, and if there is more. It is what Sophia Cavalletti (2002) described as the natural tendency to seek for God, and it is what Stonehouse (2004) described as God's initiative that makes it possible for us to respond to His "seeking love" (p. 136). Wesley described prevenient grace as "all the drawings of the Father" – a person's first desire for God, and instances of "light" or awareness of God's will (Stonehouse, 2004, p. 136). John in his Gospel described it as "the true light that gives light to everyone" (1:9, NIV).

Prevenient grace is extended to everyone and from the moment of life. Wesley reiterated the words of 2 Peter 3:9 that God was "not willing that any should to perish, but that all should come to repentance" (KJV). It is the presence of prevenient grace in the life of a child that enables them to have openness to God and an ability to develop faith at such an early age. Wesley saw this lived out in the lives of the children he engaged and believed that their faith was authentic and legitimate (Heitzenrater, 2001; Stonehouse, 2004; Willhauck, 1992). He also understood that prevenient grace needed to be nurtured and the child-like responsiveness to God's love could be lost through neglect or mistreatment (May et al., 2005; Stonehouse, 2004).

It is the grace of God "that operates before our experience of conversion" before "we give conscious thought to God or to our need of him" (Harper, 2003, p. 34). It is the love of God at work while we, as Romans 5:8 suggested, "were still sinners". Wesley believed that it is God who makes the first move toward us:

> It is not possible for men to do anything well till God raises them from the dead. ...It is impossible for us to come out of our sins, yea, or to make the least motion toward it, till he who hath all power in heaven and earth call our dead souls into life. (Jackson, 1872, Vol. 6, p. 511)

Collins (2007) suggested Wesley's writings identify five benefits of prevenient grace to humanity. The first benefit is "that a basic knowledge of God...is revealed to all" through the work of the Holy Spirit (p. 77). "All people have at least some understanding of God" through the work of prevenient grace (p. 77). Wesley also suggested that through prevenient grace God "reinscribes" a measure of the moral law on the hearts of humanity enabling them to comprehend God's holy law (p. 77). The third benefit of prevenient grace Wesley identified was the internal judge or conscience (Collins, 2007). In his sermon "On Conscience" Wesley noted of conscience: "it is not *natural*; but a supernatural gift of God, above all his natural endowments" (Jackson, 1872, Vol. 7, p. 187). The fourth benefit is "a measure of free will graciously restored" (Collins, 2007, p. 78) and the final benefit is a restraint on "human wickedness" (Collins, 2007, p. 80).

In addition to the restorative work of prevenient grace, prevenient grace is also "leading grace" "which entails *the calling* of sinners to salvation through these restored faculties" (Collins, 2007, p. 80). It creates an initial awareness of God's will and a realization that we have missed His will. It also brings a desire to please God, and it is prevenient grace that gives us the ability to choose God. "The message of prevenient grace is a message of hope. There is a way out of the human dilemma. There is a way out of our problems. God has made the way!" (Harper, 2003, p. 38). "We love him because he first loved us" (I John 4:19, KJV).

Saving grace

"Salvation is carried on by *convincing grace*, usually in Scripture termed *repentance;* which brings a larger measure of self-knowledge, and a farther deliverance from the heart of stone" (Wesley, as cited in Jackson, 1872, Vol. 8, p. 509). Prevenient grace is the beginning of the journey into salvation; salvation is not found in prevenient grace alone, but we must go on in grace into "convincing" or saving grace. Prevenient grace is the work of the Holy Spirit to restore humanity's ability to respond may be rejected. "The natural man is unholy and loves to be so; and therefore 'resists the Holy Ghost'" (as cited in Collins, 2007, p. 123). Convincing grace is the work of the Holy Spirit to lead, teach, illumine, and actively woo the spiritually dull or sleeping (Collins, 2007, p. 123). Convincing grace is also referred to as saving grace or justifying grace (Maddix, 2001; Stonehouse, 2004; Willhauck, 1992). Convincing grace, as Wesley reminded, is referred in Scripture as repentance. In his sermon, "The Way to the Kingdom", Wesley called repentance: "A change of heart from all sin to all holiness" (Jackson, 1872, Vol. 5, p. 82).

In salvation, God works through grace as suggested by Paul in Ephesians 2:8: "For it is by grace you have been saved" (NIV). Our response to that grace, or the human side of the salvation equation, is faith. "For it is by grace you have been saved, through faith" (Ephesians 2:8, NIV). Maddox and Vickers (2010) suggested:

> Wesley saw faith as 'personal trust in the atoning sacrifice of Christ for one's sins (*fiducia)* as opposed to 'faith as an intellectual assent (*assensus)*. Wesley believed that the faith that justified and therefore saved was...faith as *fiducia* or personal trust. (p. 196)

Maddox and Vickers (2010) went on to suggest that this faith is available to everyone but is conditioned on "repentance, trusting faith, and obedience" (p. 199).

Wesley proposed that this convincing or saving grace "brings a larger measure of self-knowledge" (Jackson, 1872, Vol. 8, p. 509). This knowledge is awareness that we are separated from God, that we are sinners. Wesley called for the people to "know thyself to be a sinner" (Jackson, 1872, Vol. 5, p. 82). This knowledge leads to conviction. Conviction is the feeling of sadness at the realization of the true condition of our hearts (Harper, 2003). "Conviction is a positive experience, although it may be unpleasant. It is the 'warning light of the soul' that lets us know that all is *not* well" (Harper, 2003, p. 45).

The third movement in repentance is what Wesley called a "change of our minds" (Jackson, 1872, Vol. 5, p. 83). The story Jesus told of the prodigal son is an illustration of this change of mind. The son, who chose to think of his father as dead, asked for his inheritance, left home, and squandered his wealth. When he found himself eating the food for pigs, scripture says he "came to himself" (Luke 15:17, KJV) and decided to go home. He had a change of mind, and his change of mind led to action; he went home. He turned from his life in the pigpen to life in his father's home.

Repentance leads to "trusting faith" or belief (Maddox & Vickers, 2010). Belief that possesses a confidence in God's forgiveness, and assurance that Jesus is the Son of God and your personal Lord and Savior. Wesley's doctrine of assurance was born out of his personal life experience. He shares in his journal his "Aldersgate experience" on May 24, 1738:

> In the evening, I went very unwillingly to a society in Aldersgate Street, where one was reading Luther's preface to the Epistle to the Romans. About a quarter before nine, while he was describing the change, which God works in the heart through faith in Christ, I felt my heart strangely warmed. I felt I did trust in Christ, Christ alone for salvation; and an assurance was given me that He had taken away my

sins, even mine, and saved me from the law of sin and death. (As cited in Rack, 2002, p. 144)

Wesley was criticized for teaching the doctrine of assurance, and it alienated him from some of his Anglican friends (Heitzenrater, 1995). However, Wesley believed the doctrine of assurance was described in Scripture, and he personally experienced it at Aldersgate. Maddix (2001) suggested that Wesley's key verse was Romans 8:16: "The Spirit itself beareth witness with our spirit, that we are the children of God" (KJV). Wilson (2011) in his sermon, "The Assurance of the Believer" posited:

> This is one of the great contributions of Wesley to the Christian world, this doctrine of assurance, this revitalizing of the teaching that, "God's Spirit bears witness with ours' that we are sons of God," - a teaching that was largely forgotten during the Middle Ages. A teaching to which Luther only gave partial salute and the Reformation gave secondary emphasis at best. The Council of Trent condemned this teaching of assurance and the Church of England in the 18th century banished it. Added to that, religious experience in England in the 18th century had fallen so low that the majority of people who did make a profession of being a Christian would have expressed their belief according to a popular line of that day which went something like this: 'If you seek it you won't find it; if you find it you won't know it; If you know it you haven't got it; If you've got it, you can't lose it; if you lose it, you never had it.'

> Yet, against that background, when everything was against such a doctrine, Wesley and his Methodists emerged with a doctrine of assurance, a witness of the Spirit teaching, and gave it primary importance. (p. 2)

Like prevenient grace, saving grace is a step in the journey to salvation; it too is not the final step. Wesley referred to repentance as "the porch of religion. Justification was the door. All the rooms in the house were facets of our sanctification" (Harper, 2003, p. 47). Wesley suggested we would spend a lifetime exploring and discovering all the rooms in our "house". Saving grace deals with our sinful actions, but we must go on to have our sinful nature also redeemed.

Justification and new birth

Justification is what God does for us – it is the forgiveness and pardon of sin (Collins, 2007). Grider (2002) posited of justification: "He [God] absolves us of the guilt that our acts of sin have caused. He declares us to be guiltless" (p. 362). Wesley believed that justification by faith is the heart of the gospel (Maddix, 2001). God extends convincing grace, our response is through faith, and God's response to our faith is to justify us or pardon us from our sins. God provides grace that is powerful enough to forgive us from all of our past sins and to strengthen us in any future temptation that might lead to sin. "Wesley saw no moment or event more powerful than the grace of God" (Harper, 2003, p. 59).

The result of justification is what Wesley referred to as "new birth" (Jackson, 1872, Vol. 6, p. 71). Justification is what God does for us and new birth is what

God does in us (Harper, 2003; Maddix, 2001, Wilson, 2000). Jesus told Nicodemus: "You must be born again" (Jn. 3:7, NIV). Not a physical new birth but a spiritual new birth (John 3:6). Paul described it in second Corinthians: "For if a man belongs to Christ, he is a new person. The old life is gone. New life has begun" (5:17, NLT). In his sermon, "New Birth", Wesley described it as: "that great change which God works in the soul when he brings it into life; when he raises it from the death of sin to the life of righteousness" (Jackson, 1872, Vol. 6, p. 71). In this new birth, we experience reconciliation or a restored relationship with God. The moral image is renewed. In his sermon, "The New Birth" (Sermon #45), Wesley emphasized the importance of justification and new birth:

> If any doctrines within the whole compass of Christianity may be properly termed fundamental, they are doubtless these two, the doctrine of justification, and that of the new birth: The former relating to that great work which God does for us, in forgiving our sins; the latter, to the great work which God does in us, in renewing our fallen nature. In order of time, neither of these is before the other; in the moment we are justified by the grace of God, through the redemption that is in Jesus, we are also "born of the Spirit;" but in order of thinking, as it is termed, justification precedes the new birth. We first conceive his wrath to be turned away, and then his Spirit to work in our hearts. (Burwash, 1988, p. 459)

Harper (2003) summarized:

> [Saving faith] begins in repentance and climaxes in belief. In repentance we turn from a life without Christ; in belief we complete the turn by moving to embrace Christ's way as our way. And in that process, salvation is begun. Beyond the initial commitment there will be a lifetime of development and progress. (p. 50)

Salvation is the first work of grace in which our sinful actions are forgiven, but we must go on in grace and have our sinful nature addressed. This is the second work of grace, or sanctification (Grider, 2002; Wilson, 2000).

Sanctifying grace

The "lifetime of development and progress" is the work of sanctifying grace. Wesley said that at conversion, "inward and outward holiness begins" (Jackson, 1872, Vol. 6, pp. 71-72). Wesley called Methodists to "holiness of heart and life" (Jackson, 1872, Vol. 6, p. 3) and defined holiness in his sermon "On the Wedding Garment" (Sermon #120): "In a word, holiness is having 'the mind that was in Christ,' and the 'walking as Christ walked (Jackson, 1872, Vol. 2, p. 545).

Sanctification is also termed "Christian perfection" (Grider, 2002; Harper, 2003; Maddix, 2001). Wesley viewed the doctrine of Christian perfection or sanctification as the "Grand Depositum" of Methodism (Collins, 1999; Grider, 2002; Maddix, 2001). In a letter to Robert Carr Brackenbury, Wesley wrote that the doctrine of sanctification "is the grand depositum which God has lodged with the people called Methodists; and for the sake of propagating this chiefly, He appears to have raised us up" (Jackson, 1872, Vol.13, p.154). Wilson (2000) offered a definition of sanctification in the Wesleyan tradition when he posited: "Sanctification always implies a separation, a renouncing of what we know to be contrary to the life we have received in Christ" (p. 77). There is initial sanctification and entire sanctification. Initial is the work that God begins in our life through saving grace, setting us apart and making us righteous. Entire sanctification is the result of sanctifying grace and addresses the sinful nature.

> Sin has a twofold nature – our sinful actions and our sinful nature. God first deals with our sinful actions at salvation. In this sense, all believers are sanctified initially. God also deals with our sin nature in this life through a second work of grace called entire sanctification. There is then a cleansing of the sanctified believer that continues until our physical death. This ongoing exercise of God's grace upon our lives and character is progressive sanctification. (Wilson, 2000, p. 75)

Wesley taught that our sin nature could be changed, that we did not need to be bound or held captive to sin. First Thessalonians 5:23 says: "May God himself, the God of peace, sanctify you through and through. May your whole spirit, soul, and body be kept blameless at the coming of our Lord Jesus Christ" (NIV). Wesley believed that the power of the cross not only conquered the power of our sin actions, but offered power over our sin nature (Wilson, 2000). "The essence of the New Testament is that the power of the blood of Christ not only deals with the sins we commit, but with the sin nature" (Wilson, 2000, p. 79). Maddix (2001) suggested Wesley's twofold view of grace and repentance is "an important hallmark in Wesley's doctrine of salvation" (p. 87). He went on to clarify the difference: "The first repentance is repentance of actual sin, and the later is repentance of inbred sin or carnal nature" (p. 87). Maddix (2001) also offered Wesley's description of inbred sin as "any sinful temper, passion, or affection such as pride, self-will, love of the world, in any kind of degree, any disposition contrary to the mind of Christ" (p. 87). For Wesley, entire sanctification or Christian perfection is the work of grace that deals with the power of sin, while justification addresses the guilt of sin (Maddix, 2001).

Wesley never suggested that this second work of grace or entire sanctification was the final phase but reminded the Methodists that they must continue to experience growth; sanctification is instantaneous and it is progressive. Wesley emphasized the growth before and following in the sermon, "Christian Perfection":

> By perfection I mean the humble, gentle, patient love for God and our neighbor, ruling our tempers, words, and actions. I do not include an impossibility of falling from it, either in part or in the whole. As to the manner, I believe this perfection is always wrought in the soul by a simple act of faith; consequently in an instant. But I believe a gradual work, both preceding and following that instant. (As cited in Telford, 1995, p. 141)

Wesley also wrote in *A Plain Account of Christian Perfection:* "There is indeed, an instantaneous, as well as a gradual, work of God in His children" (Parker, 1966, p. 30).

Christian perfection is an instant cleansing and a process of growth that includes radical dependence on Jesus Christ, victory over sin, equipping for ministry, and growth (Harper, 2003). Radical dependence on Jesus Christ means a full surrender to His Lordship that is continuous and deepening. Wesley believed that we could experience victory over sin. God's grace is more powerful than any temptation that we may face, and His love is more reaching than any sin we could commit. While Wesley held a very high value on grace, he never eliminated the person's free will to choose.

Christian perfection does not include spiritual infallibility, as Wesley made it clear that Christians still possess the ability to choose and therefore have the potential to sin. In addition, Christian perfection does not make one immune from difficulties or problems, in fact I Peter 5:8 would strongly suggest otherwise (Harper, 2003). Finally, it does not mean perfect in our knowledge, Wesley clarified that in his book, *A Plain Account of Christian Perfection* (Parker, 1966). Harper (2003) posited: "Wesley constantly maintained that Christian perfection is for real people in this life" (p. 82).

Harper (2003) reminded that Christian perfection is the process of being "set apart" for ministry and service to God. The expectation with Christian perfection is service. Wesley expected those who had experienced Christian perfection to: "do all the good you can to the bodies and souls of men" (Jackson, 1872, Vol. 11, p. 432).

Wesley (as cited in Parker, 1966) summarized the life of perfection: "In every thought of our hearts, in every word of our tongues, in every work of our hands, to 'show forth His praise, who hath called us out of darkness into His marvelous light'" (p. 37). Christian perfection "is simply loving God with all the heart" and having in us "the mind in us which was also in Christ Jesus" (Parker, 1966, p. 37).

The means of grace

To experience growth in grace, Wesley suggested, Christians must practice the "means of grace". In his sermon, "The Means of Grace", Wesley defined means of grace as: "outward signs, words, or actions, ordained of God, and appointed for this end – to be the ordinary channels whereby he conveys to men, preventing, justifying, or sanctifying grace" (Burwash, 1988, p. 152). Maddox and Vickers (2010) posited: "Wesley taught that believers were actively to participate in the outward means that Christ had ordained 'for conveying the grace into the souls of men' (p. 203). Wesley also taught that those seeking salvation should practice the means of grace, through which they could experience converting or saving grace.

Wesley divided the means of grace into "instituted" or those ordained by Christ, and "prudential" or those ordained by the church (Maddix, 2001, p. 86). Wesley taught five instituted means of grace or channels ordained by God and practiced as an example by Jesus Christ (Harper, 2003; Maddix, 2001). These included prayer, which Wesley called "the grand means of drawing near to God" (Jackson, 1872, Vol. 5, p. 186). It came first on his list of means of grace and included both public and private prayer. Grider (2002) suggested that prayer also included meditation: "In prayer, we speak and God listens; in meditation, *God* speaks and *we* listen" (p. 515). Searching the Scripture was Wesley's second instituted means of grace. He referenced the power of the Bible and called himself "a man of one book" (Outler, 1985). His desire was for Methodists to be "Bible

Christians" (Harper, 2003, p. 72). Fasting was a means of grace that demonstrated a commitment to spending time alone with God and the willingness to share, to a minor degree, in His suffering. Group fellowship or corporate worship, which Wesley called "conference" (Jackson, 1872, Vol. 5, p. 186), was another means of grace.

Wesley developed a small group structure for discipleship that included the formation of societies, bands, and classes for the purpose of instruction, growth, and accountability through the instituted means of grace "conference". Societies were the largest group, similar to today's congregation, and met for the purpose of presenting biblical truth in an easy to understand manner (Blevins & Maddix, 2010). Class meetings focused on a believer's behavior and bands "facilitated emotional change" (Blevins & Maddix, 2010, p. 246). "Wesley believed every Christian needed a small, intimate place to share the concerns of his or her life and to find commonality of experience and intensity of support" (Harper, 2003, p. 74).

The final instituted means of grace was the Lord's Supper. For Wesley the experience was more than symbolic, "it was an opportunity to actually commune with Christ and receive the grace of God" (Harper, 2003, p. 73). In his sermon, "Means of Grace", Wesley asked:

> Is not the eating of that bread, and the drinking of that cup, the outward, visible means, whereby God conveys into our souls all that spiritual grace, that righteousness, and peace, and joy in the Holy Ghost, which were purchased by the body of Christ once broken and the blood of Christ once shed for us? Let all, therefore, who truly desire the grace of God, eat of that bread, and drink of that cup. (Jackson, 1872, Vol. 5, p. 195)

Grider (2002) posited Wesley taught that the Lord's Supper should be received frequently and referenced I Corinthians 11:25 as support of that belief. His journals indicated that he personally received communion every four to five days (Grider, 2002).

The prudential means of grace were also considered "channels" through which the grace of God could flow and included "doing no harm, doing all you can, and attending the private and public worship of God" (as cited in Maddix, 2001, p. 86). Grider (2002) referred to these as "indirect means of grace" (p. 524) and suggested they included: discipline, service, and suffering. Wesley had a high expectation on acts of service by the Methodists, and, although he believed that salvation came through faith not works, works were an expectation of a life of faith. Maddox and Vickers (2010) suggested that Wesley did not just tell his people to "go about doing good", but he provided the means: "he set about organizing goodness" (p. 209). Wesley practiced personal discipline with his body, his words, his attitudes, and with his material possessions. In his sermon, "The Sum of Money", Wesley suggested: "Gain all you can...save all you can...give all you can" (Jackson, 1872, Vol. 6, p. 135). He did not expect more of the Methodists than he was willing to do himself.

Maddix (2001) posited that Wesley expected members in the Methodist societies to practice these means of grace. Wesley suggested that Christian growth was about faithfulness, faithfulness lived out in its practice of the means of grace.

Through the means of grace, Harper (2003) suggested: "In that divine/human encounter, the connection is made, grace flows into our lives, and we are led to greater conformity to the image of Christ" (p. 76). The purpose of the means of grace was spiritual growth, the journey to holiness and happiness (Maddox & Vickers, 2010).

Maddox and Vickers (2010) shared an incident that occurred near the end of Wesley's life and referenced his sermon, "The Unity of the Divine Being":

> The elderly John Wesley, just a few months shy of his eighty-sixth birthday, asked a crowd of Irish Methodists gathered in Dublin a classic question from an unlikely source – the Calvinist Westminster Confession: 'For what end did God create man?' One simple answer, Wesley insisted, should be 'inculcated upon every human creature: You are made to be happy in God.' Wesley then tendered advice to parents: 'Even when a child first begins to speak or to run alone, a good parent follows behind saying, many times each day, He made *you*; and he made you to be happy in him; and nothing else can make you happy'. (p. 207)

Wesleyan quadrilateral

The Wesleyan Quadrilateral is a phrase that John Wesley himself did not use, but was coined by Albert Outler in his 1964 text, "John Wesley" (Schultz, n.d.). Although Wesley never used the phrase, Schultz (n.d.) suggested that the four elements play a critical role in Wesley's theological reflections. Outler (1985) posited: "It was intended as a metaphor for a four element syndrome, including the four-fold guidelines of authority in Wesley's theological method" (p. 11). The four elements that can be seen throughout Wesley's writings as critical to the process of forming his theology are scripture, tradition, reason, and experience (Aukerman, 2004; Maddix, 2001;Outler, 1964, 1985; Schultz, n.d.).

Although a quadrilateral, it is important to note that for Wesley the four were not seen as equal (Schultz, n.d.), but scripture was unique and preeminent "and yet illuminated by collective Christian wisdom, critical reason, and heart experience" (Outler, 1985). Aukerman (2004) referred to the four elements as "complementary yet unequal sources of doctrinal and theological authority" (p. 1). Maddix (2001) cited Gunter (1997) when he posited:

> The quadrilateral is a methodology of theological reflection that places Scripture as the rule and as authoritative in a way that should not be ascribed to other components. Tradition, reason, and experience then form an interpretative or hermeneutical spiral in which the dialogical relationship among all the components continually enables the church to understand and apply scripture more accurately and effectively. (p. 79)

Outler (1985) suggested that Wesley's writings and sermons were so dependent on scripture that "the Bible was truly his second language" (p. 13). Wesley urged for scripture to be understood in light of the whole of scripture and with the understanding that the Holy Spirit is the one who brings illumination and understanding. Therefore, scripture should be approached prayerfully (Outler, 1985). He believed that if we placed ourselves in a close relationship with scripture, that

God would speak to us through it (Thorsen, 2005). Wesley saw scripture as foundational to theological inquiry and should be considered as the first or primary source for Christians who are seeking truth (Aukerman, 2004).

Christian tradition is the second element in the quadrilateral. "For Wesley, the Christian tradition was more than a curiosity or a source for illustrative material. It was a living spring of Christian insight" (Outler, 1985, p. 14). Wesley refers to tradition as "ancient church and historically developed ecclesiastical traditions" (Aukerman, 2004, p. 2) that were intended to bring clarity to scripture's theological principles. Thorsen (2005) posited that Wesley considered Christian tradition vital in the interpretation of scripture, especially with difficult, dark, or intricate passages.

Reason was the third piece of the quadrilateral. Aukerman (2004) provided Wesley's definition of reason, which was "reflecting on experience" (p. 3). It is important to note that in this definition Wesley did not refer to reason as scientific inquiry (Thorsen, 2005). He did see reason as part of our *Imago Dei* that remained. Schultz (n.d.) cited Wesley when he noted: "Reason is a unique gift from God, and God graciously continues to permit reason to function in significant ways even though sin reigns in the moral character of people" (p. 4). It should be noted, however, that Wesley did not see reason as sufficient to be used on its own without the foundation of Scripture (Aukerman, 2004; Thorsen, 2005).

Experience was the final piece of Wesley's theological method, which Outler (1985) called a "genius addition" to what was the original "Anglican triad" (p. 10). Outler (1985) went on to suggest that Wesley's Aldersgate experience and the conversion experiences he witnessed in others, were the motivating factor for Wesley amending the original triad to include experience. Wesley's was a "heart religion" and the experience piece reflected that (Aukerman, 2004). "To study the bible and not experience the power of relationship with God was a troubling thought for Wesley" (Cosby, 2001, as cited in Aukerman, 2004, p. 3). Thorsen (2005) reminded that Wesley was the first to incorporate "the experiential dimension of the Christian faith" into his theological worldview (p. 129) and that Wesley believed scriptural truth was confirmed in experience (p. 130). Like reason, however, Wesley also believed that experience was not to be used independently to establish theological ideals. Schultz (n.d.) suggested Wesley cautioned, "experience is only reliable as in harmony with the other three" (p. 4). Outler (1985) offered a summation to the fourth element in the Wesleyan quadrilateral:

> The 'experience of grace' is indeed deeply inward, but it is not a merely subjective 'religious affection.' It is an objective encounter of something not ourselves and not our own. It is in an inward assurance of an objective reality: God's unmerited favor, his pardoning mercy, an awareness of the Spirit's prevenient action in mediating the grace of our Lord Jesus Christ to the believer. (p. 15)

In his sermon, "The Witness of the Spirit", Wesley summarized the Christian experience:

> Words cannot express what the children of God experience. But perhaps one might say (desiring any who are taught of God to soften or strengthen the expression)

that "the testimony of the Spirit" is an inward impression on the soul, whereby the Spirit of God directly witnesses to my spirit that I am a child of God, that Jesus Christ hath loved me and given Himself for me – and that all my sins are blotted out and that I, even I, am reconciled to God. (Jackson, Vol. 1, p. 7)

Wesley offers a theological method that was unique to him in which Scripture was preeminent, and tradition, reason, and Christian experience were interactive aids in the interpretation of the word of God in Scripture" (Outler, 1985, p. 9). Outler (1985) went on to suggest of the quadrilateral:

The quadrilateral requires of a theologian no more than what he or she might reasonably be held accountable for: which is to say, a familiarity with Scripture that is both critical and faithful; plus, an acquaintance with the wisdom of the Christian past; plus, a taste for logical analysis as something more than a debater's weapon; plus a vital, inward faith that is upheld by the assurance of grace and its prospective triumphs, in this life. (p. 17)

Conclusion on Wesley's Theology

Outler (1964) called Wesley: "A creative theologian practically involved in the application of his doctrine in the renewal of the church" (p. 119). Wesley's desire was for the Anglican Church to find renewal through a focus on scripture in light of tradition and reason and experienced through heart transformation. A heart transformation made possible through the work of the Holy Spirit in response to God's grace that resulted in radical love for God and our neighbors. A love that could not help but be lived out in faithful service to God and our fellow man.

"Wesley's primary theological themes include his doctrine of original sin, prevenient grace, free will, justification, sanctification or holiness, and the Holy Spirit" (Maddix, 2001, p. 89). The four graces of God that Wesley addressed were prevenient, or preventing grace, which is at work in the life of the believer before they are aware of their sinfulness or need of God; convincing or justifying faith convicts the sinner and puts them in the position to seek forgiveness where they experience justification and new birth; and sanctifying grace deals with the individual's sin nature and is the work of the Holy Spirit to draw them closer to God and become more like Christ. Sanctifying grace leads the believer to Christian perfection, or perfect love for God and neighbor. The final grace Wesley suggested believers experience is glorifying grace, which is experienced at death and is the culmination of a life of faith, the restoration of the natural body, and entrance into Christ's presence.

John Wesley himself shows us the fullness of grace in his own spiritual journey. In his early life history, we see the gift of grace shaping him for one of the most effective and far-reaching ministries in human history – leading him to God, saving him in Christ, and sanctifying him through the Holy Spirit. (McKenna, 1999, p. 26)

Heitzenrater (1995) suggested that Wesley's sermon, "The Scripture Way of Salvation," provides the mature look at Wesley's theology and a single look at his soteriology, or doctrine of salvation. Heitzenrater (1995) offered this in way of summation of that message:

> Prevenient grace leads to conviction of sin, which brings repentance and fruits meet for repentance. Faith is the only condition directly necessary for God's forgiveness or justification, which is the work of Christ that results in a *relative* change in the individual, who is then 'accounted as righteous.' At the same time, regeneration (new birth) takes place. It is the beginning of sanctification, the work of the Holy Spirit that brings a *real* change in the individual, who thereby begins this process of actually becoming righteous or holy. As the believer goes on 'from grace to grace,' entire sanctification is the goal – 'full salvation from all our sins.' This Christian perfection, or perfect love, 'takes up the whole capacity of the soul' and thereby excludes all sin. (p. 220)

Wesley described what a Methodist should look like - what the result of this kind of salvation experience would be in the life of the believer in his sermon, "The Character of a Methodist":

> What, then, is the mark? Who is a Methodist, according to your own account? I answer: A Methodist is one who has 'the love of God shed abroad in his heart by the Holy Ghost given unto him'; one who 'loves the Lord his God with all his heart, and with al his soul, and with all his mind, and with all his strength.' God is the joy of his heart, and the desire of his soul; which is constantly crying out, 'Whom have I in heaven but thee? And there is none upon earth that I desire beside Thee! My God and my all! Thou art the strength of my heart, and my portion forever!' (Telford, 1995, p. 137)

Wesley lived the life he called Methodists to live and offered a message of hope with his final words: "The best of all is, God is with us!" (As cited in Collins, 1999, p. 158).

Wesley's View of Children

"By nature children of wrath, by grace children of God and the latter stronger than the former" (Wesley, as cited in Willhauck, 1992, p. 167). Wesley was a student of children, creating opportunities for observation and investing time in the study of their development and philosophical perspectives of his day (Willhauck, 1992). He came to see childhood as "significant for the human journey to God" (Willhauck, 1992, p. 266). Specifically, Willhauck (1992) posited, "Wesley studied children and their religious formation. He looked for an answer to the question of what came after infant baptism" (p. 167). Wesley, in keeping with Anglican tradition, practiced infant baptism. However, he saw infant baptism as a beginning toward a life of salvation but was not adequate alone for salvation (Willhauck, 1992). "Wesley firmly believed that a genuine and deeply religious life is possible in childhood" (Towns, 1970, p. 323). He believed that children could be recipients of God's grace and did not need to rush through childhood into adulthood in order to attain access to God's grace or the ability to pursue faith (Willhauck, 1992). Wesley held a high view of children and saw the season of childhood as valuable (Stonehouse, 2004).

"Wesley firmly believed that a genuine and deeply religious life is possible in childhood" (Prince, 1926, p. 82). Not only was it possible, but also he believed that the impact of a religious life on one's nature could be seen in very young children and could be cultivated very early (Prince, 1926). Wesley suggested that religious instruction should begin as soon as a child could reason (Heitzenrater, 2001; Stonehouse, 2004; Willhauck, 1992). Given that his mother expected her children by the age of one to understand the expectations on their sleep habits and crying responses, it is reasonable to assume Wesley would hold that the ability to reason occurs at least by the age of one (Prince, 1926). The incidents he shared of children who demonstrated a profound religious experience as early as two and three, also support Wesley's belief that the ability to reason occurs early, often earlier than most expect (Prince, 1926). Wesley reported numerous engagements with children from age two to seventeen in his journals. Willhauck (1992) posited:

> Wesley witnessed the religious precociousness of some children, and he believed the religious potential of some made it possible and preferable for all children to be encouraged to intense religious experiences of salvation. He wrote often and on the importance of teaching children. (p. 173)

One such example is from Wesley's journal of June 28, 1746:

> I inquired more particularly of Mrs. Nowens, concerning her little son. She said, he appeared to have a continual fear of God, and an awful sense of his presence; that he frequently went to prayers by himself, and prayed for his father, and many others by name; that he had an exceeding great tenderness of conscience, being sensible of the least sin, and crying and refusing to be comforted, when he thought he had in anything displeased God...When the Holy Ghost teaches, is there any delay in learning? This child was then just three years old! (As cited in Prince, 1926, p. 83)

Prince (1926) suggested Wesley's writings of the interactions he had with children demonstrated that "Wesley believed it was possible for very young children to be religious" (p. 85). Rishell (1902) concurred: "Wesley was a firm believer in the possibility of a deeply religious life in childhood of very tender years" (as cited in Willhauck, 1992, p. 167). Prince (1926) asserted that the reason Wesley accepted the possibility that children could possess a "mature religious consciousness...lay in his doctrine of grace, that when the Spirit is the Teacher there is no delay of learning" (p. 85).

Wesley (1872), in speaking of his experiences with these children and others that he had an opportunity to engage through his travels and ministry, suggested: "The experiences of many of them [children] match and in several instances surpass the experiences of their elders" (p. 75). In his journal, Wesley also shared numerous accounts of older children impacted by the revivals. Heitzenrater (2001) cited excerpts from Wesley's (1779) journal where he shared of his experience in Lowestoft, "where there had been a great awakening, especially among youth and children; several of whom, between twelve and sixteen years of age, are a pattern to all about them" (p. 296).

Willhauck (1992) suggested, "Wesley noted with envy and amazement the holiness and experience of even very young children that revealed their deep spirituality and closeness with God" (p. 266). Through his observations he came to believe that a child could experience all of the graces of God that adults could experience: prevenient, saving, sanctifying, and glorifying. A child could "repent, have faith, be reborn, and look forward to eternal salvation" (Willhauck, 1992, p. 266). Heitzenrater (2001) posited: "On the basis of firsthand observation and personal experience, Wesley presumes that a child can know God and thus be truly happy" (p. 295). Wesley did not just read about children, he studied them first hand and allowed himself to engage children through conversation and observation. Through these experiences, he came to appreciate the faith potential in children. He also began to see children in a way that most in his era did not, as developmentally different from adults but with incredible cognitive and spiritual potential. "He was a man attentive to children, sensitive to their needs, who demonstrated a tenderness and love through his active engagement" (Stonehouse, 2004, p. 133).

Wesley and the Religious Education of Children

"Make Christians, my dear, make Christians!" Wesley's told Mary Bishop, a director of a school for girls (Jackson, 1872, as cited in Anthony, 2011, p. 206). Wesley was convinced that Christians were made not born and that diligent and intentional instruction was critical in the process of Christian formation. He believed that all people, regardless of age, should be taught God's truth and provided instruction on how to live a holy life. Anthony (2011) posited that this belief caused Wesley to highly value the spiritual formation of children and to emphasize their training both in the home and at church. "Wesley was primarily concerned about the salvation of children. He believed that one of the primary means to this end was through religious education" (Maddix, 2001, p. 4).

Maddix (2001) posited: "Wesley's religious education of children follows logically from his theology" (p. 4). He believed in humanity's depravity from birth and that, as a result of sin, both children and adults lack God's natural and moral image. The result of this damaged image of God in mankind brings alienation from God (Maddix, 2001). His goal then, was to help people restore their relationship with God.

Towns (1970) suggested Wesley believed that religion and education should go hand in hand. Wesley (1872) wrote: "The grand end of education is to cure the diseases of human nature" (Vol. II, p. 310). He went to say: "The bias of nature is the wrong way; education is designed to set it right" (Vol. II, p. 459).

> Wesley was deeply convinced that the making of Christians was a process, which required devoted and diligent teaching. While never neglecting nor disparaging the importance of preaching, worship and sacraments, the Christian disciplines, Wesley recognized that persons of all ages had to be taught what Christians believe and how Christians live. Such teaching was to be both a cognitive process of didactic learning and a formative process of spiritual nurturing. (Felton, 1997, para. 2)

"He viewed education as a means of grace – as an instrument through which the Holy Spirit worked" (Felton, 1997, para. 11). Prince (1926) suggested that religious education, although critical for the Christian, did not replace conversion, rather education and conversion "supplement each other" (p. 99). "True religion ought to be instilled into children as early as possible, that education is designed to set aright the bias of nature, to cure the diseases of self-will, pride, etc." (Wesley, as cited in Prince, 1926, p. 101). Wesley went on to say, (as cited in Prince, 1926):

> Therefore to train children in the way of real religion is to regenerate them, to cure the corruption of their nature. In as much as it should begin with the first dawn of reason, before there has been any possibility of the loss of the effects of baptism, it should seem to be a regeneration process added to the regeneration received at baptism. (Pp. 101-102)

Prince (1926) offered an interpretation of Wesley's purpose for religious education:

> The goal of all work with children at home, in the schools, in the Methodist society is to make them pious, to lead to personal religion, and to insure salvation. It is not merely to bring them up so that they do no harm and abstain from outward sin, nor to get them accustomed to the use of grace, saying their prayers, reading their books, and the like, nor is it to rain them in right opinions. The purpose of religious education is to instill in children true religion, holiness, and the love of God and mankind and to train them in the image of God. (Pp. 87-88)

Prince (1926) also asserted: "Wesley's theory of religious education is in keeping with his belief that every stage of religious experience is possible in childhood" (p. 87).

Towns (1970) offered an outline of Wesley's pedagogical techniques, gleaned from his writings and instructions:

Speak to them plainly;

Secure their attention before you teach;

Use words little children may understand – the kind they use themselves;

Use illustrations from every day life;

Establish a relationship of love;

Repetition or patience is required. (p. 325)

In addition, Maddix (2001) suggested four elements that can be found in Wesley's educational practices: Emphasis on the learner, social reform, personal salvation and evangelism, and holiness of heart and life. Maddix (2001) went on to suggest: "Holiness of heart and life actually provides a broader description of transformation that encompasses his objectives of evangelism, social reform, as well as his childhood and adult educational practices" (p. 8). Holiness of heart and life, for Wesley, was the ultimate goal of religious education (Maddix, 2001).

Wesley also understood that the religious education should be appropriate to the developmental ability of the child (Willhauck, 1992). Wesley offered a warning to those entrusted with the religious education of children:

> I cannot but earnestly entreat you to take good heed how you teach these deep things of God. Beware of that common, but accursed, way of making children parrots, instead of Christians. Labour that, as far as possible, they may understand every single sentence, which they read. Therefore, do not make haste. Regard not how much, but how well, to how good purpose, they read. Turn each sentence every way, propose it in every light, and question them continually on every point; if by nay means, they man not only read, but inwardly digest the words of eternal life. (From Wesley's preface to *Lessons for Children,* 1746, pp. 3-4)

Family's role in religious education

Wesley felt that "the foundations for spiritual development must be appropriately constructed in the context of family life" (Felton, 1997, para. 11) and encouraged parents to take seriously the religious instruction of their children (May et al., 2005). In order to provide families with the tools for religious education in the home, Wesley published *Lessons for Children* (1743), which was a curriculum comprised of 200 lessons on the Old Testament. The introduction to *Lessons for Children* included "A Short Catechism for Children", which was twelve lessons on God, creation and the fall of humanity, redemption, the means of grace, hell, and heaven (Felton, 1997).

Wesley also wrote a sermon, "On Family Religion" (Sermon #94) in which he discussed the role of parents and biblical expectations of religion in the home. He based the sermon on the text "As for me and my house we will serve the Lord" (Joshua 24:15). In the sermon Wesley asks: What does it mean to serve the Lord? And who is included in your house?

He tells parents that children are "immortal spirits whom God hath, for a time, entrusted to your care, that you may train them up in all holiness, and fit them for the enjoyment of God in eternity" (Wesley, 1872, Vol. VII, p. 79). Wesley called parents to live as godly examples in front of their children and urged them to make sure that their actions matched the words of their religious instruction (Stonehouse, 2004). While his techniques included strict discipline and could by today's standards be considered severe, he also instructed the parents that everything they did in the form of rearing and education should be done "with mildness; nay, indeed, with kindness too" (Wesley, 1872, Vol. VII, p. 80). There was a balance to his approach that is difficult for us to see today. In contrast to the way children were treated and punished in the eighteenth century, Wesley was moderate in his behavior and quick to show children compassion.

Wesley's (1872) summation of the sermon included:

> You should particularly endeavor to instruct your children, early, plainly, frequently, and patiently. Instruct them early, from the first hour that you perceive reason

begins to dawn. Truth may then begin to shine upon the mind far earlier than we are apt to suppose. (Vol. VII, p. 81)

In this, Wesley encouraged the faith nurture of children at a very early age. Nurture that was to be communicated in a language children understood, repeated so that they would hear it often and come to understand it, and offered with patience.

Pastor's role in religious education of children

The heavy responsibility placed on parents for the religious instruction of their children, did not eliminate the role pastors played in the religious education of children. Wesley saw the role of children as critical to the continuance of the Methodist revival and expected that Methodist ministers would provide instruction for all of their people, including the youngest (Stonehouse, 2004). Ministers were required to visit every family in their care and while in the home spend time specifically with the children. These systematic visits were part of Wesley's expectations for ministers and overall strategy for spiritual formation. "Ministry to children was an essential part of being a Methodist preacher" (May et al., 2005, p. 103).

Wesley told ministers who felt that they did not possess the gifts required to work with children: "Gift or no gift, you are to do it, else you are not called to be a Methodist Preacher" (as cited in Felton, 1997, para. 37). Wesley went on to suggest: "Do it [teaching of children] as you can, till you can do it as you should" (as cited in Felton, 1997, para. 37). He told them to pray for the gift of teaching children and to make use of the materials he provided in the "Instructions" and "Lessons for Children".

Prince (1926) offers as way of summation, three points in Wesley's outline of the teaching work of the ministry as it relates to children. First, the preacher was expected to "revive and guide family worship" (p. 133). Secondly, the preacher was expected to teach the children themselves in the child's home. Wesley held this as critical to the point that those who were seeking to be a part of the Methodist Conference were asked: "Will you diligently and earnestly instruct the children, and visit from house to house?" (As cited in Prince, 1926, p. 134). Finally, the preachers were expected to form societies, or large groups who met for the purpose of religious instruction, made up entirely of children. Prince (1926) noted:

> Wesley provides very direct instruction for preachers to establish societies for children and suggests how each should function and what they should do: 'provide a lesson, hear the children repeat it, explain it in a familiar manner, ask often "What have I been saying?" and strive to fashion it on their hearts'. (p. 135)

Wesley realized the need for community in the development of faith and the vital role nurture and support played. In order to create this kind of environment for those seeking faith, those new to the faith, and those well established in their Christian faith, Wesley established societies, classes, and bands "where people could learn what it meant to be a Christian" (Stonehouse, 2004, p. 140). The societies, classes, and bands were used by Wesley to create a comprehensive Christian education system. The societies were the larger group, similar to our congregations today, and met for the primary purpose to present biblical truth and create a climate of where understanding could take place. Everyone was welcome to be a part of the societies, and they included believers and non-believers. The class meetings were made up of ten to twelve people and focused more on behavioral outcomes. They were considered the most influential part of Wesley's group structure in terms of life change (Blevins and Maddix, 2010). Every Methodist was a part of a class meeting. These groups were unusual in that they included both men and women, were often led by women, and were not segregated due to class or economics. The bands were the smallest group and were voluntary, homogenous groups segregated by age, gender, or marital status (Blevins and Maddix, 2010). The bands provided accountability and attention to emotional change (Blevins and Maddix, 2010). Blevins and Maddix (2010) suggested that Wesley's group formation demonstrated his theological perspective in that "Wesley believed that spiritual growth and holiness of heart and life require discipline, nurture, and accountability" (p. 75), which Wesley saw as best accomplished in the group format.

Wesley instructed the ministers to form a society when there were at least ten children, and they were to meet with the children for at least one hour every week (Minutes of 1812, as cited in Felton, 1979). Benzie (2010) posited that Wesley provided his ministers a very specific methodology for the religious education of children. "He instructed his preachers on ways to not only elicit the child's response but also on how to ensure the child did not get too stressed by the exercise and discouraged" (p. 126). Not only did Wesley make provision for children specific societies and offered guidelines for the unique instruction in those societies, Prince (1926) posited that Wesley made provision within the Methodist movement for membership of children. "They joined them as members on trial and as members in full on the same terms as their adult elders" (Prince, 1926, p. 135).

Wesley himself preached to children on occasion. One such incident is noted in his journal dated June 13, 1790 where he writes: "In the evening I preached to the children of our Sunday school, six or seven hundred of whom were present" (as cited in Towns, 1970, p. 327). Stonehouse (2004) suggested that what Wesley required of his Methodist ministers, he did himself. This included preaching to children, teaching catechism, meeting in homes with families, spending time with school children, and writing letters to children (Stonehouse, 2004).

Wesley was also quite interested in the Sunday school movement begun by Raikes (1735-1811). Prince (1926) suggested that not only was Wesley supportive of Raikes' work, but Methodists were engaged in the practice of Sunday school several years prior to the official inception of the movement. Wesley contributed financially to the Sunday school movement and said that it was "one of the noblest specimens of charity of which have been set foot in England" (as cited in Towns, 1970, p. 327). Prince (1926) posited that Wesley "saw in it a great potentiality for making Christians" (p. 92) and used every opportunity to promote it as he traveled across England.

Publications by Wesley for Children

Over his lifetime, Wesley published over 200 works. Of those several were dedicated to the instruction of children and included hymns for children, prayer books, catechism, biblical instruction, and textbooks. Children were also mentioned in his journals, and several sermons were directed at the rearing and education of children.

Wesley published the book of hymns for children with his brother, Charles. The collection of hymns for children was one of his final publications. Towns (1970) suggested that this demonstrated that "even in his old age his concern for children had not decreased" (p. 328). Felton (1997) suggested that for Wesley, "hymn singing was important to a child's spiritual development" (para. 20). An example of a Wesley hymn for children is "Gentle Jesus, Meek and Mild" (See Appendix) written for children, in a language they could understand, a tune they could easily sing, and taught a lesson they could easily grasp.

One of the works Wesley published was *Thought on the Manner of Educating Children* (1783) in which he stressed the importance of discipline and the significance of true religion to a good education (Heitzenrater, 2001). In addition to his sermon, "On Family Religion", he published a sermon titled "On the Education of Children" (1783) that reflected many of his mother's views on childhood education and specifically addressed the parent's role in the education of their children (Heitzenrater, 2001). He also wrote *A Plain Account of Kingswood School,* which included an explanation of the methods employed at the school and a defense of those methods. The book also provided an historical reflection on how and why the school was started (Heitzenrater, 2001).

In addition to Kingswood School, Wesley started the Foundery Day School in London and the Woodhouse-Grove School. He believed in a well-rounded education for all children, not just the wealthiest. This education included strong religious instruction as well as the humanities, science, history, art, and language (Heitzenrater, 2001). Heitzenrater (2001) quoted Wesley's principle for education: "Education entails the joining of knowledge and piety, wisdom and holiness" (p. 289).

The biblical narrative comprised the primary content of the publication *Lessons for Children*. This is not surprising since Wesley referred to himself as "a man of one book" quoting Thomas Aquinas's, *Homo unius libri* (Maddix, 2001). Wesley believed the Bible was the primary source of knowledge and insight and, although he also valued tradition, experience, and reason, felt the Bible should be the "first source to which Christians turn in seeking authoritative truth" (Aukerman, 2004, para. 3). Beyond giving children a biblical foundation, he also stressed the importance of testimony and personal experience. He understood that ultimately "the way to produce Christians is not by teaching doctrine, but through experiencing faith" (Wesley as cited in Willhauck, 1992, p. 269).

Conclusion on John Wesley

Wesley believed children were capable of great faith. This was based on his personal experiences with children, his personal childhood faith experiences, and his theological perspective. He saw the relationship between religion and education as critical in order to counter-act the natural condition and the external influences of the world. To that end, he constituted a Christian education approach for children that was holistic in nature and methodical in structure. It incorporated the parents, who he saw as the primary religious instructors; the Methodist preachers, who had an obligation to offer religious instruction to all of their people; the formal societies' of children that were formed whenever possible, and his established schools.

Wesley held to the conviction that teaching should not simply aim to impart information but rather "develop the power of the pupil to think, and that it should lead to the experimental knowledge of religion" (as cited in Prince, 1926, p. 132). His teaching was not just cognitive, but impacted the child physically, socially, emotionally, and spiritually as well (Stonehouse, 2004). Wesley also realized that children should not be considered the same as adults. He strongly urged parents, teachers, and ministers to speak to the children in language they understood and to take into account their developmental capabilities. However, Heitzenrater (2001) reminded: "And yet he also knew that some children had a capacity for knowledge and love that exceeded that of some adults" (p. 298).

Wesley demonstrated concern for children throughout his entire ministry through his engagement with them, his attention to their spiritual needs, and his desire to provide tools for instruction and enlightenment (Stonehouse, 2004). John Wesley died in 1791. At the time of his death, the Methodist movement totaled over one hundred thirty thousand members in Great Britain alone (Maddix, 2001), an incredible amount of growth during his lifetime. Today over seventy-five million people are impacted by ministries in the Methodist tradition (World Methodist Council, 2012). When Wesley was asked how he thought Methodism was to be perpetuated, he responded: "Take care of the rising generation; look after the children" (as cited in Willhauck, 1992, p. 196). To this end, Willhauck (1992) suggested:

> He instructed his hearers to start young, to teach children early and to continue this education throughout their lives. For Wesley knew, without benefit of a scientifically conducted survey, that a lifetime of exposure to Christian education was the most effective means to come to faith and experience the new birth. (p. 260)

Chapter Three

Methodology

The literature review revealed that faith is naturally inherent in all children and can be developed with proper nurture and guidance through childhood. The capacity for faith was consistently evident in children, and researchers and theologians alike concluded that faith is inherent in all children (Cavalletti, 2002; Coles, 1990). In addition, developmental theorists from the fields of developmental psychology and Christian education proposed that children develop faith; the development begins early and can be nurtured through relationships and experiences (Fowler, 1981; Westerhoff, 2000).

A study of John Wesley, with specific attention to his perspective on child faith formation, revealed that he believed children were recipients of God's prevenient, saving, sanctifying, and glorifying grace and were capable to respond to that grace through faith. His ontology included a belief in the depravity of humanity and the impact of sin on the *Imago Dei*, which created a bent to sin. However, Wesley saw God's grace as greater than the impact of the sinful nature. Thus, he believed humanity is able to respond to God's grace through faith. Wesley saw no difference in God's extension of grace to children or adults and their ability to respond. Wesley's epistemology saw knowledge and insight as a gift from God, initiated by Him through grace. Wesley held that humanity has an inherent desire to seek God and with proper nurture and instruction the awareness of God's grace is heightened. This heightened awareness empowers children and adults to "hear" the Holy Spirit with greater clarity and respond to God's grace with confidence.

The goal of Wesley's Christian education practices was for every person to experience "holiness of heart and life". This was evidenced in living a life that demonstrated loving God with heart, mind, soul, and strength and unselfish love for neighbor. The other unique quality of Wesley's educational practice was growth. Growth that preceded significant spiritual crises as well as seasons of growth that followed. Wesley saw faith development as a journey, in which God moves through grace, we respond in faith, and our communion or relationship with God is deepened (Harper, 2003).

Faith formation, for John Wesley, was possible in children and his personal experiences revealed that children were capable of developing a deep and abiding faith (Heitzenrater, 2001; Willhauck, 1992). However, Wesley believed the faith development in children required nurture and appropriate instruction (Stonehouse, 2004). Wesley developed high expectations for his pastors and ministry leaders in regard to child faith formation, support and instruction that included a biblical foundation, discipline, age appropriate instruction, repetition, relationship building, and experiential learning (Benzie, 2010; Felton, 1979; Prince, 1926). Wesley saw the church's role in faith formation as "nurturing and supporting human efforts to respond to the prompting of the Holy Spirit for ongoing growth in faith, including holding a person accountable for faith and life" (Matthaei, 2000, p. 28).

Prior to 1744 "Methodism was held together primarily by the personal supervision of the Wesleys" (Rack, 2002, p. 242). Methodist societies, which would relate to local congregations in the Wesleyan movement today, were multiplying and the movement was growing rapidly to the point where John Wesley did not have direct guidance and control over all that was being taught and practiced (Rack, 2002). The need for greater coordination prompted Wesley to convene the first Methodist Conference in June 1744 (Rack, 2002). The key issues noted in the agenda to be addressed were "what to teach, how to teach, and what to do" (as cited in Rack, 2002, p. 243). The agenda from the conference suggested that the ministers were encouraged to speak freely for all conference proceedings were to be kept confidential, and Rack (2002) posited, "there is in fact disappointingly little evidence about what really went on" (p. 246). The agenda provided the list of participants and the primary topics of discussion, but there is little insight as to the conclusions reached to answer the three prominent questions.

Matthaei (2000) noted that in addition to the questions explicitly mentioned in the agenda, the conference also discussed "who shall teach" and suggested that the three key questions - what to teach, how to teach, and who shall teach – need to be addressed today. Matthaei (2000) posited that "what to teach" addresses doctrine, "how to teach" and "what to do" address the practices employed in communicating the doctrine, and "who shall teach" addresses the relationships in which teaching occurs and the expectations of those who teach. The answers to the questions "what to teach", "how to teach", and "who shall teach" will help to inform what Matthaei (2000) terms "A Wesleyan ecology of faith formation" (p. 33). She defined ecology as an interconnection of "formative elements" and suggested: "The Wesleys discovered the importance of an interconnected system of instruction and nurture" used to contribute to faith formation (Matthaei, 2002, p. 33).

The research of Maddix (2001) and Willhauck (1992), as well as the writings of Blevins and Maddix (2010) and Matthaei (2000) suggested that the practices in local churches within the Wesleyan movement do not consistently align with the theological teachings of John Wesley. Although pastors and Christian educators were able to identify and confirm their support of Wesley's theological beliefs, their practices did not align with those beliefs (Maddix, 2001). Likewise, Willhauck (1992) discovered a consistency in agreement with Wesley's perspective on child faith formation, but did not see consistency in practice to support that belief. The vision for this book is to recapture Wesley's teachings and practices on child faith formation for local church nurture and instruction so that children can respond to God's grace and grow in faith.

Methodology

This book proposes to recapture Wesley's teachings and practices in regard to child faith formation through an historical qualitative study. Due to the age of the original documents and lack of access to them, a review of Wesley's documents, such as sermons, journals, writings, and publications will be conducted from primary studies. Primary studies are defined as "reliable texts of primary resources" and offer the most accurate representation of Wesley's original work compiled through "discovery, collection, comparison, and critical investigation of documents" (Heitzenrater, 1989, p. 206). This qualitative study will be conducted in order to ascertain themes in Wesley's teachings and practices that relate to child faith formation. Specific attention will be paid to biblical passages, doctrinal issues, teaching instructions, educational practices, and the requirements and expectations for teachers. The setting and audience that the teaching and practice directly related to will be noted.

Type of Study

This is an historical qualitative study that will look at archival, primary sources of John Wesley through the use of primary studies. The Wesley primary studies that will be used are those discovered through a careful examination of secondary sources, personal correspondence with Catherine Stonehouse, Dean of the School of Practical Theology at Asbury Seminary, and Randy Maddox, William Kellon Quick Professor of Wesleyan and Methodist Studies at Duke University, and through examination of Green's (1906) *The Works of John and Charles Wesley: A bibliography containing an exact account of all of the publications issued by the brothers Wesley, arranged in chronological order: with a list of early editions and descriptive and illustrative notes*. The main emphasis will be on a review of the literature to recapture Wesley's teachings and practices in regard to child faith formation. Although Wesley's writings and publications are extensive (Rivers, 2010), only the primary sources that are identified as relating to child faith formation will be reviewed. Rivers (2010) posited "with the possible exception of Daniel Defoe, Wesley was editor, author, or publisher of more works...than any other single figure in eighteenth-century Britain" (p. 145). Of Wesley's publications Rivers (2010) suggested that most were "short religious pamphlets in duodecimo format" (p. 145). Duodecimo books were small pamphlet-style books and the preferred format of many religious publications (Rivers, 2010, p. 145). Because of the small, pamphlet style of these books it is believed that many were thrown away and not retained (Rivers, 2010). Suarez (2009, as cited in Rivers, 2010) posited the folio and quartos were much more likely to have survived and "nearly half the surviving books published throughout the eighteenth century were octavos" (p. 145). Because of this lack of retention of many original publications and the extensive number of Wesley's works produced, it is difficult to quantify the number of original publications and provide a comprehensive list. Rivers (2010) identified several works that have given the greatest insight into Wesley's publications: Thomas Jackson's edited and published second edition *Christian Library* (1819-1827) and third edition of Wesley's *Works* (1829-1831), Richard Green's chronological bibliography *The Works of John and Charles Wesley* (1896, 2nd ed., Rev., 1906), and Frank Baker's *A Union Catalogue of Publications of John and Charles Wesley* (1966). Green's (1906) text identifies 397 entries of works by John and Charles Wesley and Baker's (1966) text identifies 425 total publications. Baker's (1966) collection includes "all Wesley's known original prose writings, based upon a careful collation of the editions issued during his lifetime, and showing all significant variant readings" (p. 4).

Source Selection

Personal correspondence with Dr. Stonehouse and Dr. Maddox along with the research conducted through the literature review resulted in a list of secondary sources related to John Wesley and his practices and teachings on child faith formation (See Appendix B for complete list of consulted secondary sources). Thorough examination of those secondary sources and their bibliographies resulted in a comprehensive list of primary studies. Saturation was achieved when no new primary studies were identified from the secondary sources (Richards, 2005). In addition, Green's (1906) text was consulted to determine if there were any additional primary sources, or original publications of Wesley, not represented in the primary studies or in the secondary sources. This methodical search for a comprehensive list of primary studies and additional primary sources resulted in the following list of documents to analyze in terms of Wesley's teachings and practices on what to teach, how to teach, and who shall teach:

Sermon #94, "On Family Religion" (Jackson, 1872);

Sermon #95, "On the Education of Children" (Jackson, 1872);

Sermon #96, "On Obedience to Parents" (Jackson, 1872);

"A Thought on the Manner of Educating Children" (Jackson, 1872);

"Serious Thoughts Concerning Godfathers and Godmothers" (Jackson, 1872);

"A Short Account of the School in Kingswood near Bristol" (Jackson, 1872);

"A Plain Account of Kingswood School" (Jackson, 1872);

"Prayers for Children" (Jackson, 1872);

"Prayers for Families" (Jackson, 1872);

Susanna Wesley's letter to John Wesley (Jackson, 1872);

Instructions for Children (Wesley, 1746-1754);

Hymns for Children (Wesley, 1747);

Lessons for Children (Wesley, 1746).

The review of literature resulted in one additional source, *A Token for Children* (1749). This source is a compilation of ten stories about children who faced dying. It was excluded from consideration because many of the stories pre-dated Wesley and are a second-hand telling about children with whom he had no direct contact. The primary study documents that will be addressed are available through The Wesleyan Church archives, Indiana Wesleyan University library system, Gutenberg eBooks, Google books, Wesley Center Online, and the Center for Studies in the Wesleyan Tradition at Duke Divinity School.

Richards (2005) posited that a "sample should be big enough but not such that the project cannot be completed in a timely manner or the attention given to the data sufficient to glean valuable data" (pp. 19-20). It is believed that the thirteen documents listed above will provide a broad enough sampling of the work of John Wesley in reference to child faith formation in order to get a picture of his teachings and practices in light of various contexts, audiences, and throughout his ministry. At the same time, the accumulated total of content represented in the documents is not such that should limit successful completion in a timely manner or detract from providing a thorough examination of each source.

Data Collection and Analysis

Qualitative research requires the researcher to revisit the research design and collection process throughout and make adjustments as to both as the data itself dictates (Richards, 2005). The first phase of analysis will be a quick read of the documents with notes made as to the date of the publication, the context, the audience, and the researcher's initial reaction to the document's ability to answer at least one of the questions from the research framework: What to teach, how to teach, and who shall teach. The sources will then be read thoroughly with annotations made as to the reader's reaction, points of interest, ideas about the codes and their relationships, and potential theories. The annotations will include comments, identification of summative quotes, and links to other sources (Richards, 2005). Miles and Huberman (1994) suggested that memoing, or the process of annotating, should include both conceptual and reflective remarks and occur during the entire process. The use of a "log trail" (Richards, 2005, p. 44) will include researcher's thoughts, ideas, decisions, and reactions throughout the process. Richards (2005) posited that a consistent log trail adds to the validity of the research.

Coding

The purpose of coding is data retention with the goal to "learn from data, revisit data, and look for patterns" (Richards, 2005, p. 86). Codes are "tags or labels for assigning units of meaning to the descriptive or inferential information compiled during a study" (Miles & Huberman, 1994, p. 56). Creswell (2008) suggested that the coding process helps make sense out of the text data. It is ultimately the "process of segmenting and labeling text to form descriptions and broad themes in the data" (p. 251).

The coding process will include three types of coding: descriptive, topical, and analytical coding. The descriptive coding will occur in the first skim read when information on the date, context, audience, and background of the document is noted. Topical coding will label the text in the sources according to the topics that are discussed. Codes for anticipated topics will be established prior to the coding process, with provision for addition and adjustment to codes as the coding is done (Miles & Huberman, 1994) (Appendix C). The final phase of coding will look analytically at the text, consider the meanings, and create categories that express new ideas about the data (Richards, 2005). In this phase the codes will be directly associated with phrases, sentences or paragraphs within the data. Attention will be given to the words John Wesley uses himself, looking for patterns and themes that emerge from them. Throughout the coding process memos will be created to reflect on the categories and what has been learned. Miles and Huberman (1994) suggested that notes should be made that include potential conclusions "noting regularities, patterns, explanations, possible configurations, casual flows, and propositions" (p. 11).

The material that is retrieved through careful study and examination of primary studies of Wesley's sermons, journals, and publications will be noted in regard to each of the critical questions offered for consideration at the first Methodist conference – what to teach, how to teach, and who shall teach. In addition, the researcher will note incidents in the documents when direct or indirect reference is made to the four components in the Wesleyan Quadrilateral: tradition, Scripture, reason, and experience. The research will examine if the document sources reflect any or all of these elements and note in what way they are represented.

Creswell (2008) noted that in qualitative research the work of collecting data and analyzing data often happens simultaneously, and in qualitative research the researcher returns to the data throughout the coding process in search of clarification and to extract more information. Interpretation of the data occurs throughout the process as the primary sources are read, as the collected data is reviewed in pursuit of determining codes, and as the coding process moves to identify the redundancies in the codes to finally compress the codes into themes (Creswell, 2008). The coding phase in this study will include review of source, coding of data, notation of reflections and remarks, identification of patterns and themes in data, and comparison of patterns and themes across sources with the goal to discover consistencies (Miles & Huberman, 1994).

Record Storage

The twelve primary studies will be converted into text documents and uploaded to the qualitative research computer assistant, HyperRESEARCH, a text-based manager. Miles and Huberman (1994) concluded that HyperRESEARCH offers significant assistance in the coding and theory building processes and moderate assistance in search and retrieval of codes and database management (p. 316). The predetermined codes will be established prior to the initial coding phase with the capability to edit and add codes as the coding phase occurs. As the data is coded, the software provides the capability to segment the data or identify words, phrases, sentences, and even paragraphs or "chunks" to each code. The software will provide the capability to enter various codes for the same portion of text, segment a variety of sizes of text, sort the codes, compare codes across sources, and identify trends and anomalies within the data such that classifications and categories can be identified, assertions and propositions can be formulated, and a structure implied (Miles & Huberman, 1994, p. 312). In addition, a word processor will be used to track the research log, annotations, as well as the researcher's reactions to the data and the process throughout the research.

Threats to Credibility and Transferability

The outcomes of this research have the potential to serve as a set of guiding principles for teachings and practice in Wesleyan Christian education practice today and act as a reference point in the development of curriculum for the purpose of child faith formation. However, the research is impacted by the personal experiences of the author. These personal experiences can form a bias in the selection of the primary texts to include, the reading of those texts, the interpretation of the literature, and the coding of the significant themes in the literature.

The author was born into a Pilgrim Holiness pastor's home and was raised as Bushnell (1861) suggested, as if she had always been a Christian. She spent her childhood not just attending church but with church and church life being the center of her social and spiritual culture. Her personal Christian education included attendance of age segregated Sunday school, children's worship, intergenerational worship and Bible studies, and an intensive child discipleship program called Christian Youth Crusaders. In addition to these local church Christian education practices, the author was greatly influenced by attendance at various camp meetings and Christian conferences.

The author, although a child at the time of merger, remembers the forging of the new denomination – The Wesleyan Church – through the merger of The Pilgrim Holiness and Wesleyan Methodist denominations in 1968. Because of significant family engagement in the practices and leadership of The Wesleyan Church, the author was raised not only Christian but also Wesleyan such that the teachings and practices of The Wesleyan Church were naturally accepted and seen as "normal".

The author's educational experience included an undergraduate degree in Christian Education from the Wesleyan Bible College, United Wesleyan College, and a master's degree from one of the Wesleyan universities, Indiana Wesleyan University. In addition, she is an ordained elder within The Wesleyan Church and has held ministerial roles in local churches and at the denominational headquarters. She has been an attendee and active participant in local Wesleyan church ministry her entire life and active in denominational leadership for the last twelve years.

These consistent and at times intense associations with The Wesleyan Church create within the author a bias in selection of materials to address, reflection on the materials, and goals for the research. The author has a strong personal interest in the subject of John Wesley and his views on child faith formation because of her respect for Wesleyan belief and practice as well as her focus through much of her ministerial life on children's ministry. In addition, the author's reading of texts on Wesleyan doctrine and theological understanding is influenced by her personal understanding of Wesleyan doctrine and theology forged through years of personal faith formation via direct and indirect Christian education. Finally, the author's experience as both local and denominational leader in children's ministry has forged a passion for child faith formation that may be considered unusual within Wesleyan ministry circles. This unique combination of having experienced intense Wesleyan-specific Christian education, having a deep appreciation for Wesleyan doctrine, and possessing a passionate desire to see children experience a personal and dynamic relationship with Christ creates a personal bias in both intention and interpretation.

In addition to the author's personal bias, Wesley's teachings and practices were written in the eighteenth century, which poses a threat to transferability. There is tremendous value in Wesley's teachings and practice; however, they must be understood in light of his culture and context. Eighteenth century British culture offered a context dissimilar in many ways to current American culture. Wesley was a man of his culture and context and his writings must be understood from that point of view. Therefore, adaptations for a twenty-first century context will be made that include inclusive language and insights from contemporary educational theory. Likewise, Wesley's use of the English language may require some interpretation in light of a twenty-first century American reading. Dr. Snyder (n.d.) of Asbury Theological Seminary provided a translation chart of some of Wesley's most commonly used terms with the contemporary equivalent. This chart (Appendix D) will be used in the reading of the texts to garner proper interpretation of Wesley's intention.

Triangulation for Validity

In an effort to facilitate validation of the results of the research, the author will engage data triangulation (Richards, 2005). Data triangulation will consist of comparing and crosschecking the results from multiple data sources. Richards (2005) suggested "triangulation offers multiple views or perspectives from multiple sources" (p. 21). In this study, the multiple sources will consist of the twelve selected primary studies of Wesley. These data sources, all written by John Wesley and with attention to child faith formation, will be compared in terms of date of publication, audience, and stated purpose of the writing. The study will compare analyses from multiple documents looking for commonality and consistency across timeframe, audience, and purpose for writing. In addition, the study will note any anomalies that occur within the document analysis and changes that occurred within Wesley's teachings and practices over the course of time.

Summary

God extends His grace through the work of the Holy Spirit to children and adults alike. Children are born with an ability to respond to God's prevenient grace through faith. Faith in children can be developed through environments and relationships that nurture the work of the Holy Spirit and encourage the child's receptivity to the Holy Spirit's work. Christian education in the local church setting can play a role in the nurture of child faith development.

John Wesley believed that children were recipients of God's grace and were capable of developing a strong and deep faith. He suggested that the goal of Christian education is "holiness of heart and life" or the realization of the Great Commandment: "Love the Lord your God with all your heart and with all your soul and with all your mind and with all your strength" (Mark 12:30, NIV) and the second command to "Love your neighbor as yourself" (Mark 12:31). Wesley is considered the founder of Methodism. Churches that follow the teachings of John Wesley are part of the Wesleyan movement. It is reasonable to expect that churches within this movement would not just align with Wesley's teachings but also his practices. Research has demonstrated, however, that there is disconnect between churches in the Wesleyan movement's beliefs, which align with John Wesley's teachings, and their Christian education practices (Maddix, 2001; Willhauck, 1992). Research suggested that this lack of agreement in belief and practice is due in part to a lack of literature on Wesley's Christian education teachings and practices, especially in the field of child faith development (Heitzenrater, 1989; Maddix, 2001; Willhauck, 1992).

To recover Wesley's teachings and practices on child faith development, this book will conduct historical qualitative research through engagement with Wesley primary studies. The research will attempt to answer three key questions suggested as critical to faith formation within the Wesleyan movement by Wesley and the first Methodist Conference - what to teach, how to teach, and who shall teach.

Chapter Four

Findings and Conclusions

Wesley's body of material as writer, editor, and publisher is extensive. To gain a thorough and complete sense of the man and his views would require exploration into the broader scope of his work beyond what this book has pursued. For this book's purposes, twelve works of Wesley that specifically related to the faith formation of children were considered. This author does not contend that the twelve works considered represent the full scope of Wesley's teachings and theology in general or his teachings, practices, and beliefs in regard to child faith formation specifically. They do, however, provide a glimpse into Wesley's expectations for those he suggested were responsible for the faith formation of children (who shall teach), what should be taught to children (what to teach), and Wesley's proposed methodology for the "religious education" of children (how to teach).

Wesley as Writer and Publisher

It is difficult to identify from the many publications attributed to John Wesley, which were original works as author, which were edited versions adjusted for his readership and purposes, and which were publications of another's work. Rack (2002) suggested that Wesley "silently abridged, adapted and altered pieces presented as if from his own pen" (p. 346). In contemporary culture we would see his approach as an infringement on the copyright laws, however, in the eighteenth century this was not a consideration. Wesley considered it a compliment to the original author to edit and republish someone else's work and found the issue of identifying original authorship and attributing content to the original author as a distraction from the primary purpose, which was the communication of the content and message (Rack, 2002).

Baker (2000) posited Wesley contributed to faith formation through writing through composing, by abridging, or by translating (pp. 35-36). Wesley was not unusual in this approach of writing, editing, and publishing material, as there were other individuals and groups in the seventeenth and eighteenth centuries that followed similar practices.

> If Wesley's editions are read in the wider context of what was edited, published, and distributed by members of other organizations or denominations, the importance and intrinsic interest of what he was doing remains as strong; but it becomes

obvious that to some extent he was following in the footsteps of others, and that even where there was no influence in either direction members of other denominations or groups were engaged in parallel activities. (Vickers, 2010, p. 146)

Wesley's numerous publications included his letters, diaries, and journal. "Taken together, the letters, diaries, and *Journal* of John Wesley offer us an unusually rich perspective on the private and public life of this eighteenth century figure" (Campbell, 2010, p. 130). It is estimated that Wesley wrote nearly 18,000 letters between 1721 and 1791, kept diaries from 1725 until 1791 (one week before his death), and maintained his *Journal* that chronicled his life from 1735 through 1790 (Campbell, 2010). Unlike the letters and diaries, the *Journal* was "a published literary work intended for popular leadership" that was "designed as a narrative to support Wesley's particular wing of Evangelical Revival" (Campbell, 2010, p. 130, 135).

> The *Journal* consistently offered its readers not only charming narrative of travel, witty conversations, attacks by ignorant mobs, and solemn conversations, but, a continuous narrative of divine providence, showing how God had blessed and guided John Wesley and the Methodists associated with him. (Campbell, 2010, p. 136)

Likewise, Rack (2002) posited Wesley's *Journal* is "a unique record of the public career of a tireless traveller, evangelist and observer of men and manners" (p. 351).

Wesley was a prolific writer, editor, and publisher whose influence on the Church at large and the Methodist movement in particular can be attributed in part to his extensive publications. His intentionality to publish material that even the poor in his context could access helped fuel the movement and create greater impact. He wrote, edited and published letters, sermons, thoughts, lessons, and books on a variety of topics and subjects. His breath of interest was remarkable and included works on science, history, art, poetry, theology, and education (Rack, 2010).

Excluded Documents from Research

For the purpose of this study, we have focused on twelve of his works that related specifically to the faith formation of children (Appendix E). *A Token for Children* and *Thoughts on Infant Baptism* were two pieces that addressed in some manner child faith formation but were omitted from this research project. They were eliminated because of the lack of relevance to the three questions explored and questions surrounding the authorship or timing in publication. *Tokens for Children* is a compilation of ten stories of children and their example of living faith-filled lives while dying. Prince (1926) noted that it is appears to be an abridgement of the text by James Janeway, *A Token for Children* (p. 129). While offering a wonderful testimony of God's faithfulness in the lives of the children and their ability to exercise mature faith and assurance of their salvation in the face of death, the text did not provide assistance in identifying answers to the research questions what to teach, how to teach, or who shall teach. However, *Tokens for Children* did offer support for Wesley's argument that children can experience faith formation that results in an unexpected spiritual maturity at an early age. Prince (1926) posited that Wesley "relinquish[ed] his edition of this work some time after the first Conference in favor of the *Instructions*" (p. 129). The *Instructions for Children* is a text considered in this research.

Thoughts on Infant Baptism (Wesley, 1751) was also not included in this study because of the lack of insight provided on the three questions posed for this research. The publication offered insight into Wesley's theological view of baptism in general and provided an argument for the continuation in the practice of infant baptism. This "Thought" was in response to the criticism some of the societies encountered on their practice of infant baptism. Wesley's apparent purpose in writing the document was to defend the practice. The work was an extract from an original piece by William Wall, *The History of Infant Baptism* (n.d.). In the document, Wesley (1837) acknowledged: "The baptism of infants has been a troublesome dispute almost ever since the reformation" (p. 2). Wesley (1837) responded to critiques that the practice was not in keeping with Scripture by engagement with the biblical record and a review of the practice in church history. Wesley also discussed the appropriate mode of infant baptism. Wesley concluded the document with a statement to bring unity regardless of an individual's perspective on infant baptism:

> Our brethren who reject infant baptism, as well as we who practice it, all agree in a belief of the sacred institution of this ordinance: we all agree, that children should be devoted to God, and should be partakers of all the privileges which Scripture admits, and that they should grow up under all possible obligations to duty. (Wesley, 1837, p. 23)

In the closing remarks Wesley (1837) posited, "it is a most unreasonable thing that we should be angry with each other" (pp. 23-24).

A cursory review of *Thoughts on Infant Baptism* indicated it did not provide insight into the research questions who shall teach, how to teach, and what to teach in regard to child faith formation. Because of the lack of insight from the document on the research questions and the suggestion by Wesley (1837) that infant baptism is a "lesser thing" compared with discussions on faith in Christ, love of God, and obedience to the Spirit (p. 25), *Thoughts on Infant Baptism* was not included in this study.

Research Method

The twelve works researched included three sermons, a letter, two "Thoughts" that appear to be responses to questions raised, two accounts of the school at Kingswood, and published works of prayers, hymns, lessons, and instructions written for children. They offered a variety in audience, purpose, format, and date of publication. Inquiry through secondary sources and insights provided by Dr. Maddox of the Wesley Institute at Duke University identified the most reliable primary editions of each document. A listing of each document and the source used is provided in Appendix E.

Coding Process

Each historical work was converted into a text document in order to access by the qualitative software employed for this research's purposes, *HyperResearch*. Each document was read multiple times for the purpose of coding. The first phase of coding employed descriptive codes that identified pertinent background information included in the source such as date of publication, context, purpose of writing, noted additions or changes, reference to original writings or editorial changes. In addition descriptive codes were applied to identify the type of document - publication, sermon, letter, or thought. Additionally, descriptive coding occurred to identify the direct and indirect audiences of the source - pastors, parents, teachers, the Methodist societies, children, or other. Results of the first round of descriptive coding are identified in the Appendix F, Table F1.

The second round of coding focused on topical coding and identified the research questions addressed in the document and where they were located within each source. The codes applied to the sources included "WHAT" to identify the content in the source that addressed the research question what to teach, "HOW" to identify the content in the source that addressed the research question how to teach, and "WHO" to identify the content in the source that addressed the research question who shall teach? The results of the second round, or topical phase of coding, suggested that every document studied addressed in some way the "how to teach" and "what to teach". All of the documents studied with the exception of *Prayers for Children* and *Hymns for Children* addressed the research question "who shall teach".

The third round of coding was the most time consuming and required repeated "passes" at the content in order to identify data from the documents that related to the various analytical codes. The analytical coding phase looked at the portions of text from the source documents that answered the question how to teach and applied codes of "WHN" for text that addressed when "religious instruction" of children should occur, "WHR" for text that addressed where the instruction should occur, and "MET" for text that addressed the methodology suggested or referenced including both what to do and what not to do in regard to teaching children. Data that related to "MET" was found in every document studied, data related to "WHN" was identified in every document with the exception of *Lessons for Children*, and there was no explicit data identified that related to the code "WHR" in any of the documents.

The analytical phase of coding also addressed the portions of text from the source documents that answered the question who shall teach identified with the code "WHO". Analytical codes relevant to the topical code of "WHO" included "REL" for the portions of text that identified the relationship to the child of the person responsible for the instruction and "EXP" for the portions of text that identified the expected lifestyle of the person responsible for instructing children. The results of the analytical phase of coding for "WHO" identified data in all of the documents that related to both the codes "REL" and "EXP" with the exception of *Prayers for Children* and *Hymns for Children*.

The final codes applied during the initial analytical phase of coding addressed the portions of text from the source documents that answered the question what to teach associated with the code "WHAT". Analytical codes were applied to portions of text from the source documents that related to Scripture/Bible ("BIB"), prayer ("PRA"), Christian lifestyle ("LIFE"), names and descriptions of God ("GOD"), Jesus (JES), salvation ("SAL"), Holy Spirit ("HOL"), Sin ("SIN"), human nature ("MAN"), eternity (HVN), and grace or God's work on our behalf ("GRA"). Differentiation in coding was made for Christian lifestyle ("LIFE") to identify the expectations in lifestyle after salvation and human nature ("MAN") to identify the descriptions provided of the pre-salvation person or the natural state of humanity apart from God. In addition, sin ("SIN") was used to denote the acts of people directly in conflict to God's known laws or the portions of the text that directly spoke of sin. Differentiation was also made between God ("GOD") and grace ("GRA") in which "GOD" was applied to portions of the text that provided names for God, spoke of God's character, or spoke of God's actions in general. "GRA", on the other hand, was applied to portions of text that discussed the ways in which God extended grace to humanity through His actions. Likewise, differentiation was provided through the use of codes for Jesus "JES" and salvation "SAL" to identify portions of the text that related specifically to the names and character of Jesus and others that referred to specifically the salvific actions of Jesus on humanity's behalf. Although limited in the amount of text represented by the codes for Holy Spirit ("HOL") and eternity ("HVN") these were differentiated as well from the other codes because of the unique descriptions and associations made to each that offered critical and independent examination. Because of this differentiation in the codes, there were portions of text in which code overlapping occurred in that the same text was coded in multiple ways. The insights yielded by these independent examinations, may have been lost if the text was not uniquely identified through the use of distinctive codes. The results of the analytical phase of coding "WHAT" are provided in the Appendix F, Table F2. The codes used in the descriptive, topical, and analytical phases included:

Descriptive:

Context -

Sermon	SER
Letter	LTR
Publication	PUB

Audience -

Pastors	PAS	
Parents	PAR	
Teachers	TCH	
Congregation	CON	
Children	CHD	

Topical:

What to teach	WHAT	
How to teach	HOW	
Whom shall teach	WHO	
Why teach	WHY	

Analytical: WHAT

Scripture/Bible	BIB	
Prayer	PRA	
Christian Living	LIFE	(after salvation)
Names/Descriptions of God	GOD	
Salvation	SAL	
Holy Spirit	HOL	
Sin	SIN	
Human Nature	MAN	(prior to salvation)
Grace	GRA	(acts of God on humanity's behalf)
Jesus	JES	
Heaven (eternity)	HVN	

Analytical: HOW

When	WHN	

Where	WHR	
Method	MET	
Analytical: WHO		
Relationship to child	REL	
Expected lifestyle	EXP	(of instructor)

Reports of Findings

The data collected was reviewed quantitatively and qualitatively. Frequency reports were created by document and by code to review the data quantitatively. A frequency report was generated to examine the rate of inclusion of every code for each of the documents studied. While the frequency reports identified the number of times a code was used in each document, they are not necessarily representative of the amount of data related to that code. For example, a single phrase or sentence may be identified as relating to a single code, such as in sermon 94, "On Family Religion" the phrase "As for me and my house we will serve the Lord" was coded as "BIB". Within the same document, an entire paragraph was coded with the single code "MET". The number of codes used was equal, but they are not representative of the amount of text coded – a single phrase versus an entire paragraph. A direct correlation between the results of the frequency graphs and the full amount of content related to each code cannot be made. The frequency reports simply provide an indication into the number of times content that related to that code was identified; they do not imply the amount of content or data associated with that code.

A review of the findings identified the four most frequently assigned codes were "BIB", "GOD", "LIFE", and "GRA" and the least frequently assigned codes were "WHR", "HVN", and "REL". The entire results of the frequency report for all codes in all of the documents are found in Appendix F, Figure F3. It is interesting to note Wesley's attention to content that related to the topical code of "WHAT" over his inclusion of content that related to the topical codes of "WHO" or "HOW" (Appendix F, Figure F4). Because this body of research only represents a small portion of Wesley's writings and publications, inference cannot be made to the focus of his writings and publications in general; however, in terms of his body of work that offers a primary focus on child faith formation through sermon, publication and letter or thought, it can be seen that he dedicated more text to the specific description of "What to teach" either directly – such as through the content in *Lessons* or *Instructions* – or indirectly – such as through the content in the *Prayers* and *Hymns*. Topical codes that related to answering the research question "What to teach?" in comparison to topical codes that related to the research questions "How to teach?" or "Who shall teach?" can be seen in terms of frequency in Appendix F, Figure F4.

Engagement with the coded data

Reports were also generated by code and document that included the text identified from the source document as relating to that code. These reports were used to review the data qualitatively, in the effort to extract themes from each individual document and ultimately common themes from the collection of documents. The amount of text material collected from the analytical coding related to the questions of "How to teach" (Codes "WHN", "WHR", and "MET") and "Who shall teach" (Codes "REL" and "EXP") was such that outcomes and findings could be achieved through a review of the compilation of the text material. Although the amount of text content from the analytical codes associated with "HOW" and "WHO" was limited, the research yielded valuable results. The results of that qualitative analysis are provided within the reported findings by document and by code.

Addition of sub codes

The amount of text associated with the analytical coding related to the research question "What to teach?" identified through the topical code of "WHAT" yielded a greater amount of text content than the other two questions. In some analytical coding cases, the amount of coded text was quite significant (God, grace, Christian lifestyle, and Jesus). In order to thoroughly engage the text content associated with the research question "What to teach?" another step of coding was employed. A fourth phase of coding, the second phase of analytical coding, was conducted in which each of the analytical codes associated with the research question "What" were broken down further by subtopics within the code. The sub-codes included:

God (GOD): Names, Description, and Activity;

Grace (GRA): What it is, What God does, Our response;

Prayers (PRA): Example, Purpose, How;

Bible (BIB): What taught, Description, How to Use;

Salvation (SAL): Source/means, Outcome, Our Response;

Jesus (JES): Description, Actions;

Eternity/Heaven (HVN): Heaven, Hell;

Holy Spirit (HOL): Actions, Description;

Sin (SIN): What it is, Examples, What it does;

Christian Life (LIFE): Praise, Piety, and Submission.

The code names used in the three phases of coding are listed in Appendix J and the sub-codes' names used in the fourth stage of coding are listed in the Appendix K. Reports were then generated by document, code, and sub code for qualitative analysis in order to determine common themes within the document and the collective documents. The results of that qualitative analysis are provided within the reported findings by document and by code.

Addition of why code

In addition to the descriptive, topical, and analytical codes and coding phases, an additional code was added during the process. The code "WHY" was added to identify text data that did not relate to one of the three research questions but did provide valuable insight into the author's motivation for publication or writing. The information retrieved through this additional coding phase is reported in the background report for each document when appropriate. The only frequency report provided that contains the "WHY" code is in comparison to the frequency "WHY" occurs in the documents in comparison to the other three research questions, as identified in Appendix F, Figure F4. The "WHY" was analyzed qualitatively by document and collectively with findings reported by document and by code.

Annotations

Annotations were made throughout the coding process to note the researcher's thoughts and reflections, unusual elements that were identified, summations or interpretations that occurred during the coding process, or questions that were raised during coding. The software employed for the research project, H*yper-Research*, generated reports by source and by code that identified the annotations made throughout the process. The annotations were reviewed, the questions were pursued, and summations, notes, and insights were incorporated into the reporting phase.

Findings by Documents

Reports were generated that identified the codes applied and the data associated with each code by document source. The findings from these reports by document source include an analysis of the context in which the document was published, and a brief summation of the document is provided in the following, and an engagement with each research question as connected to that document.

Descriptive Summation of Sources

Wesley used the term "religious education" in the documents reviewed to describe the faith formation of children. While the term "religious education" gave the connotation of cognitive engagement, it was clear from the works that Wesley's expectation was not just for cognitive engagement, which did play a significant role, but also an expectation that children would learn how to live or behave as Christians and possess the attitudes of Christians. For him it was a holistic transformation that was expected through the work of God's grace and the Holy Spirit made possible by Jesus Christ's death on the cross and resurrection. It was not just an accumulation of religious knowledge and biblical content, but a transformation from the natural state of humanity described as "proud, selfwilled, Lovers of the World, and not Lovers of God" (Wesley, 1746, p. 6), into the transformed and redeemed person who not only gained knowledge but thought differently (cognitive), lived differently (behavioral), and had a change of perspective (affective). In addition, this religious education was not religious in general, as understood by today's culture, but it was specifically Christian in nature, thus not just religious education, but Christian education. For our purposes, the terms of "religious education", "Christian education" and child faith formation are seen as synonymous unless specifically noted.

Chronological Comparison of Sources

Of the twelve documents examined, the earliest was the letter of Susanna Wesley to John, dated July 24, 1732. This letter was written during Wesley's time at Oxford. A series of publications and writings concerning child faith formation or what Wesley termed "religious education" occurred following Wesley's return from Georgia (1737) and the organization of the Methodist society. The first Methodist conference was held in 1744 and *Instructions for Children* was published in 1745. Following its publication in short succession were the first three editions of *Lessons for Children* (1746, 1747, 1748), *Hymns for Children* (1747), and the "Short Account of the School at Kingswood" (1749) a year following the opening of the school at Kingswood (1748). The Mid 1740's were a season where Wesley focused on the religious education of children in the school, home, and through the work of the societies. During this time, Wesley noted in his journal engagement with children who demonstrated "full assurance of faith" such as a four-year-old girl who he discussed on September 16, 1744 and "a pious boy" mentioned in June 28, 1746 (Prince, 1926, pp. 84-85). "Serious Thoughts Concerning Godfathers and Godmothers" was written in 1752 as a response to critical inquiry, the fourth installment of *Lessons for Children* was printed in 1754, and *Prayers for Children* in 1772. The *Arminian Magazine* was begun in 1778 and included four publications relating to children in 1783 and 1784: "A Thought on the Manner of Educating Children" (1783), Sermon 94 "On Family Religion" (1783), Sermon 95 "On Education of Children" (1783) and Sermon 96 "On Obedience to Parents" (1784). Also in the early 1780s Wesley wrote "A Plain Account of the Kingswood School" as a response to inquiry and need for greater details of the method and content of instruction (1781). Of the twelve documents reviewed, six were written in the mid 1740s and four in the early 1780's. *Instructions for Children*, the first three parts of *Lessons for Children* and *Hymns for Children* were published close to the opening of the school at Kingswood. It is believed these works were used as part of the curriculum at the Kingswood school

(Prince, 1926). The works were also published shortly following the organization of the Methodist society and ministers were instructed to use the resources in the societies where children were present and in the Methodist homes (Prince, 1926; Willhauck, 1992).

The publications by Wesley of the three sermons, *Prayers for Children* and "Thoughts on the Manner of Educating Children" indicated a sustained interest in child faith formation later in his life. Outler (1986) suggested this series identified a recognition that the Methodist movement had already lived beyond the typical lifespan of movements and Wesley realized the future of the movement depended on the religious instruction of the youngest generation. The first document was written to a "young" Wesley beginning his journey in ministry, the second movement of documents was written at the beginning of the formation of the Methodist movement formally, and the third movement of documents represented Wesley's final appeal to the continuation of the movement beyond his death.

Sermons

John Wesley was a preacher. "Wesley lived by preaching; he gave himself totally to mastering a practice that has a unique and lasting place in the life of the church" (Abraham, 2010, pp. 111-112). He preached from his Anglican pulpit and in the open-air fields of the countryside to miners and laborers. He preached to all classes of citizens and to all ages. It is suggested that he preached as many as 800 sermons a year and traveled up to 20,000 miles primarily on horseback to deliver those sermons (Abraham, 2010). He drew crowds up to 20,000 and although small in stature and quiet in speech, his message of salvation, hope, and spiritual transformation was heard (Abraham, 2010, Prince, 1926).

Wesley made his sermons available in print and Abraham (2010) suggested they "now serve as official standards of doctrine for much of Methodism" (p. 99). Although the style and language of the printed sermons reflect a different time and culture, the content still offers spiritual insights beneficial to readers today (Abraham, 2010). Rack (2002) posited: "Wesley's printed sermons clearly represent only the solid skeletons of discourses written down and published as pieces of systematic teaching to give a framework for Methodist doctrine" (p. 343).

Wesley's published sermons do not reflect fully his spoken or preached sermons as he was known to preach for an hour or more adding to the concise content of the printed sermon with illustrations and stories. In addition, he added content specific to the crowd he was addressing, contextualizing the sermons for the specific audience (Rack, 2002). Wesley did not use notes in his preaching and was said to have used "plain language so all could understand" (Rack, 2002, p. 343). For Wesley preaching "was a pivotal means of grace ordained by God to bring people to salvation. Abraham (2010) suggested: "Sermons are a unique form of oratory. Their aim is fundamentally spiritual. Their teleology is that of spiritual instruction and formation. This insight applies equally well to the written form of sermons; their goal is inescapably spiritual in nature" (p. 110). The research examined three sermons written by Wesley that were identified as having specific connection to child faith formation. Although the sermons were written in a language that reflected cultural implications of the eighteenth century and for a context in many ways quite different from twenty-first century North American culture, they offered valuable insights in spiritual instruction and formation.

Context and audience for sermons

The three sermons specifically addressed in this study were: "On Family Religion" (#94, Outler, 1986), "On the Education of Children" (#95, Outler, 1986) and "On Obedience to Parents" (#96, Outler, 1986). In reference to these three sermons, Body (1936) suggested that in 1766 Wesley conducted "a lone campaign, at Bristol, with a series of sermons on the education of children, all preached within a week" (p. 45). According to the literature, the sermons were preached in 1766 but Wesley did not write them out for publication until 1783. Outler (1986) suggested Wesley's motivation in writing these three sermons at this time:

> Wesley was aware that the Methodist Revival had already outlasted the normal life span of such movements, and that its future depended quite crucially on 'family religion', 'the education of children', 'obedience to parents', 'obedience to pastors', etc. Hence the sequence of Nos. 94-97. (p. 333)

Sermon 94, "On Family Religion."

The primary biblical text for the sermon "On Family Religion" was Joshua 24:15: "As for me and my house, we will serve the Lord" (KJV). Wesley asked three questions based on the text in Joshua 24:15: "First, Inquire what it is to 'serve the Lord'", "Secondly, Who are included in that expression 'my house'", and "Thirdly, What can we do, that we and our house may serve the Lord" (Outler, 1986, p. 335).

Wesley suggested that to "serve the Lord" included both outward expressions and inward expressions of service that must begin with faith in Jesus Christ. In answer to the question: "Who are included in that expression, 'my house'", Wesley answered: "every one under your roof that has a soul to be saved is under your care" (Outler, 1986, pp. 337-338). The final question Wesley addressed, "What can we do that all these may 'serve the Lord'?" was given the majority of attention and spoke to the research question "How to teach?". A summation of the way this sermon addressed the three research questions as reflected in the frequency of the various codes associated with each question can be seen in Appendix G, Figure GI.

Descriptive codes

On May 26, 1783 Wesley wrote "On Family Religion" from the text Joshua 24:15, a text Wesley had only preached from three times previously (Outler, 1986). The sermon was published in the *Arminian Magazine* in that same year (Outler, 1986; Tyerman, 1973). Wesley launched the *Arminian Magazine* in 1778 intended for "pious persons of moderate means and education, especially Methodists" (Rack, 2002, p. 349). This was a sermon and a publication. The primary audience for the sermon "On Family Religion" was parents, however, because of its publication in *The Arminian*, the greater audience would have been the members of the Methodist societies.

Why teach

Wesley asked: "What will the consequence be, if they do not adopt this resolution? – If family religion be neglected? – If care be not taken of the rising generation?" (Outler, 1986, p. 335) and concluded that if religious instruction was neglected then the "revival of religion" would end. He warned that even children of pious parents who neglect the intentionality of religious instruction will "Have neither his [God's] love in their hearts nor his fear before their eyes" (Outler, 1986, p. 335).

Who should teach

Parents were identified as the primary source of religious instruction for the children, and Wesley specifically addressed fathers and their responsibility for the spiritual care of their children. Wesley admonished parents to oversee the selection of their child's school and school instructor, employer, and future spouse. Wesley further noted that the real teacher in religious instruction is God Himself: "He alone can apply your words to their hearts; without which all your labour will be in vain. But whenever the Holy Ghost teaches, there is no delay in learning" (Outler, 1986, p.).

The expectation on lifestyle of the instructor included the indwelling of the Holy Spirit: "being endued with power from on high" (Outler, 1986, p.). Wesley suggested that without the "power from on high" the parent or teacher would not have the patience sufficient for teaching. Parents were also to "follow reason and the oracles of God; not the fashions and customs of men" (Outler, 1986, p.). They were called to be pure, "adorn the doctrine of God... Let you, your yoke-fellow, your children, and your servants, be all on the Lord's side; sweetly drawing together in one yoke, walking in all his commandments and ordinances" (Outler, 1986, p.). Wesley described the school instructors that the parents were to engage as pious who "endeavours to instruct a small number of children in religion and learning together" (cite) and God-fearing "whose life is a pattern for he scholars" (Outler, 1986, p.).

How to teach

Wesley admonished parents to teach their children "while they are young" (Outler, 1986, p.) and "early, from the first hour that you perceive reason begins to dawn" (Outler, 1986, p. 340) for he noted that the truth can begin to "shine upon the mind far earlier than we are apt to suppose" (Outler, 1986, p.).

Wesley summarized his instructions on the methodology parents should employ in the religious instruction of their children: "instruct your children, early, plainly, frequently, and patiently" (Outler, 1986, p. 340). Reminiscent of Deut. 6:5-9, Wesley instructed that parents should take every opportunity to speak of the things of God and to speak "plainly", using words the children use themselves and understand, and build on the ideas the children already possess. Wesley offered as example:

> Bid the child look up; and ask. "What do you see there?" "The sun." "See, how bright it is! Feel how warm it shines upon you hand! Look, how it makes the grass green! But God, though you cannot see him, is above the sky, and is a deal brighter than the sun! It is he, it is God that makes the grass and the flowers grow; that makes the trees green, and the fruit to come upon them! Think what he can do! He can do whatever he pleases. He can strike me or you dead in a moment! But he loves you; he loves to do you good. He loves to make you happy. Should not you then love him? And he will teach you how to love him. (Outler, 1986, pp. 340-341)

Parents were also cautioned to instruct with frequency, patience, and perseverance: "never leave off, never intermit your labour of love" (Outler, 1986, p.). In order to keep children from "evil" Wesley admonished parents to use "all advice, persuasion, and reproof" (Outler, 1986, p. 338) with kindness and as a least means correction "not till all other have been tried, and found to be ineffectual" (Outler, 1986, p.). Wesley concluded that parents who desire for their "house" to serve the Lord will need "all the grace, all the courage, all the wisdom which God has given you" (Outler, 1986, p.).

What to teach

God, also referred to as Lord, and His acts of grace on humanity's behalf are mentioned throughout the sermon such as in His role in history, His love, and His gift of salvation. Wesley reminded readers of the great things God had done for the Israelites through the telling of the story of Joshua in 15 and suggested that like Joshua they too should commit their homes to God's service: "As for me and my house, we will serve the Lord" (Joshua 24:15). Wesley called them to "serve the Lord" through belief in God's son, love for God, love for others, and obedience to God. Wesley also suggested that the readers are to engage in a Christian lifestyle characterized by: "restrain them from all outward sin; from profane swearing; from taking the name of God in vain; from doing any needless work, or taking any pastime, on the Lord's day" (Outler, 1986, p.). Fathers were admonished to "take care that every person who is under your roof have all such knowledge as is necessary for salvation" (Outler, 1986, p.), salvation made possible through the Jesus Christ, God's Son. Wesley demonstrated the value of prayer (PRA) and scripture (BIB) when he admonished parents to: "take care that they have some time every day for reading, meditation, and prayer...Neither should any day pass without family prayer seriously and solemnly performed" (Outler, 1986, p.). Parents were also admonished to not encourage their children

Findings and Conclusions 93

to seek employment not for the purpose of earning a great deal of money, but to encourage their children to "secure the possessions of heaven" (Outler, 1986, p.).

Sermon #95, "On the Education of Children."

The primary biblical text for the sermon "On Education of Children" was Proverbs 22:6 "Train up a child in the way wherein he should go: And when he is old, he will not depart form it" (KJV). Wesley acknowledged that this verse was not "to be understood in an absolute sense" but rather understood "with some limitation" as "it is a general, though not an universal, promise" (Outler, 1986, p. 347). Wesley identified two questions that he concluded must be addressed: "What is 'the way wherein a child should go'?" and "How shall we 'train him up' therein?" (Outler, 1986, p. 348). A summation of the way this sermon addressed the research questions as reflected in the frequency of the various codes associated with each question is found in Appendix G, Figure G2.

Descriptive codes

Wesley wrote "On the Education of Children" as a sequel sermon to "On Family Religion." It was published On July 12, 1783 in the *Arminian Magazine* following the publication of "Thoughts on the Manner of Educating children" (Outler, 1986). This was a sermon and a publication. The primary audience for the sermon "On The Education of Children" was parents, however, because of its publication in *The Arminian*, the greater audience would have been the members of the Methodist societies.

Why teach

Wesley suggested religious instruction was necessary to cure the "diseases" of human nature, which required "the necessity of education and tutors" (Outler, 1986, p. 349). He likened education to the medicine to cure the diseases of humanity and posited that the "grand end of education is to cure them" (Outler, 1986, p. 352) and Christian education should "teach them how to think, and judge, and act according to the strictest rules of Christianity" (Outler, 1986, p. 349). Stonehouse (2004), in reference to this sermon, posited: "Wesley believed that the best safeguard against rebellion is a deep-seated confidence in God's love. Therefore the most important goal for Christian teaching in the home, the church, and the school, is to help children grasp the greatness of God's love for them" (p. 145).

Who shall teach

Wesley identified God as the true and only "physician of souls" but posited that God chooses to use men and women to work through: "He honours men to be, in a sense, 'workers together with him.' By this means the reward is ours, while the glory rebounds to him" (Outler, 1986, p. 349). Wesley appeared to address both parents, but specifically referenced mothers and identified their role in providing spiritual care to their children when he wrote: "What can parents do, and mothers more especially, to whose care our children are necessarily committed in their tender years" (Outler, 1986, p. 352). He called mothers to be women of sense, patience, and resolution "as only the grace of God can give" (Outler, 1986, p. 355) and suggested: "For those that educate us should imitate our guardian angels; suggest nothing to our minds but what is wise and holy; help us to discover every false judgment of our minds, and to subdue every wrong passion in our hearts" (Outler, 1986, p. 349).

How to teach – when

Wesley suggested instruction of children should occur "as early as possible" and "from the first dawn of reason" and parents should "continually inculcate, God is in this and every place.... God is all in all" (Outler, 1986, p. 353). Wesley concluded religious instruction should occur: "in the morning, in the evening, and all the day beside" (Outler, 1986, p. 360), reminiscent of the biblical writer's call in Deut. 6:7.

How to teach – methodology

Wesley identified a series of "ills" in human nature and correspondingly offered responses parents should employ to deter or eliminate those "ills" from their children. The first "ill" was atheism, which Wesley suggested is encouraged in children by parents who fear God but speak little of Him in the daily life, ascribe the things of creation to "nature", and contribute good fortune to "chance" or the "wisdom of men" (Outler, 1986, pp. 352-353). Self-will was another disease that parents encourage in their children when they let them have their own way and seek after their own will, but he admonished a "wise parent" breaks their will and requires obedience. Parents are to "studiously teach them to submit to this while they are children" with "incredible firmness and resolution" (Outler, 1986, p. 354). He further contended: You must hold on still in an even course; you must never intermit your attention for one hour; otherwise you lose your labour" (Outler, 1986, p. 354).

He noted things a parent should not do in the religious instruction of their child: "feed and increase the natural falsehood of their children" and "connive" and strengthen the "ill-nature" of their children by "laughing at, or even applauding, their witty contrivances" (Outler, 1986, p. 360). Wesley also instructed "wise and kind" parents to not feed the "desires of the eyes" or the "desires of the flesh" in their children (Outler, 1986, p. 357), to not allow their children to practice "unmercifullness", to lie, or cheat. Parents were told to not encourage pride through praising the children "to their face" (Outler, 1986, p. 356) but rather to "use every means to give them a love of truth, -- of veracity, sincerity, and simplicity, and of openness both of spirit and behavior" (Outler, 1986, p. 360).

What to teach

Wesley posited that parents should teach their children to "walk in love, as Christ also loved us, and gave himself for us" (Outler, 1986, p. 360). He instructed parents to teach their children to "put away all lying" (Outler, 1986, p.359), "sow the seeds of justice in their hearts" (Outler, 1986, p. 360) and "walk in love" (Outler, 1986, p. 360). Wesley suggested parents should "teach your child as soon as possibly you can that they are fallen spirits; that they are fallen short of that glorious image of God wherein they were at first created" (Outler, 1986, p. 356) and to acknowledge that all praise and glory belong to God alone (Outler, 1986, p. 356). Wesley offered a description of God and His work of grace on humanity's behalf that parents were to inculcate on their children:

> God made you, and me, and the earth, and the sun, and the moon, and everything. And everything is his; heaven, and earth, and all that is therein. God orders all things: he makes the sun shine, and the wind blow, and the trees bear fruit. Nothing comes by chance; that is a silly word; there is no such thing as chance. As God made the world, so he governs the world, and everything that is in it. Not so much as a sparrow falls to the ground without the will of God. And as he governs all things, so he governs all men, good and bad, little and great. He gives them all the power and wisdom they have. And he overrules all. He gives us all the goodness we have; every good thought, and word, and work, are from him. Without him we can neither think anything right, or do anything right. (Outler, 1986, p. 353)

In light of that view of God, Wesley described human nature as defined by atheism, pride, love of the world, desire of the flesh, anger, lying, acting contrary to justice, and self-will but the Christian life should aim to serve, know, and love God.

Sermon #96, "On Obedience to Parents."

The primary biblical text for the sermon "On Obedience to Parents" was Colossians 3:20: "Children, obey your parents in all things" (KJV). Wesley noted that the obligations identified by the Apostle Paul in Colossians 3:20 as well as Ephesians 6:1 that draw from the fifth commandment are "extended to all ages" (p. 362). In other words, "children" is not a description of a specific age but is an address to everyone. Wesley concluded that children were to obey or honor their parents throughout their lives, that obedience and honor were not tied to an age and did not have an expiration date. This sermon addressed the research questions as identified in the frequency of the analytical codes associated with each question as noted in Appendix G, Figure G3.

Descriptive codes

The third sermon, "On Obedience to Parents" was published in the *Arminian Magazine* in the September and October issues of 1784 (Outler, 1986; Willhauck, 1992, p. 192). "On Obedience to Parents" is from the text Col. 3:20, a text Wesley had not preached from previously in public, but a text that fit in the sermon series with "On Family Religion" and "On the Education of Children" (Outler, 1986, p. 361). This sermon, as the other two, was addressed to the congregation or members of the Methodist societies through the publication, the *Arminian Magazine*. Specifically, however, the sermon addressed parents and children.

Why teach

Wesley reminded the audience of Paul's words to "obey your parents in all things" (Col. 3:20) and suggested the three reasons to do so are because it is right, it is acceptable to the Lord, and the command comes with the promise. Wesley wrote that if children obeyed their parents in all things:

> God will bless you to them, and them to you: All around will feel that God is with you of a truth. Many shall see it and praise God; and the fruit of it will remain when both you and they are lodged in Abraham's bosom. (Outler, 1986, p. 372)

He also warned that lack of obedience would result in stubbornness, misery, and damnation.

Who shall teach

Wesley's expectation for parents to carry the responsibility of the religious instruction of their children was clear, but in this sermon he offered further distinction beyond mothers and fathers to specifically "parents that fear God" and acknowledged the role of the Holy Spirit, and to "children of religious parents" (p. 371). Wesley also addressed grandmothers, admonishing them to not give their grandchildren anything that the child's mother forbids and to support the parents in their discipline.

How to teach – when

In this sermon, as in the other two, Wesley suggested that instruction should occur early: "begin this great work before they can run alone, before they can speak plan, or perhaps speak at all" (Outler, 1986, p. 367) and in reference to when to break their will: "break their will from their infancy...do it now; better late than never. It should have been done before they were two years old: It may be done at eight or ten, though with far more difficulty" (Outler, 1986, p. 370).

How to teach – methodology

He noted that parents should instruct their children "in the discipline and doctrine of the Lord" and to conquer their wills in order to "form their minds" (Outler, 1986, pp. 366 and 367). Wesley acknowledged that informing their understanding is "a work of time, and must proceed by slow degrees" however, breaking the child's will "must be done at once; and the sooner the better" (Outler, 1986, p. 367). While he admonished parents to break the child's will, which sounds harsh and cruel, Wesley was clear that the methodology employed must be done with firmness, consistency, kindness, and grace. He noted specific practices parents should avoid in their instruction such as rewarding their children for disobedience, demonstrating fondness for their children rather than true love, and encouraging their children to "adorn themselves" rather than practice simplicity in dress (Outler, 1986, p. 370). He acknowledged that godly instruction requires patience and the grace of God, and he comforted parents when he said: "this grace is sufficient to give you diligence as well as resolution" (Outler, 1986, p. 369).

What to teach

Obedience was the primary focus of what to teach in this sermon. Children were to be taught to obey, first their parents and eventually God:

> The Father of spirits has given this direction, that as the strength of the parents supplies the want of strength, and the understanding of the parents the want of understanding, in their children, till they have strength and understanding of their own; so the will of the parents may [should] guide that of their children till they have wisdom and experience to guide themselves. This, therefore, is the very first thing which children have to learn, -- that they are to obey their parents, to submit to their will, in all things. (Outler, 1986, pp. 365-366)

Humanity's natural state was described as self-focused and seeking after self-will. Self-will was referred to as the "root" of all sin and the "grand impediment to our temporal and eternal happiness" (Outler, 1986, p. 368). Wesley noted that an eternity in heaven rather than hell depended on the relinquishment of self-will to God's will through the acceptance of God's work for our salvation. The Christian life rather than a focus on self was to be characterized by obedience, love for God, and love for each other.

Susanna Wesley's Letter

Susanna Annesley Wesley was born into a Puritan pastor's household she described as a family church where "the foundations of solid piety...in sound principles and virtuous dispositions" were laid (Baker, 1982, p. 113). She was well educated, a consumer of the written word, and methodical in her thinking and writing (Edwards, 1949; Telford, 1898). She married Samuel Wesley and they had seventeen children - nine girls and eight boys of whom seven girls and three boys survived (Baker, 1982). Susanna developed her own views and practices of child rearing through the influence of Locke, Milton, and her puritan experiences (Edwards, 1949; Heitzenrater, 2001). She was the schoolmaster of the parsonage providing Christian education personally to all her children (Baker, 1982; Telford, 1898). Her grandson, Samuel Wesley, noted of her approach to Christian education "she had the happy talent of imbuing a child's mind with every kind of useful knowledge in such a way as to stamp it indelibly on the memory" (Telford, 1898, p. 15). Although her methods would be considered extreme by today's standards, they were moderate and progressive by eighteen-century culture standards. An indication that her methods were not too severe was the relationship she enjoyed with her children throughout her life: "Susanna earned her children's affection, a feeling they maintained all their lives" (Baker, 1982, p. 117). Edwards (1949) suggested that Susanna's educational practices were ahead of her time but that her greatest influencers were "theological dogma rather than theories of education" (p. 65). She believed "literally and seriously" in the fall of man rather than a child's natural innocence (Edwards, 1949, p. 65). This theological perspective provided the framework for her most notable teaching that the will of a child needed to be broken in order for the child to learn obedience to their parents and ultimately obedience to God (Edwards, 1949). Baker (1982) acknowledged the criticism Susanna faced for this principal but posited: "Harassed mothers of today may marvel that by using this principle, Susanna was successful in teaching all her children. Because it was practiced with both patience and love, her principle, however theoretically arguable, proved successful" (pp. 117-118).

Summation of letter

The letter provided a glimpse into Samuel and Susanna's household practices, child rearing, and child faith formation with an attention to the physical, mental, emotional, and spiritual growth of the children. Heitzenrater (2001) suggested that the method of education identified in the letter was typical of the eighteenth century and reflective of the work of Locke and Milton. Although "many of her specific instructions exhibit what might be called imposed formation" she did not appear to have been a severe disciplinarian by eighteenth century standards (Heitzenrater, 2001, p. 283). Two of the points evident in the letter that Susanna held in common with Locke were to conquer the child's will and the importance of education in the home (Willhauck, 1992). Her value of one on one instruction with her children was also evident as well as her attention to orderliness and obedience. As indicated in the letter, "She was a 'methodist' long before her son was – indeed, long before the critical term was coined. Perhaps he was a Methodist because she was" (Baker, 1982, p. 129). Although it appears, as Heitzenrater (2001) suggested, that Susanna imposed formation through her practices, the letter indicated she was not authoritarian or dictatorial in her approach rather was advisory and supportive (Willhauck, 1992).

> Her skill and love and patience were repaid by the responsiveness and aptitude of the children. Even more she gained their love and lasting respect. If for a time they felt they were under law they quickly passed to the condition of being under grade. She gave them not only knowledge but also a zeal for more; no merely forced obedience could have accomplished that. She survived the acid test of the good teacher that when left to themselves, freed from her control, they still had a great love of sound learning. (Edwards, 1949, p. 67)

Three significant contemporary educational thoughts were conveyed in the letter: To not punish a child more than once for an offense, to not succumb to a child's desires in order to stop their crying, and to educate girls equally with boys. Fowler (1985) noted the impact of her methodology of firmness, clarity, and consistency created a valuable sense of order and combined with her emphasis on prayer and Scripture that "provided for tangible and powerful actualization of the reality of God" (p. 174). Susanna's child faith formation practices laid the foundation for a lifetime of spiritual discipline, obedience to God's will, and thoughtful reflection of spiritual things.

Descriptive codes

Susanna wrote the letter to John in July 24, 1732 from the Epworth parsonage (Edwards, 1949; Southey, 1903; Telford, 1898). John Wesley turned to his mother for advice because of his experiences with her child rearing practices and "because she was exceptionally well read and extremely wise in the ways of both God and man" (Baker, 1982, p. 128). Heitzenrater (2001) noted "during his days as a tutor at Lincoln College, he [John] solicited from her [Susanna] a description of her techniques and rules, which he published in his journal at her death" (pp. 282-283). The letter itself indicated it was a response to Wesley's request:

> Dear Son, According to your desire, I have collected the principal rules I observed in educating my family; which I now send you as they occurred to my mind, and you may dispose of them in what order you please. (Jackson, 1872, Vol. I, p. 387)

Wesley noted his reason for entering the letter into his journal: "for the benefit of those who are entrusted, as she was, with the care of a numerous family" (Jackson, 1872, Vol. I, p. 387). The letter not only appeared in Wesley's journal of August 1742 but was also cited in numerous sermons and writings of Wesley's including the sermon "On Obedience to Parents" and in the rules for Kingswood school as noted in both "A Short Account of the School in Kingswood" and "A Plain Account of Kingswood School" (Baker, 1982; Heitzenrater, 2001; Prince, 1926).

Why teach. Susanna acknowledged the reason of the early instruction: "By this means they escaped abundance of correction they might otherwise have had" (Jackson, 1872, Vol. I, p. 387). She also suggested that the "subjecting the will" of the child should be done "at once and the sooner the better" because "by neglecting timely correction they will be overcome with stubbornness, and obstinacy. This is hardly ever conquered later" (Jackson, 1872, Vol. I, p. 388).

Who shall teach. Susanna wrote from the perspective of the home with the parents identified as the primary source of religious instruction. She identified as "cruel" parents those who allowed their children "to get habits, which they must be later broken" (cite) and called for parents to not neglect correction. She noted that it was rare to find a parent who knew what "true religion" was and who understood the nature of religion.

How to teach - when. Susanna began the formal education of her children at age five, but all of her children were taught to obey before that age: "The children were always put into a regular method of living, in such things as they were capable of, from their birth" (Jackson, 1872, Vol. I, p. 387). She continued: "When turned a year old, (and some before,) they were taught to fear the rod, and to cry softly" (Jackson, 1872, Vol. I, p. 387). The indication of these comments on when instruction of her children began was that Susanna started very early, from the moment of their birth, with strong expectations on their obedience by the age of one. Religious instruction in spiritual disciplines also began early as noted when she conveyed: "The children of this family were taught, as soon as they could speak, the Lord's prayer" (Jackson, 1872, Vol. I, p. 389) and acknowledged, "at a very early age before they could speak or walk made to distinguish the Sabbath from other days" (Jackson, 1872, Vol. I, p. 389).

How to teach – methodology

Strict routine and discipline were enforced in their mealtime habits "as soon as they were grown pretty strong" (Jackson, 1872, Vol. I, p. 388):

> They were confined to three meals a day. At dinner their little table and chairs were placed by ours, where they could be overlooked; and they were suffered to eat and drink as much as they would, but not to call for any thing...as soon as they could handle a knife and fork, they were set at our table. They were never suffered to choose their meat, but always made to eat such things as were provided for the family. (Jackson, 1872, Vol. I, pp. 387-388)

Meals consisted of one "sparing" item, eating and drinking were not permitted between meals, and supper was always served at 6:00 p.m. following family prayers. The daily routine included being washed at 7:00 p.m. and put to bed at 8:00 p.m. Likewise, communication was ordered, as were mealtimes and bedtimes. Children were never given anything they cried for but were directed to ask for what they wanted and were instructed to always say: "Pray give me such a thing" (Jackson, 1872, Vol. I, p. 390). "Taking God's name in vain, cursing and swearing, profaneness, obscenity, rude, ill-bred names, were never heard among them" (Jackson, 1872, Vol. I, p. 390) and they never used each other's given names without adding the title of brother or sister.

The strict routine was carried beyond the child's sleeping and eating routine to their spiritual practices as well. The Lord's Prayer was said at rising and bedtime and when they were older "a short prayer for their parents, and some Collects; a short Catechism, and some portion of Scripture, as their memories could bear" were added (Jackson, 1872, Vol. I, p. 389). They were taught to be silent during family prayers and even before they could speak to ask for a blessing immediately following "which they used to do by signs" (Jackson, 1872, Vol. I, p. 389). Susanna mentioned that when the family returned to their rebuilt house after the fire, singing the Psalms was done daily in the morning and evening and before and after school. In addition, they read a chapter from Psalms and the Old Testament in the morning and a chapter form Psalms and the New Testament in the evening. Following the reading of Psalms and chapter in the Old Testament, the children would retire for "private prayers" (Jackson, 1872, Vol. I, p. 391).

Susanna also followed a rigorous routine in the formal education of her children. They were all taught to read at age five and the school hours were from nine until noon and from two until five. All of the children learned their letters in a day or a day and a half and then began to read starting with the first chapter of Genesis. "As soon as they knew the letters, they were put first to spell, and read one line, then a verse; never leaving, till perfect in their lesson" (Jackson, 1872,

Vol. I, pp. 390-391). The school day followed strict rules of quiet without loud talking or playing permitted: "Rising out of their places, or going out of the room, was not permitted, unless for good cause; and running into the yard, garden, or street, without leave, was always esteemed a capital offense" (Jackson, 1872, Vol. I, p. 391).

How to teach – break the will

Of all the methodology she employed, the one most noted was her prescription: "In order to form the minds of children, the first thing to be done is to conquer their will, and bring them to an obedient temper" (Jackson, 1872, Vol. I, p. 388). Susanna suggested that when the will of a child was brought to obedience, then "childish follies and inadvertences may be passed by. Some should be overlooked and taken no notice of, and others mildly reproved" (Jackson, 1872, Vol. I, p. 389). She noted, however, that willful transgressions should never be overlooked but chastised "as the nature and circumstances of the offense require" (Jackson, 1872, Vol. I, p. 389). She identified the value in conquering the will of children "because this is the only strong and rational foundation of a religious education" (Jackson, 1872, Vol. I, p. 389). When a child was brought to the point where they surrender their self-will, they were "capable of being governed by the reason and piety of its parents, till its own understanding comes to maturity, and the principles of religion have taken root in the mind" (Jackson, 1872, Vol. I, p. 389). Susanna identified true religion as doing the will of God.

How to teach – observed by-laws

Susanna argued that her strict routine and methodology provided her children necessary personal discipline and called parents "cruel" who would "permit their children to get habits, which they know must be later broken" (Jackson, 1872, Vol. I, p. 388). As a form of summation to her methodology of instruction, Susanna provided a list of eight "by-laws" the family observed. They appear in their entirety in Appendix H but are summarized as follows:

If a child was charged with a "fault" and confessed their guilt with a promise to "amend", they would not be "beaten" for the offense;

"No sinful action, as lying, pilfering, playing at church, or on the Lord's day, disobedience, quarrelling, & etc." was ever left unpunished (Jackson, 1872, Vol. I, p. 392);

No child was ever "beaten" for the same offense twice;

Every act of obedience was noticed and rewarded;

If a child was obedient, but their action was not well done, the child would be commended for their obedience and instructed "with sweetness" on how to do better in the future;

A child could never take or borrow something that belonged to someone else without permission;

No gift that was given freely could be taken back, unless it was given conditionally and the conditions were not met;

No girl was taught to work until she was taught to read and then her time for work must never be greater than the time allotted for reading. (Jackson, 1872, Vol. I, pp. 392-393)

Susanna's consistency in discipline and yet fairness in response was evident in these by-laws.

What to teach

Scripture played a critical role in the education and instruction of the Wesley children. They were taught to memorize the Lord's Prayer and to read from the Bible. Together they read chapters in Psalms, the New Testament and the Old Testament daily. They memorized portions of scripture and a short catechism and sang songs from the Psalms. Not only did Scripture play a valuable role in Susanna's child faith formation, but prayer was a fundamental element in their daily routine as well. They held daily family prayers and were expected to engage in personal times of prayer and reflection. The letter mentioned a "short prayer for their parents" that the children memorized and prayed daily as well as the Lord's Prayer. In addition to Scripture and prayer, they were taught to respect the Sabbath and engaged in worship services both in their home and in the church. The frequency of codes contained in the data of Susanna Wesley's letter to John Wesley is identified in Appendix I, Figure I1.

Serious Thoughts Concerning Godfathers and Godmothers

Wesley responded to objections raised over the practice and role of godfathers and godmothers in a brief writing titled "Serious Thoughts Concerning Godfathers and Godmothers. It was published independently as a pamphlet, as part of a larger compilation, and was included in Wesley's journal. It was dated "Athlone, August 6, 1752" in Wesley's journal (Jackson, 1872, Vol. X, p. 309). The article was also published as an independent pamphlet but with limited information as to the full title, authorship, or printer provided (Green, 1906). In addition to the limited information on the printed pamphlet, Green (1906) noted an error in the dating on the pamphlet: "Dated at end, Athlone, Aug. 1732, obviously an error for Aug. 6, 1752, on which date Wesley was in Athlone" (p. 77). The date of August 6, 1752 and the location of Athlone align with the notation in Wesley's journal. "Serious Thoughts Concerning Godfathers and Godmothers" was also printed as part of a larger work collected by Wesley and printed by E. Farley in 1758 titled *A Preservative Against Unsettled Notions in Religion*.

Summation

In "Serious Thoughts Concerning Godfathers and Godmothers", Wesley referred to godparents as "witnesses" whose role was "to watch over those souls in a peculiar manner, to instruct, admonish, exhort, and build them up in the faith" (Jackson, 1872, Vol. X, p. 506). Wesley also noted that the godparents were "a kind of spiritual parents to the baptized, whether they were infants or at man's estate; and were expected to supply whatever spiritual helps were wanting either through the death or neglect of the natural parents" (Jackson, 1872, Vol. X, p. 506). He identified infant baptism as part of the baptism practices in the ancient church and noted that Tertullian referred to godparents as "sponsors" (Jackson, 1872, Vol. X, p. 506).

The three objections to the practice of godfathers and godmothers posed in the publication included:

(1.) There is no mention of godfathers and godmothers in Scripture;

(2.) That many undertake this without ever considering what they undertake, or once seriously thinking how to perform it;

(3.) That no serious man [or woman] would undertake it, because it is impossible to perform it. (Jackson, 1872, Vol. X, p. 507)

In response to the first objection, Wesley acknowledged that Scripture does not include any reference to godparents "it is undoubtedly true...and therefore it cannot be said they are absolutely necessary" (Jackson, 1872, Vol. X, p. 507). Wesley suggested that although not biblically necessary godparents are "highly expedient" in the faith formation of a child when they are chosen well. Wesley also concurred with the second objection and held the parents responsible for the poor selection: "It is altogether the fault of those foolish parents who will, on any account whatever, either desire or suffer these to be sponsors for their children, that do not take care of their own souls" (Jackson, 1872, Vol. X, p. 507). He counseled parents to select individuals as godparents who "truly fear God" (Jackson, 1872, Vol. X, p. 507). The third objection Wesley contributed to ignorance of the role of godparents and a lack of understanding of the liturgy. The liturgy contained a response by the godparents that was misunderstood to suggest, "the sponsors themselves undertake or promise, that the child shall 'renounce the devil and all his works, constantly believe, God's holy word, and obediently keep his commandments'" (Jackson, 1872, Vol. X, p. 508). Wesley protested that the godparents or sponsors did not make the promise but it was the infant that made the promise as suggested in the liturgy: "This infant must for his part promise" (Jackson, 1872, Vol. X, p. 508). Wesley offered a further explanation that he did not include the troubling questions in the liturgy but "the compilers of our Liturgy inserted them because they were used in all the ancient Liturgy" (Jackson, 1872, Vol. X, p. 508). The godparents' role was not to promise that the child would "renounce the devil and all his works" but to remind the child that through their infant baptism they (the child) renounced the devil and his works.

Descriptive codes

The document "Serious Thoughts Concerning Godfathers and Godmothers" was a publication and the audience identified as the members of the Methodist societies at large but specifically parents and potential godparents.

Why teach

Wesley noted the motivation for instruction is to lay "a foundation of holiness and happiness" that will last "even to your late posterity" (Jackson, 1872, Vol. X, p. 509). He concluded the document with the promise that if the foundation of "holiness and happiness" is laid "then it may justly be hoped, that not only you and your house, but also the children which shall be born, shall serve the Lord" (Jackson, 1872, Vol. X, p. 509).

Who shall teach

Wesley identified the godparents' and parents' role in the faith formation of children and instructed parents to "Regard not whether they [the godparents] are rich or poor" but do select godparents who "truly fear God" (Jackson, 1872, Vol. X, p. 507). Wesley described parents as "wise and kind" who selected godparents that "truly fear and serve God" and to not regard if they are "rich or poor" (Jackson, 1872, Vol. X, p. 508). As in other documents studied, Wesley identified God as the true source of instruction and inspiration in the faith formation of children. He admonished parents and godparents to proceed "with all the wisdom and power God hath given you" (Jackson, 1872, Vol. X, p. 509).

How to teach

"Serious Thoughts Concerning Godfathers and Godmothers" identified that instruction should occur "as soon as he [she] shall be able to learn, what a solemn vow, promise, and profession he [she] hath here made by you" (Jackson, 1872, Vol. X, p. 508). Wesley called for godparents to perform their duties "faithfully, with all the wisdom and power God hath given you" (Jackson, 1872, Vol. X, p. 509). Wesley also identified the methodology of instruction embarked by the godparent: "you do undertake to see that he [she] be taught the things a Christian ought to know and believe" and to bring the child up "to lead a godly and a Christian life" (Jackson, 1872, Vol. X, p. 508).

What to teach

Wesley identified "the creed, the Lord's Prayer, and the Ten Commandments, and all other things which a Christian ought to know and believe to his [her] soul's health" (Jackson, 1872, Vol. X, p. 508) as critical for a child's religious instruction. The godparents were expected to remind the child of the promise they made at their baptism to "renounce the devil and all his works, constantly believe, God's holy word, and obediently keep his commandments" (Jackson, 1872, Vol. X, p. 508). Frequency of the research codes as they relate specifically to the document "Serious Thoughts Concerning Godfathers and Godmothers" is found in Appendix I, Figure I2.

A Thought on the Manner of Educating Children

"A Thought on the Manner of Educating Children" was a short work included in Wesley's journal (Jackson, 1872, Vol. XIII). It was printed in 1783 and appeared in the Arminian Magazine in 1783 (Prince, 1926). The short work was written at the end of Wesley's life and indicated his awareness of a child's faith formation potential and his continued commitment to that endeavor (Prince, 1926).

Summation

As in the previously addressed document, Wesley wrote in response to direct criticism; criticism he faced regarding the educational practices at Kingswood schools and the schools run by Miss Bosanquet and Miss Owen (Jackson, 1872, Vol. XIII, p. 474). The objections centered on the severe discipline and forced religion that were said to characterize these schools and the supposed results of religious indifference by the students (Rack, 2002, pp. 33-354). Wesley identified the specific elements objected to as:

> Bringing them up too strictly; to the giving them more religion than they liked; to the telling them of it too often, or pressing it upon them whether they will or no. He thought that the common methods that are used in those that are called religious schools, of talking about divine things continually, and daily pressing it upon children, did abundantly more harm than good; especially if any severity were used. (Jackson, 1872, Vol. XIII, p. 474)

Wesley compared the educational preference of the criticizer with that of Rousseau found in *Emilius,* which Wesley described as "the most empty, silly, injudicious thing that ever a self-conceited infidel wrote" (Jackson, 1872, Vol. XIII, p. 474). Wesley reflected on the possibility of this man's point of view being correct, but concluded "I doubt the fact; nay, that is not enough, I totally deny it" (Jackson, 1872, Vol. XIII, p. 475). However, Wesley acknowledged "Yet, I allow that what is commonly called a religious education frequently does more hurt than good" (Jackson, 1872, Vol. XIII, p. 475). He concluded that when this is the case it is either the "religion wherein they are instructed, or the manner of instructing them, be wrong" (Jackson, 1872, Vol. XIII, p. 475).

Descriptive codes

The document was identified as a publication and the audience was the members of the Methodist societies at large but specifically parents and teachers.

Why teach

Wesley identified the purpose of Christian education when he noted: "The bias of nature is set the wrong way: education is designed to set it right" (Jackson, 1872, Vol. XIII, p. 476).

Who shall teach

Wesley noted both parents and teachers or "instructers" as responsible for the religious instruction of children. The document did not include a description of the expected lifestyle of the parents but offered insight into that of the teachers. It is worded in a way to suggest that the expected lifestyle for instructors was the same as the parents:

> Then let them [the children] be delivered to instructers, (if such can be found,) that will tread in the same steps; that will watch over them as immortal spirits, who are shortly to appear before God, and who have nothing to do in this world but to prepare to meet him in the clouds, seeing they will be eternally happy, if they are ready; if not, eternally miserable. (Jackson, 1872, Vol. XIII, p. 477)

Wesley also posited that parents and must "understand the nature of religion" and "know what true religion is" (Jackson, 1872, Vol. XIII, p. 476).

How to teach - when

Wesley posed the question: "But does it follow, that we ought not to instill true religion into the minds of children as early as possible?" and answered the question with the response "we should do it with all diligence from the very time that reason dawns" (Jackson, 1872, Vol. XIII, p. 476). Later in the document he also addressed when the behaviors associated with the child's corrupt nature should be addressed: "From the moment we perceive any of those evil roots springing up" (Jackson, 1872, Vol. XIII, p. 476). Wesley concluded this "Thought" with an address to parents and a plea to "let all that have children, from the time they begin to speak or run alone, begin to train them up in the way wherein they should go" (Jackson, 1872, Vol. XIII, p. 477).

How to teach – methodology

Wesley also addressed the methodology that should be employed in the religious instruction of children. He noted that one of the reasons religious education "does more hurt than good" is a lack of understanding on the part of the teacher on how to instruct children. He identified errors in the methodology that included a "lack of government" by the instructor or the inclination to "habitually lean to this or that extreme" (Jackson, 1872, Vol. XIII, p. 476). By "extreme" Wesley suggested teachers "either give children too much of their own will, or needlessly and churlishly retrain them" and "use no punishment at all, or more than is necessary" (Jackson, 1872, Vol. XIII, p. 476). He then identified a means of instruction that offered better results in the faith formation of children. These included: "with all diligence", "laying line upon line", and with "all pains and care" (Jackson, 1872, Vol. XIII, p. 476). Wesley also noted that the "roots" of evil should be rooted out but with "mildness, softness, and gentleness" (Jackson, 1872, Vol. XIII, p. 476). He added an additional note, however, if this method was not productive "then we must correct with kind severity" (Jackson, 1872, Vol. XIII, p. 477). Wesley's first direction was to instruct with kindness and gentleness and reserved the Proverbs 13:24 approach when these tactics did not work.

What to teach

Wesley suggested that "true religion" could be misunderstood to be: "barely the doing no harm, the abstaining from outward sin; some, the using the means of grace, saying our prayers, reading good books, and the like; and others the having a train of right opinions, which is vulgarly called faith" (Jackson, 1872, Vol. XIII, p. 476). In contrast, Wesley posited that "true religion" should be described as "consisting in holy tempers, in the love of God and our neighbour; in humility, gentleness, patience, long-suffering, contentedness in every condition, to sum up all, in the image of God, in the mind that was in Christ" (Jackson, 1872, Vol. XIII, p. 476). Frequency of the research codes as they relate specifically to the document "A Thought on the Manner of Educating Children" is found in Appendix I, Figure I3.

"A Short Account" and "A Plain Account" of the School in Kingswood

Wesley included in his journal several writings that acknowledged the purpose for starting the school in Kingswood, the management of the school, and the educational practices employed at the school. Felix Farley of Bristol printed "A Short Account of the School in Kingswood" in 1749, with a second edition printed in 1758 (Green, 1906). The date identified with the publication "A Short Account of the School in Kingswood" in Wesley's journal was 1768 (Jackson, 1872, Vol. XIII, p. 283), followed in the journal by "A Plain Account of Kingswood School" identified as "printed in the year 1781" (Jackson, 1872, Vol. XIII, p. 289). Wesley's journal contained three separate documents that referenced this "New House" in Kingswood. The first document, "A Short Account of the School in Kingswood," was published earlier and separately, while there was no record of the other two documents published other than as part of Wesley's journal (Green, 1906). "A Short Account of the School in Kingswood" was printed one year after the opening of the school. It described Wesley's educational practices while the "Plain Account" included a more robust discussion on the educational practices and "discussed some of the finer points of his philosophy of education" (Willhauck, 1992, p. 207). Wesley identified in the "Plain Account" document his motivation in writing:

> I have long taken it for granted, that it would be quite sufficient to publish the bare rules of that school, and to se down simply the method therein pursued, in as few

words as possible [such as is provided in "A Short Account"]. I supposed the reasons whereon those rules were grounded were not only so strong, but so obvious, that every person of common understanding must discern them as well as myself. However, after above twenty years' trial, I am convinced this was a supposition not to be made. What is as clear to me as the sun at noon-day, is not so clear to every one. At length, therefore, I judged it needful to enlarge a little upon the nature of that institution; to lay down the grounds of those rules, and the reasons of what is peculiar in our method. (Jackson, 1872, Vol. XIII, p. 289)

Rack (2002) noted that there were four schools in Kingswood by 1749, but Wesley was most attentive to the school he called "New House" (p. 355). This school opened in 1748 with six instructors or masters and 285 students (Green, 1906). It was suggested that "Wesley gave much time and attention to this school for many years" and wrote many books for use at the school (Green, 1906, p. 61). Wesley's stated motivation for starting the school was his frustration with the educational practices of schools in his day, including those providing supposed Christian education (Jackson, 1872, Vol. XIII, pp. 289-292). Stonehouse (2004) posited: "Wesley held a very negative view of schools for children in his day and the options open to Methodist parents" (p. 145). He took issue with both the content of the instruction as well as the character of the teachers. Wesley identified five concerns with the schools in his day, but a singular concern was foundational to them all – "a total lack of religion and religious motive" for Wesley "religion and education must go together" (Body, 1936, p. 47).

Summation

In "A Short Account of the School in Kingswood" Wesley identified the purpose of his educational design, the resources used in each of the eight classes, what was taught, the cost of the education, and how students were selected. He concluded the document with the rules of the house that included sleeping, eating, and waking schedules. Buckroyd (2001) suggested that the daily schedule resembled that of Herrnhut; the Moravian school in Germany Wesley visited.

> He had learnt that in education the Moravians studied to 'amend the wills' of their scholars 'as well as their understanding; finding by experience, that when their will is moved they often learn more in a few hours than otherwise in many months. (Body, 1936, pp. 50-51)

Wesley also developed an appreciation for Comenius and an understanding of the practical application of his teachings at Herrnhut (Body, 1936). Body (1936) posited that for Comenius "education was not merely a means to eradicate natural sin, but to build up a moral control over man. Knowledge, virtue and piety, in this order of acquisition, were to be the aims of education" (p. 49). The "amend the wills" philosophy of the Moravians and Comenius' work were reflected in Wesley's methodology and description of the educational practices at Kingswood.

In "A Plain Account" Wesley provided his inspiration and motivation for his educational practices at the Kingswood school, his strategy in selection of the site of the school, the process of admission, selection of teachers, and expectations of the students' parents. He addressed the educational errors in other schools and noted how his school differed. He also compared the education provided at Kingswood with that provided at Oxford and Cambridge. He restated his purpose for the instructional method employed at the school and listed the "general rules" of the school (Jackson, 1872, Vol. XIII, p. 294). The rules included a description of the daily and weekly schedule and the associated behavior of the children. Wesley also provided a glimpse of the courses taught and the authors read (Jackson, 1872, Vol. XIII, pp. 294-295).

Descriptive codes

The documents, "A Short Account of the School in Kingswood" and "A Plain Account of Kingswood School" were both identified through the descriptive coding phase as publications. The intended readers were not specifically identified, but because of the inclusion in Wesley's journal and his stated motivation for printing, it is assumed the intended readership were the members of the Methodist societies at large.

Why teach

Wesley identified the purpose of the education provided at Kingswood school when he wrote: "Our design is, with God's assistance, to train up children in every branch of useful learning" (Jackson, 1872, Vol. XIII, p. 283). He further expounded: "It is our particular desire, that all who are educated here may be brought up in the fear of God; and at the utmost distance, as from vice in general" (Jackson, 1872, Vol. XIII, p. 284) and concluded: "Whoever carefully goes through this course will be a better scholar than nine in ten of the graduates at Oxford or Cambridge" (Jackson, 1872, Vol. XIII, p. 289). From this description it appeared his motivation was to provide God-inspired instruction that resulted in students who were both God-fearing and excellent scholars. In the "Plain Account" Wesley reiterated his statement also found in the "Short Account": "It is our particular desire, that all who are educated here may be brought up in the fear of God; and at the utmost distance, as from vice in general" (Jackson, 1872, Vol. XIII, p. 294) and added:

> Our first point was to answer the design of Christian education, by forming their minds, through the help of God, to wisdom and holiness, by instilling the principles of true religion, speculative and practical, and training them up in the ancient way, that they might be rational, Scriptural Christians. (Jackson, 1872, Vol. XIII, p. 293)

In this document, Wesley placed the primary emphasis on the formation of students who are "rational, Scriptural Christians" in whom religion and education are fully integrated.

Who shall teach

Wesley described his search for masters or teachers who were "sufficient" in their knowledge of the course of study they were to teach and teachers who possessed:

> The fear of God...who were truly devoted to God; who sought nothing on earth, neither pleasure, nor ease, nor profit, nor the praise of men; but simply to glorify God, with their bodies and spirits, in the best manner they were capable of. (Jackson, 1872, Vol. XIII, p. 292)

Stonehouse (2004) conjectured that Wesley "placed great importance on the character of the schoolmaster and all the adults who worked at the school. For effective education, Wesley realized that the teachers' lives needed to demonstrate what they taught" (p. 146). Wesley noted that only children whose parents agreed to the school's rules were considered for admittance, and parents who desire that there children not be "almost, but altogether, Christians" (cite).

How to teach – when

In both documents, Wesley identified the accepted age of students between six and twelve years old with emphasis provided in the "Plain Account": "One of these rules was, that 'no child shall be admitted after he is twelve years old.' The ground of this rule was, a child could not well before that age be rooted either in bad habits or ill principles" (Jackson, 1872, Vol. XIII, p. 293). Instruction was only provided to boarders, therefore, the instruction occurred at school.

How to teach – methodology

The methodology and design of the instruction provided at Kingswood was described in detail in both accounts. In the "Short Account", Wesley identified that only boarders were accepted, and they were taught "reading, writing, arithmetic, English, French, Latin, Greek, Hebrew, history, geography, chronology, rhetoric, logic, ethics, geometry, algebra, physics, music" (Jackson, 1872, Vol. XIII, p. 283). Wesley also noted the daily schedule of the students and the general rules of the house that included the time the children rose, how they spent their private morning time, and the details of their day by the hour. The daily schedule described a strict routine with a focus on spiritual disciplines, study, and instruction. Every day followed an identical schedule, except for Sunday. The diet reflected a similar consistency in routine and included specific foods for each day of the week, water as the only beverage, and nothing to eat between meals.

Wesley reiterated the rules in the "Plain Account" with a bit more perspective on why or how each rule of the house was engaged. An example was a description of the work the students employed: "On fair days they work, according to their strength, in the garden; on rain days, in the house. But particular care is taken that they never work; alone, but always in the presence of a Master" (Jackson, 1872, Vol. XIII, p. 294).

Wesley provided the list of books read in each course of study and the way in which the books were presented – from easiest to hardest (Jackson, 1872, Vol. XIII, p. 295). Heitzenrater (1995) posited: "The severity of the daily schedule matched the rigor of the academic discipline" (p. 168) and Willhauck (1992) posited: "The severity of his method was not based on an ignorance of children [which could be assumed by the severity of the schedule and expectations] but on an attempt to help children to realize their potential" (p. 22). One rule that would appear severe and not respective of childhood developmental needs was Wesley's exclusion of "play-days" in the schedule; no play was allowed on any day. In defense of that rule, Wesley quoted a German proverb: "'He that plays when he is a boy, will play when he is a man'" and suggested the allowance of play would instill an action that would have to be unlearned as an adult (Jackson, 1872, Vol. XIII, p. 294).

What to teach

In the "Short Account" Wesley listed the actual book titles in each of the eight classes, which included some of his own compositions such as *Instructions for Children* and *Lessons for Children* as well as classics such as Milton's *Pilgrim's Progress*, Law's *Christian Perfection* and *Serious Call* and Lewis's *Hebrew Antiquities*. He also identified works the students were required to translate or transcribe from Latin, Greek, and Hebrew. The children engaged Scripture through their daily schedule in personal reflection and in the reading of the Hebrew Bible and Greek New Testament. They also engaged prayer as part of their daily schedule with reference to a "short form" of prayer the children prayed daily until they could pray "in their own words" (Jackson, 1872, Vol. XIII, p. 285). Wesley desired for the students to have the "thoughts of God," the "fear of God," and to know the "oracles of God". Frequency of the research codes as they relate specifically to the documents "A Short Account of the School in Kingswood" and "A Plain Account of Kingswood School" is found in Appendix I, Figure I4 and Figure I5.

Concluding remarks of Kingswood School

Wesley identified both excitement and frustration with the school in Kingswood and eventually his goals for the school were not realized (Rack, 2002; Stonehouse, 2004). In another document in Wesley's journal (Jackson, 1872, Vol. XIII) that related to his work at the school at Kingswood titled "Remarks on the State of Kingswood School", Wesley noted:

> My design in building the house at Kingswood was, to have therein a Christian family; every member whereof, children excepted, should be alive to God, and a pattern of all holiness...And almost as soon as we began, God gave us a token for good; four of the children receiving a clear sense of pardon. But at present the school does not in any wise answer the design of the institution, either with regard to religion or learning. (Jackson, 1872, Vol. XIII, p. 301)

Wesley blamed the failure of achieving a "Christian family" at Kingswood on the teachers and staff. "The rules were not kept", "the masters were never right: either they were solemn and earnest and the boys ridiculed them, or they were adequate teachers but lacked piety and management skills" and ultimately the "religion" was found "wanting...except for the revival of 1768-1773" (Rack, 2002, pp. 358-359).

Hymns for Children

The influence of the German Moravians at Herrnhut was seen not only in the rigorous schedule Wesley instituted at Kingswood School, but also in his inclusion of hymns as part of a child's faith formation. Wesley noted in his Journal of August 1738 a citation from the Moravian constitution: "Our little children we instruct chiefly by hymns; whereby we find the most important truths most successfully insinuated into their minds" (Telford, 1827, Vol. 1, p. 135). Although Wesley offered no additional remarks to this citation in his Journal, Buckroyd (2001) suggested that Wesley understood the value of hymns as a teaching tool with children (p. 61) and Maddox (2008) suggested: "This precedent likely encouraged the Wesley brothers to provide hymns specifically for use by children" (p. 1).

Contextual analysis

John and Charles Wesley wrote and published a series of pamphlets that were titled *Hymns for Children*. There were at least three unique collections of hymns for children published between the 1740's and 1790. The first known published in 1747, a collection of 100 hymns in 1763, an abridged publication of that in 1787, and a reprint in 1790 with an added preface (Buckroyd, 2001; Green, 1906; Maddix, 2008).

The first publication is thought to be dated around 1747, although the pamphlet contained no author, date, or printer's name (Buckroyd, 2001; Green, 1906). It was in a pamphlet style with twelve pages of hymns for children and several prayers. The collection contained nine hymns all adopted from other works: Five hymns from *Hymns and Sacred Poems* (Wesley, 1742), two from *Hymns and Sacred Poems* (Wesley, 1740), and two from *A Collection of Psalms and Hymns* (Wesley, 1741) attributed to Isaac Watts and Samuel Wesley Jr. In addition, *Hymns for Children* contained a series of exhortations and prayers for children with some attributed to Thomas Ken and John Lewis (Maddox, 2008). Another publication that contained one hundred hymns was published in 1763 with an abridgement of that collection published in 1787. A new volume of *Hymns for Children* was published in 1790 that included a preface by John Wesley that provided "a clear indication of his approach to hymnody in relation to young people" (Buckroyd, 2001, p. 62). Wesley (1790) wrote:

> There are two ways of writing or speaking to children; the one is, to let ourselves down to them; the other, to life them up to us. Dr. Watts has wrote in the former way, and has succeeded admirably well, speaking to children as children, and leav-

ing them as he found them. The following hymns are written on the other plan; they contain strongly manly sense, yet expressed in such plain and easy language, as even children may understand. But when they do understand them, they will be children no longer, only in years and stature. (preface)

Prince (1926) noted that the preface aligns with the remarks in the *Instructions for Children* and *Lessons for Children* and "indicates Wesley's conviction that teaching should aim not simply to impart information but to develop the power of the pupil to think, and that it should lead him to the experimental knowledge of religion: (p. 132). Prince (1926) also identified the 1790 collection as one of the final publications of Wesley's and suggested that Wesley was committed to the faith formation of children even in his final days of ministry.

Question of authorship. There is some doubt as to the compiler and publisher of the 1747 printing of *Hymns for Children*. Green (1906) questioned the inclusion of one of the prayers ("At Lying Down in Bed") and suggested it was uncharacteristic of other Wesley writings. Buckroyd (2001), however, believed that the doctrinal and theological content of the collection suggested Wesley's involvement and noted the way *Hymns for Children* complemented *Instructions for Children* – a known work by John Wesley. "It [*Hymns for Children*] would appear to complement the *Instructions of Children* and together these books could have formed part of an educational program for children set up by John in the 1740's as a response to a perceived need" (Buckroyd, 2001, p. 77). In addition, Maddox (2008) proposed: "There are strong reasons to believe that John Wesley was the anonymous collector of this volume...There is little reason to doubt that John is the editor" (p. 1). Maddox (2008) identified as a primary argument the other catechetical materials John Wesley developed for children during that time period. He also noted that John Wesley had used Thomas Ken's work in other publications and recommended readings. The short bedtime prayer Green (1906) identified as "troublesome" Maddox (2008) identified as possibly a "poetic distillation of Ken" by Wesley (p. 1). Of the various publications of hymns for children, Maddox (2008) posited that John Wesley was the publisher of the 1747 and 1787 documents and Charles Wesley the source of the 1763 collection. Maddox (2008) concluded that John Wesley was the most likely source for the 1787 collection because of Charles's declining health at that time. The preface of the 1790 collection identified John as the publisher.

Purpose and use. Buckroyd (2001) asserted that the purpose of the hymns was for use at Kingswood School and in Methodist homes and that the content and approach parallels other works for children by Wesley of that time. These works included *Instructions for Children* (1745), *Lessons for Children* (1746, 1747, 1748), *A Token for Children* (1749) and textbooks written for Kingswood school in the 1750's. Buckroyd (2001) further asserted that the number of hymns included in the publication provided "a fixed hymn morning and evening, a daily hymn which fits into an overall plan for the week" (p. 70). Based on the work and findings of Maddox (2008) and Buckroyd (2001), this book focused on the 1747 publication of *Hymns for Children* (Maddox, 2008) as the original source but included for review the unique content from the 1790 preface.

Summation of Hymns for Children (1747)

The first hymn, (Hymn 1) began with the line "Gentle Jesus, meek, and mild" (Maddox, 2008, p. 1) and offered a request by the child to God for a relationship with Him based on the example of Jesus. The second hymn (Hymn 2) also identified Jesus' example as one to emulate, this time in response to earthly things and spoke of salvation through Christ's redemptive work. The fourth hymn (Hymn 4) was an anthem to Jesus the "lover of little children" and "loving Saviour". The other hymns focused more on God's provision as creator (Hymn 3), architect of salvation (Hymn 5), and God's eternal nature (Life and Eternity). There was a "Hymn for Sunday" that offered praise and celebration to God, "A Morning Hymn" that called for a relationship with God made possible through Jesus' work and "An Evening Hymn" that served as a prayer of confession.

The collection also included "An Exhortation for a Child" that instructed the child that their "chiefest care" was "to serve and glorify God" (Maddox, 2008, p. 10) and referenced Eccl. 12:1 and 2 Timothy 2:22. *Hymns for Children* also included "Directions for a Child" that told the child how they should approach prayer: "look on your souls as undress'd, 'till you have said your payers" (Maddox, 2008, p. 10). Beyond the exhortation and direction, *Hymns for Children* included prayers for morning, evening, "At Lying Down in Bed", and prayers for grace before and after meals. Buckroyd (2001) proposed that the language used in *Hymns for Children* was reflective of Wesley's era where it was assumed that children could grasp adult religious concepts from an early age. She posited: the hymns "assisted in the transfer of established patterns of thought and behavior from adults to children" (p. 77), which would have been considered a reasonable goal in the eighteen century. In light of contemporary educational theory, the language of the hymns could be deemed inappropriate for children in their tone and imagery.

Engagement with codes

Data was identified that only related to the research question what to teach. The preface to the 1790 hymnal included data related to how to teach, however, the 1747 edition contained no data that suggested why children should be taught, the methodology of instruction that should be employed, or who should be doing the instructing.

Descriptive codes. *Hymns for Children* (1747) was a publication intended for children, although the content and language by today's standards might suggest otherwise. The broader audiences were parents, teachers, and pastors for their use in faith formation of children.

Why teach. The 1747 publication of hymns contained no indication as to why religious instruction of the children should be provided.

Who shall teach. The 1747 publication of hymns contained no indication as to who was responsible for the religious instruction of the children.

How to teach. Although not explicitly defined, the question of when instruction should occur was suggested as daily and routinely through the inclusion of daily prayers prays for morning and evening and prayers for before and after mealtime.

What to teach – sin, humanity, Christian life. Sin was described as "contrary" to and "forbidden" by God and referenced as bringing "uneasy strife" ("Hymn I", Maddox, 2008, pp. 1-2). Human nature, or a person in their natural state before salvation, was described as a "poor and guilty worm" ("Hymn II", Maddox, 2008, p. 3), and "traveling to the grave" (Life and Eternity, p. 7). In contrast, the Christian life was described as "free from sin's uneasy strife" ("Hymn I", Maddox, 2008, p. 1). The request was to have a mind like Christ's, to be meek, gentle, mild, loving, humble, and obedient. There was a call to praise and serve God, to trust Him, do His will, and follow in His footsteps. The author described changes in mind ("Prepossess my tender mind"), changes in behavior ("Let me in thy footsteps tread"), and in attitude ("Let me cast the world behind") (Hymn II, Maddox, 2008, p. 3) that should exemplify the Christian life. There was a call to posses a transformed heart and to desire a relationship with God - "Give me thine only self to know...Open the intercourse between My longing soul and thee" ("A Morning Hymn", Maddox, 2008, p. 8). The goal of the child's life was advanced to "serve and glorify God" ("An Exhortation for a Child", Maddox, 2008, p. 10).

What to teach – God, salvation, Jesus, Holy Spirit, eternity. God was identified as the child's Father, friend, and redeemer. He was described as holy, eternal, almighty, loving, good, and merciful. God is called "the Eternal Word" and "Creator." God's grace was said to provide provision, protection, and rest. Jesus was the focus of many of the hymns. He was described as the "Lamb of God", gentle, meek, and mild. Jesus was said to be the "lover of children," humble and obedient, a "loving Saviour", "Lord of Sabbath", the "all restoring Word", and the "all-atoning Lamb." Significant data was also identified in relation to salvation. The work of salvation was attributed to Jesus: "Ransom'd by the bleeding Lamb. Jesus, this be all my boast, Thou hast sav'd a sinner lost, thou hast spilt thy noble blood Me to make a child of God" ("Hymn II", Maddox, 2008, p. 3). The result of salvation was that the child was forgiven, became "an heir of heaven" and possessed a purified heart. Heaven was described as "above" and the home of God. The "Spirit" of God was said to bring grace, insight, and the ability for the child to learn and understand.

What to teach – Bible and prayer. The hymns, prayers, and instructions identified the role of prayer in the child's life. The child was called to begin their day in prayer, pray anywhere, and always pray from the heart. In the "Directions for a Child" they were told to "Never omit prayer"" (Maddox, 2008, pp. 10). The prayers provided for morning, evening, at bed, before meals, and after meals offered examples of prayer for specific occasions. It appeared the child was expected to memorize these prayers and recite them daily. "Directions for a Child" also suggested prayers were to include praise and thanks, a call for forgiveness, and a request for blessing. The primacy of prayer in the child's Christian life was established through the hymns, prayers, and instructions contained in the *Hymns for*

Children. Buckroyd (2001) posited "these prayers provide a short but complete pattern for the child". Frequency of the research codes as they relate specifically to the document *Hymns for Children* is found in Appendix I, Figure I6.

Lessons for Children

Wesley wrote and published a four-part guide of selections of Scripture from the Old Testament and the Apocrypha with a few explanatory footnotes and references titled *Lessons for Children* (Wesley, 1746, 1747, 1748, 1754). The entire Old Testament is represented in part except for the books of Ruth, Song of Solomon, and Lamentations, and the Minor Prophets: Hosea, Joel, Amos, Obadiah, Jonah, Micah, Nahum, Habakkuk, Zephaniah, Haggai, Zechariah, or Malachi. Prince (1926) proposed Wesley did not include the New Testament "because he felt that all of it should be read" (p. 126) but Prince (1926) questioned why Wesley would not have included the story of Jonah. The first volume (Part I) of *Lessons for Children* was printed in 1746, the second volume (Part II) in 1747, and the third volume (Part III) in 1748. Of the first three volumes, no author or printer was identified in the material. The fourth volume (Part IV) was published in 1754 and identified as printed in London by Henry Cock. Thomas Cordeux of London published a second edition that included the entire work with all four parts in a single volume in 1816 (Green, 1906).

Summation

The "Lessons" provided the Old Testament in a narrative format that was intended as a tool of instruction with children. The preface to the first volume addressed the parents and schoolmasters with instructions on how to use the "Lessons". Children were identified as the intended users of the texts: "I have endeavoured in the following Lessons to collect the plainest and the most useful portions of Scripture, such as children may the most easily understand, and such as it most concerns them to know" (Wesley, 1746, p. 3). Wesley (1746) noted that he had included in the same order and with the same words the biblical text "wherein they were delivered by the Spirit of God" (p. 3) and had included additional words only when they were necessary for explanation. The Preface in Part I was dated February 24, 1745-6.

Green (1906) suggested that the "Lessons" were "prepared with much painstaking and care" and that they form a "really valuable lesson-book for the young" (p. 45). For this research, the content of the preface to the Lessons was coded with the desire to identify if Wesley provided any attention to the three research questions within that original content. The biblical passages that made up the majority of the content of the "Lessons" were seen as relating to the analytical code "BIB" or Scripture/Bible as a whole, but the actual content of each biblical passage was not coded independently. Rather, the biblical passages were attributed to Wesley's engagement with the question what to teach and identified as relating to the code for Bible and Scripture (BIB). Based on the content of "Lessons", Wesley suggested Scripture should be taught – not words about Scripture but the actual words of Scripture in a form that the children themselves could read and engage. The role of the lessons in the home, church, and school and the fact that it was comprised almost exclusively of biblical text demonstrated Wesley's desire for children to engage the Scripture and his grasp of the impact of that engagement on the child's faith formation. The desire for children to read Scripture themselves was reminiscent of his mother's use of Scripture to teach Wesley and his siblings to read.

Summation, part I. The first volume contained 54 lessons from the first five books of the Bible, those attributed to Moses (Tyerman, 1872). The Scripture was written in a narrative format with the elimination of book, chapter, and verse. The corresponding book, chapter, and verse information was contained in a footnote. Some of the lessons contained a title that was descriptive of the content, such as lesson 6, "of Cain and Abel" (Wesley, 1746, p. 10). Lesson one began with the creation account of Genesis 1:1: "In the beginning God created the Heaven and the Earth" (p. 5). The creation account continued through lesson four with lesson five telling the story of the Serpent and the fall. Lesson six was the story of Cain and Abel. The lessons continued throughout volume one in such a manner of narrative style and similar length concluding with lesson 54 that told the story of Moses' death in Deut. 33:1-34:12. In all, volume one covered Genesis 1:1 through Deuteronomy 34:12. For a complete listing of biblical texts and corresponding lessons, see Appendix L. There were a few notations made throughout volume one that offered clarification of a word used in the biblical text such as in "Lesson V Fall of Men": "The Devil is the Serpent" (p. 8) or in "Lesson XIV. Of Abraham's Intercessions for Sodom: "namely, The Three One God, that is, either god himself, or Angels, in the Form of Men" (p. 19). These notations are included in the footnotes and identified in the text by a corresponding symbol.

Summation, part II. Volumes two through four did not include a preface, but began immediately with the first lesson. The format was the same as the first volume. Volume two (1747) began with "Lesson I: The Israelites pass over Jordan" from the biblical text of Joshua 1:1 – 3:17. The book of Joshua was covered in the first four lessons followed by the book of Judges beginning with the story of Gideon. The stories from I Samuel were covered in detail and concluded with the story of Saul's death (I Samuel 31:1 – 2 Samuel 1:27). Volume two contained 57 lessons and covered portions of Scripture from Joshua 1:1 through 2 Chronicles 33:20. Volume two concluded with six lessons on the destruction of Jerusalem. For a complete listing of biblical texts and corresponding lessons for *Lessons for Children Part II*, see Appendix L.

Summation, part III. The third volume, *Lessons for Children Part III* (1748) included lessons from the biblical text of Ezra, Nehemiah, Esther, Job, Psalms and Proverbs (Ezra 1:1 through Proverbs 31:30). Tyerman (Vol. 2, 1872) noted in regard to *Lessons for Children* in general but specifically in reference to part three: "The whole of the above were class books in Kingswood school" (p. 29). For a complete listing of biblical texts and corresponding lessons for *Lessons for Children Part III* (1748), see Appendix L.

Summation, part IV. The fourth volume, *Lessons for Children Part IV* (1754) included only 35 lessons and was the shortest of the four volumes. It was published several years after the initial three. Part four covered the biblical text from Ecclesiastes 1:1 and concluded with Ecclesiasticus 51:30. It is not known why Wesley included the Book of Ecclesiasticus as part of this collection. The Book of Ecclesiasticus is not part of the Hebrew Cannon but was accepted as canonical by the Catholic Church and written by a Jewish scribe, Sirach of Jerusalem (Gigot, 1909). None of the lessons in this volume contained a title or description. For a complete listing of biblical texts and corresponding lessons for *Lessons for Children Part IV* (1754), see Appendix L.

Descriptive codes

Lessons for Children Part I-IV (1746, 1747, 1748, 1754) were publications printed, distributed, and intended to be used by children in the home, church, and school. It was Wesley's attempt to make biblical text approachable to children. He took significant biblical texts from the Old Testament and wrote them in a way that read more like a story in narrative format to create an ease of reading for children and provide them the opportunity to engage the Old Testament biblical text in a way they could understand (Wesley, 1746, p. 1). The broader audiences were parents and teachers, as identified in the preface to the first volume, as well as ministers who were instructed by Wesley to visit the homes, spend time with the children, and instruct them although ministers were not explicitly noted (Tyerman, Vol. 2, 1872).

Why teach

Wesley identified the role of "Lessons" in a child's religious instruction: "The following lessons to reflect the plainest and most useful portions of scripture, such as children may the more easily understand, and such as it most concerns them to know" (Wesley, 1746, p. 3).

Who shall teach

The preface to the "Lessons" in part I was addressed to "Parents and School Masters" who were called to "commend themselves" and their children to the Lord and to acknowledge that it is He alone that "giveth the increase" (Wesley, 1746, p. 3).

How to teach

Lessons for Children Part I (Wesley, 1746) included a preface addressed "To All Parents and School-Masters" (p. 3) that spoke to the method of instruction parents and teachers should employ when providing religious education:

> Beware of that common, but accursed, Way, of making Children Parrots, instead of Christians. Labour that, as far as is possible, they may understand every single

Sentence which they read. Therefore, do not make Haste. Regard not *how much,* but *how well,* to how good Purpose, they read. Turn each Sentence every Way, propose it in every Light, and question them continually on every Point. (Wesley, 1746, p. 3)

The instructions indicated Wesley's desire for the children to read the Scripture themselves with parents and teachers to guide in that reading with patience so that the child truly grasped the meaning: "If by any means, they may not only *read,* but *inwardly digest* the Words of Eternal Life" (Wesley, 1746, p. 4). Wesley (1746) added that the instruction should be done with "all Diligence" (p. 4). Wesley (1746) acknowledged in the preface of Part I that the goal could only be attained if the parent or teacher "commend both yourselves and your little ones to Him" because "He alone giveth the Increase" (p. 4).

What to teach

The rest of *Lessons for Children Part I* (Wesley, 1746) and the entirety of *Lessons for Children Parts II, III, and IV* (Wesley, 1747, 1748, 1754) are devoted to the biblical text and exclusively related to the research question what to teach and the analytical code for Scripture (BIB). Scripture was referred to as "Bread" that is "delivered by the Spirit of God" (Wesley, 1746, p. 3). A detailed outline of each of the volumes and the corresponding biblical references, by lesson, and with title when included can be seen in Appendix L.

A summation of the biblical stories contained in *Lessons for Children Part I* (Wesley, 1746) included: Creation, the Fall, the flood, Tower of Babel, Abraham, Sodom and Gomorrah, Isaac, Jacob, Joseph, Moses, the Israelites flight from Egypt and journey, Balaam, and "Exhortation to Obedience" from Deuteronomy. *Lessons for Children Part II* (Wesley, 1747) included: Jericho, Joshua, Gideon, Samson, Samuel, Saul, David and Goliath, David's flight from Saul, David as King, Solomon, Elijah, Ahab, Naaman, Elisha, Jehu, Hezekiah, Josiah, destruction of Jerusalem. The biblical stories and texts contained in *Lessons for Children Part III* (Wesley, 1748) included: Rebuilding of the Temple, Ezra, Esther, and selections of Psalms and Proverbs. The final volume, *Lessons for Children Part IV* (Wesley, 1754) contained texts from Ecclesiastes, Isaiah, Jeremiah, Ezekiel, Daniel, Solomon, and Ecclesiasticus that included biblical narratives of Nebuchadnezzar, Daniel, and the fiery furnace. Frequency of the research codes as they relate specifically to the document *Lessons for Children* is found in Appendix I, Figure I7.

Instructions for Children

Instructions for Children was written by Wesley in 1745 and printed in London by M. Cooper. There were at least seven known editions printed between 1745 and 1760 (Green, 1906). For this research, the 1746 edition was used. The "Instructions" were a catechism developed by Wesley to be used by children. Prince (1926) noted: "Wesley gave *Instructions for Children* chief place among the textbooks for children in the home" (p. 125). They were translated in Latin and used at the school at Kingswood (Green, 1906; Rack, 2002) and in the 1748 Minutes of Conference, the "Instructions" were identified as "curriculum proposed for the school at Kingswood" (Buckroyd, 2001, p. 63). In addition, they were to be used by ministers as a tool for instruction. Wesley called for the "Instructions" to be in every Methodist home and for ministers to commit them to memory (Prince, 1926; Rack, 2002). In a letter "to a young disciple" dated "Bristol, September 8, 1773," Wesley admonished: "The *Instructions for Children* contain the best matter that we can possibly teach them [children] (Jackson, 1872, Vol. VII, p. 94). In addition, Wesley mentioned the "Instructions" in an address to ministers following the conference of 1766. Wesley had called for "a thorough reform of the preachers" that included an expectation to visit and instruct the children:

> The sum is, go into every house, in course, and teach every one therein, young and old, if they belong to us, to be Christians inwardly and outwardly. Make every particular plain to their understanding. Fit it in their memory. Write it on their heart. Read, explain, and enforce the rules of the society; the *Instructions for Children*; the fourth volume of sermons; and Philip Henry's method of family prayer. (Tyerman, 1872, Vol. II, p. 582)

"Instructions" adapted from French work

Green (1906) noted that *Instructions for Children* was "chiefly translated from the French of Abbe Fleury and M. Poiert" (p. 34). Fleury and Poiret were French church historians and Fleury a tutor to the children of Louis XIV (Willhauck, 1992, p. 199). Maddox (Personal correspondence, June 19, 2012) identified the first portion of *Instructions* as "loosely dependent" upon Claude Fleury's *Grand Catéchisme Historique* (1683). In this "Historical Catechism", Fleury made use of the narrative style to highlight Scripture and developed a series of questions about the biblical text. Wesley admired this approach and borrowed the biblical narrative format for his work in "Lessons" and the catechesis question and answer style for his "Instructions" (Willhauck, 1992). The second portion of the *Instructions* were an edited translation of Pierre Poiret's *Les Principes Solides de la Religion et de la Vie Chrétienne, appliqués a l 'Education des enfans* (1705) (Maddox, Personal correspondence, June 19, 2012). Body (1963) contended: "So highly did he [Wesley] think of the work of these Frenchmen that he prefixed to it a short catechism, which was to be used instead of the church catechism, thus making the *Instructions* a complete manual of Christian education" (pp. 66-67). In spite of Wesley's use of someone else's work as part of this critical piece in his religious educational scheme for children, Prince (1926) posited: "Although it is not an original work of Wesley's, it is an accurate presentation of his theology" (p. 127).

Format of "Instructions"

The format of the "Instructions" was designed with children in mind and in a form they could easily understand and use. The sentences were short, generally only a line or two. Each lesson contained a series of questions and the corresponding brief answer. An example from the first section, lesson twelve: "1. Where will Believers go after Death? To Heaven" (Wesley, 1746, p. 9). There were six sections of varying length in this single publication with a total of 58 lessons. The tone of the work was imperative (Prince, 1926). The preface was addressed "To all Parents and Schoolmasters" (Wesley, 1746, p. 3), as was the preface to *Lessons for Children, Part I* (1746). Wesley (1746) described the document as "true Principles of the Christian Education of Children" (p. 3). Although he did not give direct credit to Fleury and Poiret, he did admit in the preface that a significant portion had been translated from French but with a change to the form and structure. Wesley (1746) concluded the preface with a statement of the "Instruction's" goal: "And you will have the Comfort of observing, that by the Same Steps they advance in the Knowledge of these poor Elements, they will also grow in Grace, in the Knowledge of God, and of our Lord Jesus Christ" (p. 4).

Summation

Instructions for Children (1746) was divided into six sections that each addressed a different topic. Some of the sections were in the question and answer format and others contained content without the catechesis style. Wesley did not attribute a topic heading to the first section but did to sections II through VI, and only section I contained lesson titles.

Summation, section I. The first section contained twelve lessons on God, creation and the fall, "the Redemption of Man", the means of grace, hell, and heaven. Section I, Lesson I and II titled "Of God" began with the question "How many Gods are there?" (Wesley, 1746, p. 5) and the answered: "One: Who is God the Father, God the Son, and God the Holy Ghost. These three are One" (Wesley, 1746, p. 5).

Summation, section II. Section two consisted of six lessons related to the subtitle "*Of GOD, and of the Soul of Man*" (Wesley, 1746, p. 10). Lessons one through five responded to the single question: "Do you know what God is?" (Wesley, 1746, p. 10) and lesson six addressed the question: "Do you know what your Soul is?" (Wesley, 1746, p. 12).

Summation, section III. Section three contained eleven lessons that related to "How to regulate our Desires" (Wesley, 1746, pp. 13-19). Wesley (1746) defined "Desire of the Soul" as the "heart, or the Will" (p. 13). This section of the *Instructions* included eight lessons that called the child to give up self-will and surrender to the will of God. Lessons nine through eleven addressed the nature of prayer and began with the question: "What do you mean, when you pray to God, in the Name of Jesus Christ?" (Wesley, 1746, p. 17): Prince (1926) posited of these lessons that they give the "form of prayer as a guide" and noted that Wesley "sets down the desires that should be voiced every time prayer is offered" (p. 127). Lesson eleven included the Lord's Prayer and described it as "The best Prayer in the World" (Wesley, 1746, p. 18).

Summation, section IV. Section four was titled "*How to regulate our Understanding*" (p. 19) and contained eight lessons on belief. Wesley acknowledged in lesson two that only God "can open the Eyes of our Soul, to see and know spiritual Things" (Wesley, 1746, p. 19). He responded to the question "What do you believe of God" (Wesley, 1746, p. 22) in lesson six with the Apostle's Creed.

Summation, section V. Section five was titled "How to regulate our Joy" (Wesley, 1746, p. 24) and contained nine lessons that defined joy, spoke of the source of our joy, and gave reasons why we should rejoice. The section concluded with the first line of lesson seven: "Joy was made for God" (Wesley, 1746, p. 28).

Summation, section VI. Section six was titled: "How to regulate our Practice" (Wesley, 1746, p. 30) and included twelve lessons on the expectations of a Christian life. The first line of lesson one offered the reminder: "Our Body and our Life belong to God" (Wesley, 1746, p. 30) and defined the Christian life as one that seeks to do God's will. Lesson four asked: "What are the Ten Commandments of God?" (Wesley, 1746, p. 32) and listed them. Lessons five through seven offered further explanation of each of the commandments and lesson eight identified the three commands that are the full sum of the ten: "To love God...To love Jesus Christ himself...To love our Neighbour" (Wesley, 1746, p. 35). These three were further expounded in the lessons that follow. The final lesson, lesson twelve, was an exhortation to parents and concluded with: "Train up the precious Souls of their Children, wholly by the Rules of Jesus Christ. They shall be blessed by them for ever in heaven and shall together bless God to all Eternity" (Wesley, 1746, p. 39).

Descriptive codes

Instructions for Children (Wesley, 1746) was a publication printed, distributed, and intended to be used by children in the home, church, and school. It was used as a text at the school at Kingswood, by parents in the home who were instructed to have their children memorize them, and by ministers when they visited children in their home or established societies of children (Rack, 2002). It was a text written for use by children, but the broader audiences were parents and teachers, as identified in the preface as well as ministers, although not explicitly noted, who were instructed by Wesley to visit the homes, spend time with the children, and instruct them (Tyerman, Vol. 2, 1872). Wesley (1746) noted in the preface: "And altho' the great Truths herein contained, are more immediately address'd to Children, yet are they worthy the deepest Consideration, both of the oldest and wisest of Men" (p. 3).

Why teach

Wesley (1746) desired for children to not just know the Scripture but understand it and concluded the preface with the intended result of the "Instructions": "By this Means they will learn to think as they learn to read" (p. 4).

Who shall teach

The preface addressed parents and teachers and called them to have the contents of the *Instructions for Children* in their own hearts and minds but acknowledged, as did other Wesley documents, that it is God alone who "giveth the increase" (Wesley, 1746, p. 4).

How to teach

Data was identified in the preface that related to when instruction should occur: "as soon as ever they can distinguish Good and Evil" (Wesley, 1746, p. 3). In addition, the method of instruction was discussed in the preface that resembled the methodology described in the "Lessons" preface: "let them not read or say one line, without understanding and minding what they say" (Wesley, 1746, pp. 3-4). Wesley (1746) continued:

> Try them over and over; stop them short, almost in every Sentence. And ask them, 'What was it you said last?' Read it again, 'What do you mean by that?' So that, if it be possible, they may pass by nothing till it has taken some Hold upon them. (p. 4)

What to teach

Because of their format and intended purpose as a catechism for children, the bulk of the material covered in "Instructions" was associated with the research question what to teach.

What to teach – Bible. Wesley (1746) provided a description of the Bible, the role of the Bible, and commands in the Bible in section six. The Bible was described as God's Word (Section 5, Lesson 7), God's "undefiled" Law, "the Law of Love", and "The Testimony of the Lord" (Section 6, Lessons 8, Wesley, 1746, p. 35). It was said to give wisdom and light, and was right, pure, clean, true, and endured forever (Section 6, Lesson 8). The Ten Commandments were specifically addressed (Section 6, Lessons 4-7) and described as "wonderful and holy" (Section 6, Lesson 8, Wesley, 1746, p. 35), "The Spring of Life, the Light of the Heart, the Treasure of Souls," and "Life everlasting" (Section 6, Lesson 8, Wesley, 1746, p. 35, citing John 12:50). In addition to the Ten Commandments, Wesley identified the Great Commandment as the summation of the Ten Commandments (Section 6, Lesson 8) specifically with a call to "love God", "love Jesus", and "love our Neighbor" (Wesley, 1746, p. 35).

What to teach – prayer. Data was also identified within "Instructions" that related to prayer. Wesley (1746) provided a description of how to pray and offered The Lord's Prayer as an example (Section 3, Lesson 11), which was identified as "the best Prayer in the World" (p. 18). The readers were warned to check their desire or heart before praying to make sure they were rightly motivated (Section 3, Lesson 8), to put their trust and confidence in Jesus Christ "For God would not hear us at all, but for the Sake of the Blood of Christ shed for us" (Section 3, Lesson 9, Wesley, 1746, p. 17), and to pray in Jesus Christ's name (Section 3, Lesson

10, p. 18). Wesley (1746) also addressed what the children should pray for: "to give you his light, and to open the Eyes of your Soul" (Section 4, Lesson 4, p. 21), "true understanding", "an humble, submissive, simple and obedient Heart", and to pray for parents and "superiors" (Section 6, Lesson 9, p. 36), neighbors, friends, and self (Section 6, Lesson 10).

What to teach – Christian life. A significant portion of the text described the Christian life (LIFE) and how the child should think, behave, and feel. "Instructions" suggested that those who have been "saved from sin" should desire nothing but God and to do His will (Section 1, Lessons 5, 6, 7, Section 3, lessons 2) desire "nothing but what is good" (Section 3, lesson 1, Wesley, 1746, p. 13), and desire to know God (Section 4, lesson 1). They should desire "to praise and honor him as he deserves, and to please him in every thing" (Section 3, Lesson 5, Wesley, 1746, p. 15). In addition, they should desire God's grace, a meek spirit, and a thankful heart, (Section 3, Lesson 7). The children were called to seek forgiveness, be thankful, offer praise to God for what He has done, and to bless the Lord (Section 3, lesson 8). They were also called to believe and trust in what God had told them (Section 4, Lesson 2, Lesson 8), to "see God in all Things", to obey their parents, and to "walk continually in his [God's] presence" (Section 4, Lesson 5, Wesley, 1746, p. 21 and Lesson 8). "Instructions" called the child to rejoice in God, His will, and His gift of eternal life and joy (Section 5, Lessons 1, 2, 3); to be content with what they have been given, (Section 5, Lessons 3 & 4); to acknowledge that "all this comes from God" (Section 5, lesson 5, Wesley, 1746, p. 26); and to "rejoice in the Lord always" (Section 5, lesson 7, Wesley, 1746, p. 28). Wesley (1746) admonished the children to "beware of the Love of Money" (Section 5, lesson 6, Wesley, 1746, p. 27) and to fear the Lord (Section 5, Lesson 11). The child was to practice obedience (Section 6, Lesson 1), give God the glory in all things (Section 6, Lesson 2, 3, 5), and obey the commandments (Section 6, Lessons 5, 6, 7, & 8). They were to "Live in Peace", "desire nothing fine" (Section 6, Lesson 10, Wesley, 1746, p. 37) and to not be "comfortable" in the present world (Section 6, Lesson 12, Wesley, 1746, p. 39). In summation, Wesley (1746) admonished the child to "always live and act, as being in the Presence of God" (Section 6, Lesson 9, Wesley, 1746, p. 36).

What to teach – humanity and sin. Wesley (1746) asked how, why, and where God made man. He offered: "out of nothing", "To know, love, and be happy in God forever", "and In the Garden of Paradise" (Section 1, Lesson 3, 4, p. 6). The result of breaking God's command was described as "Sin and Guilt, and Pain and Death" (Wesley, 1746, p. 6), and human nature was said to be "without his Grace" (Section 2, Lesson 4, Wesley, 1746, p. 11), "spoiled and destroyed by sin" (Section 2, Lesson 5, Wesley, 1746, p. 12 and Section 3, Lesson 4), and "Evil" (Section 2, Lesson 4, p. 11 and Section 3, lesson 3). Without salvation we are said to be "unworthy of his Grace and Blessings" (Section 3, Lesson 8, Wesley, 1746, p. 16) and under the "wrath" and "curse" of God (Section 3, lesson 9, Wesley, 1746, p. 17). Humanity was said to be "blind" with "foolish and false Conceptions" (Section 4, Lessons 2, 3, & 4), as well as weak, ignorant, foolish, and wicked (Section 4, Lessons 5, 7, 8; Section 5, Lesson 1). Humanity was described as being "drawn into Hell" (Section 6, Lesson 1, Wesley, 1746, p. 30) and deserving of punishment (Section 6, Lesson 11). Sin (SIN) was said to have "spoiled and destroyed" our souls (Section 2, Lesson 5, Wesley, 1746, p. 12) but Jesus Christ "the Eternal Son of God" offered to save us from our sin (Section 1, Lessons, 5, 6, 7, Wesley, 1746, p. 6).

What to teach – Jesus, salvation, Holy Spirit, and eternity. The *Instructions* provided an explanation of the process by which we are saved beginning with Jesus's life, death, and resurrection. Repentance was described, and Wesley suggested that we are called to faith through the work of the Holy Spirit (Section 1, Lessons 5, 6, 7; Section 3, lessons 9; Section 4, Lessons 8; Section 5, Lessons 8). Wesley (1746) instructed the child to ask God to forgive their sins (Section 3, Lesson 8) and "really believe in him [Jesus Christ]" (Section 3, Lesson 9, p. 17 and Section 5, lesson 8). Salvation is only possible through Jesus Christ who is the Son of God (Section 1, Lessons 5, 6, 7; Section 2, Lesson 3). Jesus "lived and died and rose again, to buy Forgiveness for us" and to show us how we are to live (Section 4, Lesson 7, p. 22; Section 5, Lessons 2, 3). He did this because he loved us (Section 4, Lesson 8). The Holy Spirit (HOL) was said to restore "fallen Man to the Image of God" (Section 4, Lesson 6, Wesley, 1746, p. 22) and enlighten our understanding and fill us with peace and joy (Section 4, Lessons 6, 7, 8 and Section 6, Lessons 8, 9). Wesley (1746) posed the question: "Where will Believers go after Death" with the answer given, "To Heaven" (Section 1, Lesson 12, p. 9). Heaven was described as "A Place of Light and Glory" (Wesley, 1746, p. 9) filled with joy and happiness (Section 1, Lesson 12; Section 5, lesson 7), where God is continually praised (Section 3, Lesson 5; Section 6, Lesson 12). The *Instructions* speak of "The Resurrection of the Body" (Section 4, Lesson 6, p. 22) and suggested, "after the Body is dead and risen again, we shall live together in eternal Glory [Heaven]" (Section 4, Lesson 7, Wesley, 1746, p.16; Section 2, Lesson 5). In contrast to heaven, hell was described as "a dark bottomless Pit, full of Fire and Brimstone" where "unbelievers" go (Section 1, Lessons 10, 11, Wesley, 1746, p. 8) and live in "everlasting Perdition" (Section 6, Lesson 1, Wesley, 1746, p. 30) and eternal punishment (Section 6, Lessons 9, 11, 12).

What to teach – God and grace. The *Instructions* also suggested that God "will keep us by his Power, and defend us against every Thing that would hurt us" (Section 2, Lesson 5, Wesley, 1746, p. 12). This is done through God's grace (Section 3, Lessons 1, 3, 6). Grace was defined as "The Power of the Holy Spirit, enabling us to behave and love and serve God" (Section 1, Lessons 8, 9, Wesley, 1746, p. 7). God was described as a spirit who is everywhere, knows everything, and can do "Whatever he will" (Section 1, Lessons 1, 2, p. 5). God is the creator of everything and loves everything He created (Section 1, Lessons 1, 2; Section 3, lesson 6; Section 4, Lessons 6, 7; Section 5, Lesson 2). God is eternal, invisible, good, wise, happy, merciful, forgiving, and "True" (Section 2, lesson 2, Wesley, 1746, p.10; Section 5, Lesson 2). There is only one God (Section 1, Lessons 1, 2; Section 2, lesson 4) who is the source of everything that is good (Section 2, lesson 4, Section 3, Lesson 2; Section 5, Lesson 5). God is "power, Wisdom, Goodness itself" (Section 3, Lesson 5, Wesley, 1746, p. 15; Section 4, Lesson 5) and deserves to be praised (Section 3, Lesson 6; Section 5, Lessons 2, 3, 6, 7). God is the "Redeemer" (Section 4, lesson 8, Wesley, 1746, p. 23), "happy and glorious in himself" (Section 5, Lesson 2, Wesley, 1746, p. 25), and the "wise Physician of our Souls" (Section 5, Lesson 4, Wesley, 1746, p. 26). His will is for us to please Him (Section 6, Lesson 2), and he was said to be "continually looking upon you" (Section 6, Lesson 9, Wesley, 1746, p. 36). He alone "can open the Eyes of our Soul, to see and know spiritual Things" (Section 4, Lesson 2, Wesley, 1746, p. 20) and is three in one "God the Father, the Son and the Holy Spirit" (Section 4, Lesson 8, Wesley, 1746, p. 23). Frequency of the research codes as they relate specifically to the document *Instructions for Children* is found in Appendix I, Figure I8.

Prayers for Children

Prayers for Children was published in 1772, and originally printed by William Pine of Bristol and included in the 1812 edition of Wesley's collected *Works* with the addition of the names of the days and weeks and with Wesley's name attributed following the preface (Green, 1906). Wesley also wrote prayers for families and adults, but the *Prayers for Children* specifically identified needs of children and their expected responses to God (Prince, 1926). In response to this pamphlet of prayers specifically for children, Green (1906) posited: "Wesley paid very great attention to the preparation of books for the young, and in many ways sought to promote their best welfare" (p. 160). The publication included a preface addressed to "My Dear child" (Jackson, 1872, Vol. XI, p. 259) that outlined when and how the child should engage the prayers. The selection began with prayers for the "Lord's Day" providing two prayers a day (morning and evening) through Saturday, prayers for "Grace" before and after meals, and "A Prayer for Relations, Friends, & etc. to be used after Morning and Evening Prayer" (Jackson, 1872, Vol. XI, p. 272). The prayers concluded with a recitation of The Lord's Prayer and contained significant phrases of Scripture throughout. Other than the preface, they were not written with words of instruction but with the expectation that the child would recite them as they had been written. Prince (1926) noted that the prayers called for an attitude of reverence for God, a sense of corruption of human nature, receptivity to spiritual things, a desire to become more spiritual, and deep sincerity with reoccurring petitions that include pardon, strength against temptation, God's blessings on studies, an openness to understanding, and an advancement in the means of grace (p. 131). Prince (1926) posited that Wesley's theology is seen throughout the prayers such as in the line:

> Give me oh Lord the highest learning to know thee and that beset wisdom to know myself. O Lord do thou teach me the meaning of the new birth that I a child of wrath may become a child of grace. (Jackson, 1872, Vol. XI, p. 267)

Summation

Wesley admonished the child how often and from what position they should pray and offered a warning of how not to pray in the "Preface" to the prayers:

> My Dear Child, -- A lover of your soul has here drawn up a few prayers, in order to assist you in that great duty. Be sure that you do not omit, at least morning and evening, present yourself upon your knees before God. You have mercies to pray for, and blessings to praise God for. But take care that you do not mock God, drawing near with your lips; while your heart is far from him. God sees you, and knows your thoughts; therefore, see that you not only speak with your lips, but also pray with your heart. And that you may not ask in vain, see that you forsake sin, and make it your endeavor to do what God has shown you ought; because God says, "The prayers of the wicked are an abomination unto the Lord.' Ask them of God for the blessings you want, in the name, and for the sake, of Jesus Christ; and God will hear and answer you, and do more for you thank you can either ask or think. (Jackson, 1872, Vol. XI, p. 259)

Summation – Lord's day prayers. In the prayer, "Lord's Day Morning" the child acknowledged who God is, what He has done, and the purpose of the Lord's Day. In response to what the child would experience on that Lord's Day, they were directed to ask for a blessing from God's Word, the means of grace they will experience, and from the worship they will engage. The "Lord's Day Evening" prayer offered thanks for those experiences of the day that included "thy house is open to me, the bread of life offered me, the word of salvation preached, and thy Spirit striving with me" (Jackson, 1872, Vol. XI, p. 261).

Summation – other prayers. The daily morning prayers offered praise for God's protection through the night and sought protection from temptation throughout the day. The evening prayers offered thanksgiving and praise for the blessings of the day; forgiveness for any sins committed during the day, and sought protection through the night. The prayers for before and after meals were brief in comparison to the morning and evening prayers and sought blessing on what they will eat and offered thanks for what they had received. The prayer for relations and friends sought a blessing on family, friends, enemies, and "all mankind" (Jackson, 1872, Vol. XI, p. 272). Prince (1926) suggested this prayer made a "provision for the social element in prayer" (p. 131). In general the "Prayers" offered an acknowledgement of who God is and what He has done and offered a form of praise and thanksgiving for what God had done for them and in them.

Descriptive codes

Prayers for Children (Wesley, 1772) was a publication printed, distributed, and intended for use by children in the home. While it was a text written specifically to children, as suggested by the preface, the broader audience would have been the parents who possessed the responsibility of teaching the prayers to their children and encouraging their daily recitation.

Why teach

The preface provides limited insight as to role the prayers play in the religious instruction of the child: "in order to assist you" and "God will hear and answer you, and do more for you thank you can either ask or think" (Jackson, 1872, Vol. XI, p. 259).

Who shall teach

The prayers are only addressed to children: "My dear child" (preface) and there is no explicit instruction on who is responsible for the religious instruction of the child.

How to teach

Wesley provided instruction in the preface to the prayers on how to teach, or rather how the child should use the prayers. The child was admonished in the preface to not mock God by saying one thing with their mouth and having a different attitude in their heart. They were told to ask God "for the blessings you want" in the name of Jesus (Jackson, 1872, Vol. XI, p. 259). The children were directed to pray daily and both morning and evening as demonstrated by the inclusion of two prayers for every day of the week titled either "morning" or "evening. In addition, the child was provided prayers for before and after mealtime.

What to teach – prayer and Bible. Because of the nature of the text and the fact that each of the elements contained in it are prayers, prayer was expected and exemplified. Every prayer concluded with a recitation of the Lord's Prayer, was addressed to God, and was offered in Jesus' name. The continued use of the Lord's Prayer as closing to every prayer, identified the value of that particular prayer, Wesley's desire for the children to commit it to memory, and the value of Scripture. In addition, scripture was interspersed throughout all of the prayers, but without notation of book, chapter, or verse. The biblical phrases were interspersed in such a way as to become part of the natural communication of the child, which was typical of Wesley's personal communication style. In speaking of Wesley's style of speaking and writing, Wall (2010) posited: "One easily senses the authority he grants the words of Scripture by noting the distinctive phraseology in the sermons. Most include long strings of different Bible verses cobbled together, one glossing the other to express Scripture's sense in Scripture's phrase" (p. 114). Wesley noted of himself "the Bible is my standard of language as well as sentiment. I endeavor not only to think but to speak the oracles of God" (Telford, 1931, Vol. 5, p. 8). The child was also taught the value and purpose of the Bible when they were instructed to pray the prayer "Lord's Day Morning," in anticipation of engagement with the scriptures on that day:

> Save me from all hardness of heart and contempt for Thy Word; increase my love to it, and enable me to hear it meekly, and to receive it with pure affection, and to bring forth fruit unto good living. Open my understanding to receive thy truth in the love thereof. Set it so powerfully upon my heart, and root it so deep in my soul,

that the fruits thereof may be seen in my life, to thy glory and praise. May I always so hear, read, mark, learn, and inwardly digest thy word, that it may be a savor of life to my soul. (Jackson, 1872, Vol. XI, p. 260)

What to teach – God. Every prayer began with an address to God. He was described as the "Almighty God, Maker of all mankind, in whom we live and move, and have our being, who makest the outgoings of the morning and the evening to rejoice" (Lord's Day Morning, Jackson, 1872, Vol. XI, p. 260). He was also described as merciful, good, gracious, everlasting, "Giver of all good things", (Tuesday Evening, Jackson, 1872, Vol. XI, p. 264) "gracious Preserver of all mankind" (Monday Evening, Jackson, 1872, Vol. XI, p. 262), watchful and does not sleep (Tuesday Evening), the "Fountain of all goodness" (Wednesday Morning, Jackson, 1872, Vol. XI, p. 265), the "only true God...blessed Sun of Righteousness" (Thursday Morning, Jackson, 1872, Vol. XI, p. 267), and our guide. Every prayer was offered "through Jesus Christ" who was described as redeemer, Lord, Saviour, Lamb of God, and "Son of the Father" (Tuesday Evening, Jackson, 1872, Vol. XI, p. 264).

What to teach – humanity and sin. In the prayers, the child was led to refer to himself or herself as "a lost sheep" (Monday Evening, Jackson, 1872, Vol. XI, p. 262) and unworthy. As one who lives "in the midst of a sinful world" (Saturday Morning, Jackson, 1872, Vol. XI, p. 270), is "bound with the chain of my sins" (Wednesday Evening, Jackson, 1872, Vol. XI, p. 266), and can do nothing on their own. The prayer for Friday morning gives a glimpse of Wesley's view of humanity when the child is led to pray: "I am taught by thy word, that I am by nature born in sin and a child of wrath, and that except I am born again I cannot see the Kingdom of God" (Jackson, 1872, Vol. XI, p. 268). Sins are described as "offenses, which I have from time to time most grievously committed, by thought, word, and deed, against thy divine Majesty (Jackson, 1872, Vol. XI, p. 268). The child is encouraged in the prayers to confess their sins, turn from their sin, seek God's forgiveness, and be redeemed by God's grace from them.

What to teach – Jesus, salvation, and Holy Spirit. The prayers acknowledged that Jesus Christ is the source of the child's salvation and identified salvation as "new birth" (Friday Morning, Jackson, 1872, Vol. XI, p. 268). Jesus was repeatedly called "Blessed Savior" and "Redeemer", "Lamb of God", and God's Son and every prayer was offered in Jesus' name. Through the prayers the child acknowledged their sinful nature, sought forgiveness of their sins, and turned from their sinful ways (Friday Morning and Friday Evening). There was reference to the Trinity in the repeated phrase that suggested the child give thanks to "Christ my Redeemer, with thee and the Holy Ghost," and the Holy Ghost was attributed with daily renewal of the child. Salvation was referred to as "redemption" and washing. The child was instructed to pray the description of salvation reminiscent of the words of scripture: "Wash me thoroughly from my wickedness, and cleanse me from all my sins. Turn thy face from my sins, and put out all my misdeeds. Create in me a clean heart, O my God, and renew a right spirit within me" (Jackson, 1872, Vol. XI, p. 269).

What to teach – grace. Significant data was connected to the code for grace. Through the prayers the child was led to seek God's grace and to give thanks for God's grace. God's grace was identified as enabling the child to walk in "holiness and righteousness'" (Friday Evening, Jackson, 1872, Vol. XI, p. 269) and filling their heart with love (Lord's Day Evening). God, through His grace, provides protection from the "dangers in the night season" (Lord's Day Evening, Jackson, 1872, Vol. XI, p. 261) and the "temptations of the world" (Monday Morning, Jackson, 1872, Vol. XI, p. 262). Through grace, God instructs, reforms, and saves; He grants rest, hope, help, joy, and comfort (Monday Evening) and the ability to worship, serve, believe, fear and love Him (Tuesday Morning). Through the "Prayers" the child attributed to God the ability to know Him, to live a holy life, to love His name, and to gain everlasting life (Tuesday Evening, Wednesday Morning).

What to teach – eternity. Heaven was referred to as the place Jesus had gone to prepare (Tuesday Evening) and the "everlasting Kingdom" (Friday and Saturday Morning). The "Prayers" addressed what happens at death: "for my last sleep in death, my departure out of this mortal state" (Wednesday Evening, Jackson, 1872, Vol. XI, p. 266) and suggested "when I lay down my body in the grave, my soul may rise to life immortal" (Saturday Evening, Jackson, 1872, Vol. XI, p. 272). Heaven was called eternal and the home of Jesus, God, and the angels. "Prayers" offered a summation to the topic of eternity: "When the trumpet shall sound, and at last call me from the sleep of death, let me be caught up into the clouds to meet the Lord in the air, and so for ever be with the Lord" (Lord's Day Evening, Jackson, 1872, Vol. XI, p. 261) and live in "fullness of joy" (Tuesday and Thursday Evening).

What to teach – Christian life. Significant data was also collected connected with the code for Christian life. The "Prayers" described the life the child was called to live, as a child of God. The Christian life was to include worship, service, praise, humility, obedience, and love for God, family, and others. The child was to seek to do the Lord's will, please the Lord in all things, and increase in "faith, hope, and love" (Wednesday Morning, Jackson, 1872, Vol. XI, p. 265). The child prayed for wisdom, understanding, a desire to bless the Lord's Name, and to do good. The prayers offered a description of the child was to pray for:

> Make me just and honest in all my dealings. Let me not bear any malice or hatred in my heart. Keep my hands from picking and stealing, my tongue from evil speaking, lying, and slandering; keep my body in temperance, soberness, and chastity. (Jackson, 1872, Vol. XI, p. 263).

And to be "obedient and faithful" to Him and to their parents.

Finally, the prayer for "Lord's Day Morning" described how the child should observe the Sabbath: "Set apart this day for holy uses, to engage me in thy service, wherein consists my honor and happiness" and refers to it as "thy day" (Jackson, 1872, Vol. XI, p. 260). Note that the code for prayer in this document was only used to identify data specifically related to instructions on prayer as opposed to coding each individual prayer, which would have greatly increased the frequency of the code "PRA" in the final report. Frequency of the research codes as they relate specifically to the document *Prayers for Children* is found in Appendix I, Figure I9.

Findings by Research Questions

In addition to reports produced by document that addressed the four research questions and associated codes for that specific document, reports were also produced for each research question that looked at the codes associated with that specific question and contain data representative of all of the research documents. The following findings provide a summation by research question representative of all the documents studied.

Descriptive Codes

The larger audience for all the documents as suggested by the location and form of their printing and distribution were people involved in the Methodist Societies. In the sermons parents, children, and grandparents were specifically addressed. In "Thoughts on Godparents" parents and godparents are specifically addressed. "Lessons" and "Instructions" identified parents and teachers as the intended audience. "Hymns", Instructions", "Lessons", and "Prayers" were written for the use of children but through the guidance of parents, teachers, and ministers.

Why Teach

Wesley suggested that religious instruction of children was necessary for the continuation of the revival movement beyond the current generation (On Family Religion), to "cure the disease" of human nature and "set right" the bias of human nature (On Education of Children), and to lay a foundation of "holiness and happiness" (thoughts on godparents) for a lifetime of faith formation.

Who shall Teach

The research question, who shall teach, had the least amount of coded data associated with it. The codes used in reference to the research question who shall teach included identification of the person who was to teach or instruct the child (REL) and the expected lifestyle of the instructor (EXP).

Relationship to child (REL)

Data that related to the analytical code representative of material that identified the person responsible for the religious instruction of the child, was identified in all of the documents except *Hymns for Children* and *Prayers for Children*. The other documents explicitly mentioned parents, teachers, instructors, or godparents in some form. Beyond these the documents identified God as the true source of the instruction and posited that without the work of the Holy Spirit, transformational instruction was not possible.

Expected lifestyle of instructor (EXP)

Data that related to the analytical code representative of material describing the expected lifestyle of the person responsible for the religious instruction of the child, was identified to some extent in all of the documents studied, with the exception of *Hymns for Children* and *Prayers for Children*. The documents carried the expectation that those entrusted with the religious education of children were to be people who feared God, who understood and knew "true religion" or biblical Christianity, and who served the Lord. There was the expectation that the instructor possessed the knowledge or understanding of the things of God and lived in a way that complemented that knowledge, and the instructors in the school at Kingswood were also expected to possess knowledge of the subjects they were to teach. Parents were called to "adorn the doctrine of God our Savior" in both their lives and their home (Sermon 94) and in the *Instructions for Children* parents and teachers were called to have the biblical knowledge "engraved" on their hearts, which is reminiscent of the call in Deut. 6. Parents were to select teachers for their children whose primary desire was to prepare the children to "meet him [God] in the clouds" (Wesley, 1746, pp. iiii-iv). The instructors at Kingswood Schools were to be "truly devoted to God" and called to "glorify God with their bodies and spirits, in the best manner they were capable of" (Jackson, 1872, Vol. XIII, p. 292). However, Wesley acknowledged that even the most God-fearing and pious parent or teacher was incapable of providing the kind of religious instruction that resulted in true transformation, rather it was only through the work of the Holy Spirit in the life of the instructor and in the life of the child that transformation could be attained: "He alone giveth the increase" ("Lessons", Wesley, 1746, p. iv), "He alone can apply your words to their hearts"(Sermon 94, Outler, 1986, p. 345) and "God not man is the physician of souls" (Sermon 95, Outler, 1986, p. 349).

How to Teach

The data collected that related to the research question how to teach included data that related to when the instruction should begin (WHN), the location for the religious instruction of the children (WHR), and the suggested methodology of the instruction (MET).

When instruction should occur (WHN)

Data that related to the analytical code representative of material describing the timeframe for when religious instruction should begin was identified to some extent in all of the documents studied, with the exception of *Lessons for Children*.

There was a consistent call in the documents for religious instruction to begin early in the life of a child. Susanna Wesley's letter suggested she began at the moment of birth and held fairly high expectations on obedience by the age of one. In his other publications, Wesley identified "as soon as reason dawns" (Sermons 94) as a timeframe for instruction to begin. This was additionally clarified to include "while they are young" (Sermon 94), from infancy (Sermon 96), as soon as a child is able to learn ("Thoughts" on Godparents), by the time they can speak or run on their own ("Thoughts" on Educating Child), and when they can distinguish between good and evil ("Instructions"). In the publications on the instructional methodology employed at Kingswood School, Wesley noted they only accepted children between the ages of six and twelve and highlighted that in this as well, the younger the child the better the possibility of meeting the religious instructional goals.

There was data collected that related to when instruction should occur not only in the life of the child but also in the child's day. Wesley provided prayers for morning and night of each day of the week and prayers for before and after meals. In Susanna's letter she spoke of prayers, hymns, and meditation being a part of the daily routine in the morning and at night, and Wesley provided a description of the school day in the "Plain Account" that included morning and evening prayers and Bible study. The collection of hymns also included prayers for before and after meal and for morning and evening. The indication from the documents and materials Wesley produced for children was that he expected practices that contributed to a child's faith formation to be engaged daily.

Where instruction should occur (WHR)

There was no data identified that explicitly described the location where religious instruction of children should occur. Implicitly the location was identified through the general context such as in the sermon "On Family Religion" that declared the theme "as for me and my house, we will serve the Lord" (cite). In addition, Wesley's expectation that Methodist families and ministers would provide religious instruction in the home was evident in his provision of the "Instructions", "Lessons", and "Prayers" for that purpose. In both *Instructions* and *Lessons for Children* the parents were specifically addressed in the preface and encouraged to use the materials with their children. Likewise, Methodist pastors were expected to provide religious education of children when they visited children in their homes and through the formation of societies comprised of children (Tyerman, Vol. II, 1862). Wesley also expressed the expectation that Methodist families would provide religious education for their children as part of their formal educational experience, such as the one provided at Kingswood School. The documents that relayed the schedule and curriculum of the school identified the role of religious instruction alongside instruction in the arts, languages, humanities, history, and mathematics. Finally, because Wesley preached sermons, devoted portions of his journal, published in the *Arminian Magazine*, and printed for distribution publications that specifically addressed the faith formation of children with an intended audience broader than parents, teachers, and ministers, one can appreciate the vital role child faith formation played for Wesley in the overall spiritual formation of the people called Methodists.

Methodology of the instruction (MET)

Data that related to the analytical code representative of material describing the proposed methodology for religious education of the child was detected in every document reviewed. In the case of the preface to *Instructions and Lessons for Children* engagement of the specific document with the child was addressed. In the case of the sermons, a suggested method of religious education in general was prescribed and the publications related to the school at Kingswood identified methodology consistent with the school instruction.

It could be assumed from the tone and language of his mother's letter and description of instruction at Kingswood School that Wesley employed and suggested a form of religious education that was rigid, harsh, and brutal. The phrase "breaking the will" and the reference to "spare the rod, spoil the child" (Prov. 13:24) in those documents and others might lend the reader to see a methodology that included extreme physical discipline and unreasonable expectations. Wesley's methodology, however, understood in light of the whole scope of his teachings as presented in these twelve documents, suggested a religious educational methodology that was far gentler and more reasonable than anticipated.

> It is possible that Wesley's theories look, on paper, more strict and deadening than they actually proved in practice, and we know that, as he himself grew in worldly wisdom and in knowledge of children, the sternest of his decrees were repealed. (Body, 1936, p. 143)

How to teach methodology – break the will. Wesley did instruct parents and teachers to break the will of the child. "Break their will the first moment it appears. In the whole art of Christian education there is nothing more important than this" (Sermon 95, Outler, 1986, p. 354). His theology saw human nature as being self-focused, self-determined, and following after one's own will. In his "Thought on the Manner of Educating Children" Wesley (1783) posited: "Scripture, reason, and experience jointly testify, that in as much as the corruption of nature is earlier than our instructions can be, we should take all pains and care to counteract this corruption as early as possible" (Jackson, 1872, Vol. XIII, p. 476). Wesley felt it was foundational in the transformation process for a child to change the focus of their desire from selfish and self-focused to other focused. Submission and obedience were the critical first step in a child's move away from self-centeredness to God-centered living. Parents were petitioned to command obedience or honor in an effort to move a child from their self-willed ways to an attitude of submission with the ultimate desire for them to live a life submitted to the will of God.

How to teach methodology – correction. Wesley admonished parents to restrain their children from evil with not just "advice" but with "persuasion and reproof" and with "correction" (Sermon 94) and noted that correction should be used last "not till all other have been tried and found to be ineffectual" (Outler, 1986, p. 342). A further caution against physical discipline was seen in the sermon "On Obedience to Parents" when Wesley warned "instead of restraining them with a strong hand; speak (though as calmly as possible, yet) firmly and peremptorily" (Outler, 1986, p. 370).

How to teach methodology – early, plainly, frequently, patiently. In the Sermon "On Family Religion", Wesley also posited religious instruction should be done early, in a language the child understood, frequently, and patiently. The sermon "On the Education of Children" called parents and teachers to provide instruction that resulted in a confidence in God's love and the sermon "On Obedience to Parents" urged parents to be firm and called for consistency and gentleness. The document, "Thoughts on the Manner of Educating Children" suggested diligence on the part of the instructor and advised the instructor to lay down "precept upon precept" with mildness, softness, and gentleness. It is noted that only when that approach to instruction did not work, the instructor was challenged to rely on the Proverb 13:24 approach. Godparents are called to meet their obligations with faithfulness and godly wisdom.

How to teach methodology – routine and relational. The methodology engaged by Susanna Wesley, as noted in her letter and outlined at the Kingswood School, included routine, consistency, rigor, and fairness. Both Susanna and John referred to parents as "cruel" who indulged their children and permitted behavior that would later need to be corrected. Susanna demonstrated instruction that was personal, identified unique techniques used with her various children, and identified the relational nature of her instruction by employment of one on one religious instruction time. John also highlighted the relational aspect of the religious instruction at the school at Kingswood and the "Lessons" called for the parent to allow the child time to read, reflect, and digest the Scripture so that they could truly understand it. Likewise "Instructions", included a question and answer or question and reflection routine between instructor and child, leading the child through a deeper engagement with the content to a richer understanding. Wesley specifically warned against teaching just for the outcome of memorization of facts, "beware of that common, but accursed way of making children parrots, instead of Christians" ("Lessons", Wesley, 1745-6, p. 3) and cautioned instructors to not be in a hurry but to deliberately and attentively engage the child.

The types of publications Wesley created for children and the format they took suggested his expectation on consistency, frequency, and rigor but through a personal, one on one relational experience between the parent, teacher, or pastor and the child.

What to Teach

The coding phase that addressed the research question what to teach was the most robust and represented the largest amount of collected data. In addition, because codes were employed that contained slight variation in interpretation or meaning there was data that was "double coded" or coded to reflect more than one association.

The data collected was associated with the explicit items specifically identified as critical to teach as part of a child's faith formation as well as data that reflected Wesley's implicit instruction of what to teach. An Example of explicit instruction is found in the *Instructions for Children* (Section IV, Lesson VI) that directed the child to memorize the Apostle's Creed. Implicit instruction occurred within the *Prayers for Children* and *Hymns for Children* as they were directed to memorize and recite names for God, offer thanks to Jesus for His gift of salvation, and plead for protection by the Holy Spirit through the use of the prayers and hymns. A complete list of the analytical codes and sub codes associated with the research question what to teach are listed in the Appendix J and K.

God (GOD)

Data that related to the analytical code "GOD" representative of material that was associated with the names or references of God was identified in all the documents studied. Identification of names for God beyond the direct title of "God" or Lord were noted in *Hymns for Children*, *Instructions for Children*, and *Prayers for Children*, with the greatest variety of descriptive names attributed to God found in *Instructions for Children*.

God – names. A variety of descriptive names were used to refer to God that included Father, friend, eternal Word, Creator, Holy Lord, Almighty, Maker of Heaven and Earth ("Hymns"), Maker of All Things, Redeemer, wise Physician ("Instructions"), Father of angels and men, Preserver of all mankind, Father of all mercies, Giver of all good things, Fountain of all goodness, Sun of Righteousness, Author and giver of life, Savior, and The Holy One ("Prayers").

God – description. In the "Instructions", God was described as a Spirit who is everywhere, knows everything, does whatever He wills, and loves everything he has created. He was said to be invisible, powerful, wise, happy, good, swift, true, and merciful. The document suggested God is the only source of wisdom and goodness, that He is worthy of our praise, and greater than we can think. The "Instructions" described God as our gracious creator who is ever watchful and present, suggested we can only come to know God through His revelation, and identified Him as "infinite goodness", true, worthy, and our guide.

God – actions. The "Hymns" described the actions of God as including creation, redemption and, preservation of our bodies and souls. The document suggested that God gives grace, brings awareness, and forgives sins. "Hymns" also identified God as the joy-giver who deserves our praise and that He will eventually serve as our judge. *Prayers for Children* acknowledged God's sovereignty over all of creation, His protection in our life, His graciousness through His blessings, and His compassion at work in our lives through providing safety. Likewise, the *Hymns for Children* acknowledged that all the blessings we receive daily are gifts from God who is our creator and redeemer.

Grace (GRA)

Data that related to material describing the gracious work of God in our lives and in creation, was identified to some extent in all of the documents studied, with the exception of the documents relating to the school at Kingswood and

"Thoughts Concerning Godfathers and Godmothers". God's grace was referred to in Susanna's letter (1742) only in the closing poem as a description of God.

Grace – what it is. In "Thoughts on the Manner of Educating Children" God's grace was considered the source of humanity's transformation and there was a reference to the role of the "means of grace" in that transformation. The indication was that these are two different things. The grace of God is a free gift and the "means of grace" are actions such as prayer and participation in the sacraments that result in the reception of God's grace and ultimately transformation. The sermons identified grace as responsible for growth, transformation, and change. Sermon 96 "On Obedience of Children" suggested that God's grace is sufficient to meet all of our needs and in every other instance grace is attributed to a work of God on our behalf. The biblical narrative in *Lessons for Children* contains numerous stories of the work of God's grace. In the *Hymns for Children* God's grace was counted as responsible for the child's protection from the night and from "youthful lusts" (Maddox, 2008, p. 10). The *Instructions for Children* provided a vivid description of grace in Section I, Lessons VIII & IX with the response to the prompt, "What is grace": "The Power of the Holy Spirit, enabling us to behave and love and serve God". Additionally the child was instructed to seek grace through "constant and careful Use of the Means of Grace" (Wesley, 1746, p. 7). The "Means of Grace" included "The Lord's Supper, Prayer, Searching the Scriptures, and Fasting" (Wesley, 1746, p. 7) and the child was instructed to practice the "Means of Grace" "To his Life's End" (Wesley, 1746, p. 8). *Instructions for Children* also identified actions of God on our behalf that are indirectly attributed to grace. These include keeping, defending, and delivering us from danger; and helping us, providing good things, and enabling us to produce good "fruit".

Grace – what God does and our response. The *Prayers for Children* attributed the child's preservation through the night and day that is both physical and spiritual to the grace of God. His grace had made them His child, guided them throughout their life, and it was through God's grace that they had received blessings. The "Prayers" taught that through God's grace the child was enabled to live a holy life, love "all mankind", worship and serve God, praise God, and "seriously apply my heart unto wisdom, and work out my salvation with fear and trembling" (Jackson, 1872, Vol. XI, p. 270).

Human nature (MAN)

Data that related to material describing human nature prior to the work of God's grace in salvation that results in transformation, was identified to some extent in six of the documents studied, with the greatest response in *Instructions for Children* and *Prayers for Children*.

In *Hymns for Children* humanity was described as "A poor, guilty worm" (Maddox, 2008, p. 3) and a feeble mortal who is "travelling to the grave" (Maddox, 2008, p. 7). In Susanna's letter it was suggested that humanity's natural inclination is to self and it was posited: "Self will is the one grand impediment to our temporal and eternal happiness" (Jackson, 1872, Vol. I, p. 389). The letter continued with suggestions on how the impediment of self-will should be subdued. Sermon 95 "On the Education of Children" described natural humanity as "his [or her] own god" and suggested that humanity worships his or herself (Outler, 1986, p. 350). The sermon identified common malaises of humanity that must be addressed in order for spiritual transformation to occur. These included pride, "love of the world" (Outler, 1986, pp. 350-351), anger; "a deviation from truth (Outler, 1986, p. 351) that brings with it revenge; self-will; and Wesley identified "to speak or act contrary to justice" (Outler, 1986, p. 352) as consistent in everyone. Wesley noted: "All human creatures are naturally partial to themselves, and when opportunity offers, have more regard to their own interest or pleasure than strict justice allows" (Outler, 1986, p. 352). *Prayers for Children* suggested that humanity is unworthy of God's goodness, grace, and blessings because humanity has followed its own desires, offended God's laws, and sinned. The child was directed to pray "I am young, and cannot discern between good and evil" (Jackson, 1872, Vol. XI, p. 268) and "I am nothing, and can do nothing, of myself" (Jackson, 1872, Vol. XI, p. 271).

Instructions for Children provided the greatest insight into human nature through a series of questions in Section I, Lessons three and four that addressed the "Of Creation and Fall of Man". These included "How did God make Man?" "Why did God make Man?" and "Where did God put the first Man and Woman?" The answers identified humanity as made from dust with the purpose "To know, love, and be happy in God forever" (Wesley, 1746, p. 6). The lessons explained the command God gave to the man and woman, their response, and the consequences of that first sin. "Sin and Guilt, and Pain and Death" (Wesley, 1746, p. 6) were those consequences and attributed to all humanity. Humanity was said to be "proud, selfwilled, Lovers of the World, and not Lovers of God" (Wesley, 1746, p. 6). Section II in "Instructions" offered further descriptions of humanity as evil with nothing good. Man was said to contain a soul that is eternal, but does not desire God, and is "spoiled". The concept that humanity is naturally self-willed and not capable of good apart from God was reiterated in Section III. Section III also contended that humanity is "nothing but Sin" (Wesley, 1746, p. 14) and deserves Hell. The document posited that sin makes us "brittle" and prone to "break in Pieces", unworthy of God's grace, and "under the Wrath and under the curse of God" (Wesley, 1746, p. 14). In Section IV of "Instructions" humanity was described as blind to God and the things of God. This blindness made humanity incapable of reason and the ability to know God. "The Natural Man discerneth not the Things of the Spirit of God" (Wesley, 1746, p. 21) but rather finds them foolish. Without the light of God to illumine understanding, it is not possible for humanity to see its "Weakness, Ignorance, Folly and Wickedness" (Wesley, 1746, p. 21). The Fall turned humanity's desire away from God and the things of God and made humanity "guilty, wicked and miserable" (Wesley, 1746, p. 21). Section V continued this description of humanity apart from God and noted: "Men are poor, ignorant, foolish Sinners, that will shortly rot in the Earth" because everything of the Earth is perishable (Wesley, 1746, p. 24). The final section in the "Instructions", Section VI "How to Regulate our Practice", described humanity as possessing "deadly Vices of Covetousness, Pride and Sensuality" (Wesley, 1746, p. 30) because our will is inclined to its own "profit". The section suggested this corrupt nature "softly" draws humanity into Hell and apart from God "You deserve Punishment" because of that corrupt nature (Wesley, 1746, p. 30). Throughout "Instructions" humanity apart from God was described as sinful, deserving of nothing good but God's judgment and punishment.

As *Instructions for Children* described the extreme sinfulness of humanity, in contrast it described the light, love, and goodness of God. Although the description of humanity was difficult and perhaps frightening for a child to read, Wesley offered hope through the grace of God: "he will keep us by his Power, and defend us against every Thing that would hurt us" (Wesley, 1746, p. 12).

Sin (SIN)

Data that related to material that defined sin, described the consequences of sin, gave examples of sin, and offered a "cure" for sin was identified to some extent in eight of the documents studied that included, the sermons "On Family Religion" and "On Obedience to Parents", the letter of Susanna Wesley, the "Plain Account of the Kingswood School", *Hymns for Children, Instructions for Children,* "Thoughts on the Manner of Educating Children", and *Prayers for Children*.

Sin – what it is. In *Hymns for Children*, sin was defined as contrary to God, forbidden by God, and evil. The *Instructions for Children* suggested that Adam and Eve's original sin hurt all of humanity and the consequence of that sin was guilt, pain, and death. "Instructions" noted that sin has spoiled ours souls and requires punishment. Because of sin, "Instructions" contended, humanity desires to follow his or her own will and despise God's will. *Prayers for Children* noted that humanity is "bound to the chains of sin" (Jackson, 1872, Vol. XI, p. 266). Sins are described as "manifold" and committed "by thought, word, and deed" (Jackson, 1872, Vol. XI, p. 263).

Sin – examples and cure. "Instructions" also provided practical examples of sin that included lying, calling someone names, disobedience, or striking another person. "Instructions" noted that only God can provide the cure for sin and the child was directed to: "ask of God to forgive our past Sins, for the Sake of his Son who died for us, and to keep us from them for the Time to come" (Wesley, 1746, p. 16).

Jesus (JES)

Data that related to material relating to a description of Jesus or the actions of Jesus was identified to some extent in six of the documents studied, with significant response in *Hymns for Children, Prayers for Children,* and *Instructions for Children*. There were no codes for "Jesus" assigned to text in the writings of the school at Kingswood, Susanna Wesley's letter, sermon 96 "On Obedience to Parents", the preface to *Lessons for Children*, or in the "Thoughts Concerning Godfathers and Godmothers". It was worthy to note that not only did these documents not include data that related to a description of Jesus or His actions, but also a search revealed that none of the documents even contained the name of Jesus.

Jesus – description. In the *Hymns for Children* (1747) Jesus was described as the "Lamb of God" who is gentle, meek, and mild. Jesus is also called the "Lover of little children", a loving Saviour, "the all-restoring Word", our hope, salvation, "The life, the truth, the way", "All atoning Lamb", and "Lover of lost mankind". Through the "Apostles Creed" that was incorporated into Section IV of the "Instructions", the child is led to recite they believe:

> Jesus Christ, his only Son, our Lord, Who was conceived by the Holy Spirit, born of the virgin Mary; suffered under Pontius Pilate, was crucified, dead, and buried, he descended into Hell. The third Day he rose again from the Dead. He ascended into Heaven, and siteth at the Right hand of God the Father Almighty. From thence he shall come to judge the Quick and the Dead. (Wesley, 1746, p. 22)

Jesus – actions. In the *Hymns for Children* (1747) it was noted that Jesus was "once a little child" who lived in humility, never sought His own desires, and serves as our example in obedience and love. The *Instructions for Children* identified Jesus as the "Eternal Son of God" who provides salvation from our sin. Jesus is said to have "lived and died and rose again" (Wesley, 1746, p. 6). "Instructions" additionally called for the child to repeat of Jesus: "The Son of God was made Man, lived and died and rose again, to buy Forgiveness for us, and to show us how we ought to renounce our own Will and Desires, and to give ourselves up to the holy Will of God" (Wesley, 1746, p. 23). Jesus is said to have taken on humanity's nature and that He loves us, gave Himself for us, wants to take us to Heaven forever, and wants to dwell in our heart.

Jesus – response. In the *Prayers for Children*, children were instructed to pray in the name of Jesus and He was repeatedly referred to as "Jesus Christ, my Redeemer" and "Jesus Christ, my Lord and Savior". Jesus was acknowledged as deserving of our praise, and the "Lamb of God" who "takest away the sins of the world" (Jackson, 1872, Vol. XI, p. 264). The children were also instructed in the "Instructions" to pray "in the Name of Jesus Christ" as He stands before God's "Throne" and offers our "desires, as his own, to God" on our behalf (Wesley, 1746, p. 17). In *Hymns for Children*, the child was instructed to ask Jesus to give them a loving mind, an obedient heart, and seek for Jesus to "live Thyself within my heart" (Maddox, 2008, p. 2) and sanctify them "to thy service" (Maddox, 2008, p. 12)

Salvation (SAL)

Data that related to material describing the means of our salvation, our response to the gift of salvation, and the outcome of salvation was identified to some extent in eight of the documents studied, with the greatest response in *Hymns for Children*. There were no codes for "SAL" assigned to text in the documents "A Short Account of the School at Kingswood", the preface to *Lessons for Children*, Sermons 95, or the "Thoughts" concerning godparents.

Salvation – source. The *Hymns for Children* identified Jesus as the source of our salvation through His life, death, and resurrection. The hymn, "A Morning Hymn" included the clarification: "No! My best actions cannot save" and noted that only Jesus' blood can bring salvation (Maddox, 2008, p. 8) The order of salvation was provided in *Instructions for Children* and began with the question: "By whom are we to be saved from Sin?" (Wesley, 1746, p. 6). The response was Jesus Christ who lived, and died, and rose again and through whose death we can find "Forgiveness of Sins, and Holiness and Heaven" (Wesley, 1746, p. 6). The "Instructions" continued with a question and answer response to salvation that outlined the plan or process of salvation that contained the question and response: "When does God forgive our Sins? When we repent and believe in Christ" (Wesley, 1746, p. 6). (A complete list of the questions and answers Wesley used to describe the process of salvation can be found in Appendix M).

Salvation – outcome. It was posited that the outcome of salvation was they became a child of God and "an heir of heaven" who is "Free from the world" and sin (*Hymns for Children*). The "Instructions" suggested that "if we really believe in him [Jesus]" that God is "reconciled to us"; we enjoy forgiveness of sin, and gain a "true Knowledge of all the Things of God" (Wesley, 1746, p. 17). Not only was it suggested that the child who believes and loves God saved from their sin, the child was saved from "all sinful Tempers and Words and Works" (Wesley, 1746, p. 6) that included pride, self will, sinful Words, love of the world, and sinful works through the grace of God, the work of Jesus Christ, and the ministry of the Holy Spirit.

Salvation – response. In the *Prayers for Children*, salvation was referred to as "new birth" in which "a child of wrath may become a child of grace" (Jackson, 1872, Vol. XI, p. 268). It was suggested that the Lord reveals our sinful nature, makes us sorry or "grievous" for our sins, and leads to the "fountain opened for sin and uncleanness" where we can "wash and be cleansed" (Jackson, 1872, Vol. XI, p. 268). The child was directed in the prayer to ask the Lord to not grant them rest "till I find redemption in thy blood, even the forgiveness of all my sins" (Jackson, 1872, Vol. XI, p. 268). In another prayer ("Friday evening") this washing and cleaning was attributed to God's mercies and the result of salvific cleansing was suggested to be "a clean heart" and "a right spirit" that enabled us to "walk before thee henceforth in holiness and righteousness" and ultimately to "bring me to thy glory" (Jackson, 1872, Vol. XI, pp. 269-270).

Holy Spirit (HOL)

Data that related to material that included text about or in reference to the Holy Spirit, was identified in *Instructions for Children, Prayers for Children, Lessons for Children, Hymns for Children,* "On Obedience of Children" and a single inclusion in the document, "Thoughts on the Manner of Educating Children". The name of the Holy Spirit was not identified at all in the sermons "On the Education of Children" or "On Family Religion", the articles about Kingswood school, the letter of Susanna Wesley, or the "Thoughts" concerning godparents.

Holy Spirit – description and actions. The reference to the Holy Spirit in *Prayers for Children* suggested the Holy Spirit is with us, guides us, and renews us. The Holy Spirit was also identified as deserving praise along with Jesus. In the *Instructions for Children*, the child was instructed that the Holy Spirit "works in us, enlightening our Understanding, and filling our Souls with a divine Peace and Joy" (Wesley, 1746, p. 23). The Holy Spirit was attributed with giving understanding of the "Truths of God" and bringing restoration through belief in the Holy Spirit, as well as in God. The Holy Spirit was also identified as a member of the Trinity: "these three are one, God the Father, the Son, and the Holy Spirit" (Wesley, 1746, p. 23).

Eternity (HVN)

Data that related to material that addressed eternity, heaven, or hell was identified in *Prayers for Children* and *Instructions for Children*. The word "Heaven" was not found in "Serious Thoughts Concerning Godfathers and Godmothers," "Thoughts on the Manner of Educating Children," or "A Short Account of the School at Kingswood". A single incident was found in "A Plain Account of the Kingswood School" inside a direct quote from St. Augustine and in Susanna Wesley's letter: "Heaven or hell depends on this alone" (Jackson, 1872, Vol. I, p. 389).

Eternity – heaven. *Lessons for Children* included Old Testament biblical passages that referenced Heaven such as Elijah's chariot ride to Heaven and throughout the biblical text that comprised the various "lessons" of the Old Testament. Sermon 94 "On Family Religion" referred to "our Father who is in Heaven" and the treasures that are stored on earth or in Heaven. Sermon 95 "On the Education of Children" referred to Heaven as the sky and as a place other than earth. *Hymns for Children* identified those who were saved as "heirs" of heaven and heaven as our inheritance. The *Prayers for Children* concluded with the "Lord's Prayer" which begins with the phrase "Our Father, who art in Heaven". *Prayers for Children* also identified Heaven, as a place where Jesus lives that is everlasting and filled with joy and pleasures. "Prayers" also identified heaven as following death: "When I lay down my body in the grave, my soul may rise to life immortal" (Jackson, 1872, Vol. XI, p. 272) and in connection with Jesus's return to earth: "when the trumpet shall sound, and at last call me from the sleep of death, let me be caught up into the clouds to meet the Lord in the air, and so for ever be with the Lord" (Jackson, 1872, Vol. XI, p. 261).

The *Instructions for Children* offered the most robust description in Section I, Lesson XII "Of Heaven". It was identified as the place where believers go after death, a place of "Light and Glory" where people live in "Joy and Happiness" free from "Want, or Pain, or Sin" (Wesley, 1746, p. 9). "Instructions" posited that in heaven our bodies will be spiritual "swifter than Lightning and brighter than the Sun", and we will find enjoyment in God whom we will see "Face to Face" (Wesley, 1746, p. 9). In heaven people will spend their time singing praises to God forever and ever. Likewise it was suggested that the angels in heaven spend their days praising God and singing "Holy, Holy, Holy, Lord God of Hosts!" (Wesley,

1746, p. 15). As was noted in reference to *Prayers for Children*, *Instructions for Children* also included references to Heaven in connection with Jesus' return to earth and our physical resurrection of the body after death: "And at that Day he [Jesus] will restore in Glory [Heaven] both our Bodies and Souls, and all that we had committed to his Charge" (Wesley, 1746, p. 12) and in the text: "And after the Body is dead and risen again, we shall live together in eternal Glory" (Wesley, 1746, p. 23).

Eternity – hell. There was also mention of hell in a few of the documents. Within Susanna's letter hell was referenced in contrast to heaven, and the *Instructions for Children* provided a greater description in Section I, Lessons X and XI, "Of Hell". There it was described as the place where "unbelievers" go after death, a "dark bottomless Pit, full of Fire and Brimstone" where people spend their time "weeping and wailing and gnashing of Teeth" with tormented souls and bodies (Wesley, 1746, p. 8). The torment of the bodies, "Instructions" contended, will be through "lying in burning and flaming fire" and the torment of the souls will be through having a sense of God's wrath (Wesley, 1746, p. 8). In hell, unbelievers will be tormented by "their own Consciences, the Devils, and one another" and there will be no rest for all of eternity (Wesley, 1746, p. 8).

Christian lifestyle (LIFE)

Data that related to the analytical code "LIFE" representative of material describing the Christian life was identified to some extent in seven of the documents studied. The preface to the *Lessons for Children* did not contain data explicitly descriptive of the Christian life, however, the biblical content that comprised the "Lessons" did contain both direct and indirect engagement with Christian living. Likewise, the two documents related to the school at Kingswood did not speak explicitly of Christian living but the rigor of the schedule and the course of instruction were designed to set an example and foster habits conducive to Christian living. The "Thoughts" concerning godparents and the manner of educating children also did not contain explicit reference to Christian living; however, the end goal was for the child to live a Christian life.

A significant amount of data was coded from the remaining sources and fell into three general categories related to Christian living: praise, piety, and surrender.

The Christian life – described. The "Hymns" identified things that should be a part of the child's Christian life and a description of that life. The Christian life was described as simple and free from sin. Christian living was to include serving, loving, and following after God's will. In "Instructions" a Christian life was described as "Good, Wise, Just, True, full of Love, and of Power to do well" (Wesley, 1746, p. 12); a happy life in which the child desired only God and to do good. The Christian life was defined as a content life of obedience in which the person "sees God in all Things" (Wesley, 1746, p. 21). A person who lives the Christian life was holy, gave to the poor, and served the Lord. The "Instructions" pressed the child to "deny ourselves in all things", to possess a spirit of charity and penitence, and to "aim at being made conformable to our crucified Savior" in all things (Wesley, 1746, p. 30). The child was commended to never swear falsely, use the Name of God irreverently, kill or hurt anyone, steal, or to think of himself or herself as better than someone else. They were to honor their parents, speak the truth, to pray daily, to read God's Word, and to participate in public worship. The "Instructions" offered two summative responses to the Christian life. The first was in Section VI, Lesson VIII where the child was called to "love God", "love Jesus Christ", and "love our Neighbour". The second was in Section VI, Lesson IX: "always live and act, as being in the Presence of God" (Wesley, 1746, p. 36). *Prayers for Children* also described the Christian life as humble, righteous, loving, obedient, seeking after things that are right, and pleasing to God. The Christian life resulted in an increase in "faith, hope, and love" (Jackson, 1872, Vol. XI, p. 265) and embraced "temperance, soberness and chastity" (Jackson, 1872, Vol. XI, p. 263). It was to strive to keep God's commands, to increase in godly wisdom, and to draw near to God through prayer and praise. The "Prayers" offered as a summation: "whatever I do to the glory of thy name" through a cleansed heart, inspired by the Holy Spirit that "perfectly" loves God and magnifies His name (Jackson, 1872, Vol. XI, p. 264).

The sermons also address Christian living. In Sermon 96 "On Obedience to Parents" the child was called to obey their parents, do what they asked and not do whatever they forbid. Sermon 94 "On Family Religion" suggested the Christian life was identified as one that loved and served God and others. Sermon 95 "On the Education of Children" called for parents to help their children to "make God their end in all things; and inure them, in all they do, to aim at knowing, loving, and serving God" (Outler, 1986, p. 359).

The Christian life – praise. The *Hymns for Children* repeatedly called the child to offer praise and glory to God. In the "Exhortation for a Child" within the "Hymns", the child was exhorted to make it their "chiefest care to serve and glorify God" (Maddox, 2008, p. 10). The nature of every hymn was expressed as a poem of thanks, praise, and glory to God, explicitly stated in many but implicitly stated in all. The *Instructions for Children* also commended the children to offer praise to God, to thank Him, and to "rejoice and delight in him alone" (Wesley, 1746, p. 26) with "Joy unspeakable and full of Glory" (Wesley, 1746, p. 28).

The Christian life – prayer. Prayer was identified as a critical element in the Christian life through the inclusion of prayer in the daily routine at Kingswood school and in the Wesley household. Wesley's provision of prayers for morning, evening, and meals as well as hymns that included prayers indicated the expectation of the child to engage in prayer as part of the Christian lifestyle. Additionally, the inclusion of Bible reading in the daily routine at Kingswood school and in the Wesley household, as well as the expectation that children would be led by their parents, pastors, and teachers to read the scripture as provided in the *Lessons for Children,* demonstrated the value of scripture to the Christian life.

The Christian life – submission. The final component of a Christian life that can be seen throughout the documents was submission. The "Hymns" directed the child to seek to be lowly and live not for their own desires but for God's alone.

The child was called to "delight" in doing God's will and exhorted to flee his or her personal desires. The "Prayers" likewise compelled the child to give his or herself to God "wholly" and to be "entirely devoted" to Him. The "Instructions" posited the child must be saved from self will, which is accomplished through a "Heart continually says, "lord, not as I will, but as thou wilt" (Wesley, 1746, p. 7). The child was instructed to desire God through a "meek and quiet Spirit, a contended, humble, thankful heart" (Wesley, 1746, p. 16) and told, "His Glory should be our supreme, absolute, and universal End" (Wesley, 1746, p. 31). The "Instructions" provided a summative description of the Christian life: "To desire him alone, to rejoice in him always, and to love him with all thy Heart and with all thy Soul" (Wesley, 1746, p.33).

Prayer (PRA)

Data that related to material describing prayer, was identified to some extent in five of the documents studied, with the greatest response in *Instructions for Children* and *Prayers for Children*. Due to the nature of the document, *Prayers for Children* contained the greatest engagement with the subject of prayer. There were no codes for "prayer" assigned to text in "A Plain Account of Kingswood School", the preface to *Lessons for Children*, Sermon 95 "On the Education of Children," or Sermon 96 "On Obedience to Parents".

Prayers – examples. Wesley taught the significance of prayer in the faith formation of the child through his instructions to parents and teachers. They were instructed to engage the child in the act of praying, and Wesley provided specific examples of prayers for children. The *Hymns for Children* included a prayer for morning, at "Lying Down in Bed", and before and after meals. The *Prayers for Children* contained a morning and evening prayer for the child to pray every day of the week, as well as prayers for mealtime, and on behalf of others. Children were expected to memorize and recite the "Lord's Prayer "following every daily prayer and the "Lord's Prayer" was identified in the *Instructions for Children* as "The best Prayer in the World" (Wesley, 1746, p. 18). Following that description, the children were also expected to memorize the prayer.

Prayers – how to. Children were instructed to pray from the "heart" and to "never omit prayer" either in the morning or evening ("Hymns"). The child was commended to praise and thank God in their prayers, to ask for His grace and mercy, and to seek pardon or forgiveness from sins ("Instructions"). The child was also instructed to ask God for wisdom, understanding, and an obedient, humble, and submissive heart ("Instructions"). In the *Instructions for Children*, Wesley posited that children should pray to God through the name of Jesus Christ, to make sure there was alignment between the child's heart and their lips, and to pray earnestly. Susanna's letter identified the value of family prayer and parents were instructed in the sermon "On Family Religion" to set time aside every day for prayer as a family. Susanna's letter also identified the role of the "Lord's Prayer" and personal prayer was an expectation of a child's daily routine.

Scripture/Bible (BIB)

Data that related to material describing scripture or the Bible, was identified to some extent in all of the documents studied except "A Plain Account of the Kingswood School", with the greatest response in *Instructions for Children* and *Lessons for Children*. Due to the content and nature of *Lessons for Children*, that source contained the greatest engagement with scripture. "A Plain Account" did not explicitly address scripture reading and the use of the Bible, however, children were taught the biblical languages and "meditation" was part of their daily routine.

Bible - how to use. Scripture, as with prayer, played a valuable role in the faith formation of children and was considered an expected focus in their Christian life. Parents were commended, as with prayer, to engage as a family in Scripture reading and meditation ("On Family Religion") and Susanna noted the use of Scripture in teaching her children to read. The child was instructed to seek the ability to "hear, read, mark, learn and inwardly digest" God's Word in *Prayers for Children*. The "Prayers" identified not only the child's engagement with scripture but their affection of it and the result of "good living" because of that engagement:

> Open my understanding to receive thy truth in the love thereof. Set it so powerfully upon my heart, and root it so deep in my soul, that the fruits thereof may be seen in my life to thy glory and praise. (Jackson, 1872, Vol. XI, p. 260)

Bible – what taught. Wesley's writing style interspersed scripture verses and phrases with his own in such a way that in the "Instructions", "Prayers", and "Hymns", the child was reciting scripture, committing it to memory, and engaging in the meaning of God's Word through the recitations, prayers, and hymns. The *Instructions for Children* included a list of the Ten Commandment, detailed descriptions of each command, and suggested the practical impact of that command on the child's life. *Lessons for Children* was a narrative representation of large portions of the Old Testament. Wesley identified the purpose behind this approach was to make the Word accessible to children so they could understand and come to know the Scripture, which he described as "delivered by the Spirit of God" (*Lessons for Children*, Wesley, 1746, p. 3). A complete listing of the biblical texts contained in the "Lessons" is provided in the Appendix H. The biblical text for the sermon "On Family Religion" was Joshua 24:15: "As for me and my house we will serve the Lord", the text for sermon 95 "On the Education of Children" was Proverbs 22:6: "Train up a child in the way he should go: And when he is old, he will not depart from it", and the text for Sermon "On Obedience to Parents" was Ephesians 6:1: "Children obey your parents in the Lord, for this is right" (KJV).

Bible – description. The Bible was referred to in *Instructions for Children* as the "Law of God", "Spring of Life", "Light of the Heart", "Treasure of Souls", and the "Testimony of the Lord". It was described as wonderful, holy, undefiled, sure, right, pure, true, righteous, and "sweeter also than Honey and the Honey comb" (Wesley, 1746, p. 36). Wesley posited that scripture teaches, gives light, endures forever, and shows the way to our great "reward" ("Instructions"). Wesley also contended that the "Rules" or expectations found in the Word of God are easy to follow with the grace of God but ridiculous to the world ("Instructions"). The child was guided to pray: "Make thy Word a light unto my feet, and a lamp to my path" ("Prayers", Jackson, 1872, Vol. XI, p. 268) and called to love and admire God's Word ("Instructions").

Conclusion

Wesley provided a glimpse of his objectives, methodology, content, and outcomes in the practices and expectations of his religious instruction of children for the purpose of child faith formation through the twelve documents studied. The documents represented original works of Wesley, personal correspondence to Wesley, and revised works all produced and provided for the purpose of instruction or explanation in regard to child faith formation. The two documents related to the school at Kingswood were in response to questions about the school's routine and purpose; the *Instructions for Children, Lessons for Children, Prayers for Children* and *Hymns for Children* were written to be used by children as curriculum at the school at Kingswood, in Methodist societies comprised of children, and in Methodist homes; "Thoughts" on godparents and the education of children were in response to criticism of practice, and the three sermons were printed as part of a series in the "Arminian Magazine" along with "Thoughts on the Manner of Educating Children".

Objectives of "Religious Instruction" (Why Teach)

Wesley saw the natural condition of humanity as apart from God, depraved, and in need of reconciliation and restoration. The goal of religious instruction was to "set right" humanity's natural condition to one of obedience, faithfulness, and love in a restored relationship with God, a renewed heart, a transformed mind, and Christ-like behavior. Without the work of salvation, humanity was destined for an eternity apart from God but through the work of salvation humanity was provided the hope of heaven. The goal of religious instruction was transformation through salvation and formation through discipleship. Transformation and formation that impacted the child's mind, attitude, and behavior as the child grew in grace and the love of God, through the work of Jesus Christ, and the indwelling of the Holy Spirit. Wesley was also concerned about the continuation of the revival movement beyond the current generation and saw the religious instruction of children as critical in the continuance of revival.

Responsibility of "Religious Instruction" (Who Shall Teach)

Wesley specifically identified parents as the primary spiritual caregivers of their children. In the documents he also identified the role of instructors or teachers, ministers, and godparents. Because of the broad distribution of the documents to the greater Methodist societies, it can be inferred that he also attributed responsibility of child faith formation to all. Wesley was clear to identify God as the true source of instruction and transformation through the indwelling of the Holy Spirit both in the life of the instructor and in the life of the child.

Wesley held high expectations for the life style of those responsible for the religious education or faith formation of children. He described them as "God fearing" parents and instructors who saw their primary purpose to glorify God and help the child come to know Him and experience His love. Wesley expected the instructors to know, understand, and live a life representative of biblical Christianity. Wesley also acknowledged that ultimately Christian education and faith formation are not the work of the godliest of parents or instructors but the work of God alone through the power of the Holy Spirit and called for instructors to be led by the Spirit as they served the Lord.

Methodology of "Religious Instruction" (How to Teach)

Wesley called parents and instructors to begin instruction early, to speak plainly, and to offer instruction frequently and patiently. He identified a methodology of instruction that was daily and routine, encompassing the whole of a child's life including their sleeping, waking, playing, and learning. The methodology was also holistic in that it encompassed a child's whole world, taking into account the impact of the home, school, and church. The instruction included informal moments where parents were told to help the child see God in the everydayness of life, integrated moments where the child was led to see God and His work through science, math, language, and literature; the instruction included intentional experiences with prayer, Scripture, and worship; and the instruction included direct teaching through question and answer catechesis, sermons and creeds, and memorization of prayers, hymns, and scripture.

Although called to "break" a child's will in order to teach submission and obedience, Wesley's methodology required the instructors to be gentle, kind, and personal in their engagement with the child; to be consistent, orderly, and faithful in their discipline and instruction; to know the child well enough to provide personalized instruction that was on their own level, in their own language, and built upon what they already knew; and Wesley always expected the instructor to employ grace and love. Wesley understood that this method of instruction was not easy to engage and posited: "It requires no small resolution to begin and persist herein. It certainly requires no small patience, more than nature ever gave" (Sermon 96, Outler, 1986, p. 370) but promised: "But the grace of God is sufficient for you; you can do all things through Christ that strengtheneth you. This grace is sufficient to give you diligence, as well as resolution" (Outler, 1986, p. 370).

Content of "Religious Instruction (What to Teach)

The twelve documents engaged for this study suggested Wesley emphasized teaching about God, grace, Jesus, salvation, the Holy Spirit, Christian living, and eternity. He also taught about the Bible, prayer, humanity, and sin. Wesley offered a variety of names and descriptions of God that provided a broad and comprehensive perspective of who God is, what God has done in the past, and how God is involved in our lives today. The incredible greatness of who God is and what He has done, the wickedness of humanity apart from God but the potential for reconciliation, salvation, transformation, and formation through Jesus's birth, death, and resurrection and the work of the Holy Spirit, and the assurance of the believer that offers hope for an eternity in heaven with God were themes throughout all of the writings. In summation to the research question "what to teach", the whole of the documents provided a response to four key questions: Who is God? Who are we? What has God done? How are we to respond?

Outcomes of "Religious Instruction"

The identified outcomes of the religious instruction for the faith formation of children recognized within the documents included the experience of repentance and forgiveness of their sins and for the child to experience freedom, joy, and the hope of heaven. Outcomes of the instruction also included for the child to desire to obey, know, worship, and serve God; engage daily in prayer, Scripture, and praise; live a life characterized by love for God and love for others; and ultimately spend eternity in Heaven. In addition, Wesley desired that through investment in the faith formation of children, the revival movement that began with him and the children's parents would continue beyond the present generation. Please find attached in Appendix N "A Schematic for the Religious Instruction of Children for the Purpose of Child Faith Formation Based on the Writings of John Wesley".

Chapter Five

Interpretations, Implications, and Recommendations

This book sought to rediscover Wesley's teachings and practices on child faith formation and identify insights relevant for the Christian education of children in the Wesleyan movement today. Wesley realized that the future of the Methodist movement required intentionality in the "religious education" of children. The same realization is ours today, we must:

> Tell the children-to-come the praises of the Lord, and of His power and the great things He has done... So the children-to-come might know, even the children yet to be born. So they may rise up and tell it to their children. Then they would put their trust in God and not forget. (Psalm 78:3-8 NLT)

John Wesley was an eighteenth century Anglican minister who desired to see revival sweep through the church. He called the people back to a deep and abiding faith in Jesus Christ and urged them to "go forward" in their faith formation (Rotz & Lyon, 1999, Sermon #106, para. 20). This book focused on the three research questions specifically in the realm of child faith formation asking: Is there evidence in Wesley's writings and publications that related specifically to child faith formation that reveal answers to the questions of how to teach children, what to teach children, and who shall teach children and are those insights relevant today? Wesley held a high view of children and believed that every stage of faith formation was possible during childhood (Prince, 1926). Wesley spent time engaging children through his work in schools, through personal visitation of children in their homes, and through engagement with children that were part of Methodist societies. Although Wesley had no children of his own, his appreciation of children and attention to them was evident in his writings and publications. Wesley was a prolific writer and publisher, having published hundreds of duodecimo style tracts, which were small in size and inexpensive to print and distribute in order to get the message and tools of the Methodist movement into the hands of the common people (Rivers, 2010). Twelve of those works were selected for examination in an attempt to fill the gap in literature, to recapture Wesley's beliefs and practices about child faith formation, and to provide answers to the research questions (Heitzenrater 2001; Maddix, 2001; and Willhauck ,1992)

Findings

The twelve documents studied provided a glimpse into Wesley's teachings and practices of child faith formation, what he referred to as "religious" instruction or education. The twelve documents included published sermons, reports on the educational practices of the school at Kingswood, responses to critics, and documents developed for children. The scope of the documents offered a variety in publication date, audience, purpose of publication, and focus of education. Although none of the documents independently provided a thorough response to the three research questions, a comprehensive response was provided through the cumulative impact of the twelve documents.

Who shall Teach

In response to the research question who shall teach children in the process of their faith formation or as Wesley termed, religious instruction, response can be seen as to the individuals who were responsible for the instruction and their expected lifestyle.

Who shall teach – relationship

Wesley believed in the primary responsibility of the parents for the faith formation of their children even to the point where parents were called to actively oversee the selection of the child's school instructors, employers, and marriage partners. While the authority of the religious education or child faith formation laid squarely on the shoulders of the parents with both fathers and mothers being addressed in the scope of the documents, instructors or teachers of the children beyond the parents also included ministers, Godparents, grandmothers, and caretakers in general were also addressed with responsibility for the spiritual care of children. Because of the intended readership of most of the documents, it can be inferred that Wesley held everyone within the Methodist societies responsible for the faith formation of children.

Who shall teach – lifestyle

Wesley also addressed the expected lifestyle of those responsible for the religious instruction of children. He knew, as contemporary research has documented (NSYR, 2011), that it is not just what the parents and instructors say that informs the education of a child but it is how they live that informs as well. Wesley called for the parents and instructors to have the knowledge of God in their own minds and hearts and for their lifestyle to be representative of what they knew and believed. Parents and teachers were called to be "God-fearing" and live a life according to God's will in humble obedience and submission in which scripture and prayer were an integral part of their daily life. In the preface to the "Instructions" parents and teachers were called to have the lessons on their own hearts, reminiscent of the call of Moses to the people of Israel in Deuteronomy 6, acknowledging that unless the instructors both knew in their minds and their hearts the teachings their instruction would be ineffective. Wesley asserted that ultimately God was the true source of all instruction and called for parents and instructors to "lift up" their hearts to God as they sought prayerful support and intercession from the Holy Spirit for it is "He alone [that] giveth the Increase" (*Lessons*, Wesley, 1746, p. 4).

How to Teach

In response to the research question how to teach children, answers were found that related to the timing or when the instruction should occur, where the instruction should occur, and the method that should be employed in religious instruction.

When instruction should occur

Wesley admonished that instruction should occur early such as in Susanna's letter where it stated "from the moment of birth" (Jackson, 1872, Vol. I, p. 387). He believed that it would be very difficult, if not impossible, to right the "wrongs" of human nature later in a child's life. Not only did he suggest early but he suggested instruction should occur daily and routinely in a way that encompassed every aspect of a child's life – from sleeping, waking, eating, playing, formal education, and engagement with the means of grace. Wesley saw the impact of every aspect of a child's life on their formation, reminiscent of the Deuteronomy 6 text.

Where instruction should occur

The question of where instruction should occur, while not explicitly stated in any of the documents, was obvious in the expectation and audience addressed. In keeping with the understanding that faith formation should encompass every aspect of a child's day (including their sleeping), religious education or faith formation should occur in every environment the child finds him/herself: the home, the school, the church, and "along the road" (Deut. 6:7, NIV). The sermon "On Family Religion" described what it means for a house to serve the Lord and called for all of the practices in the home to be reflective of the things of God. The documents on the schools in Kingswood described daily school schedules that were representative of the integration of faith and instruction through the practices conducted and the instructional materials used. The sermon "On Family Religion" and "Serious Thoughts concerning Godfathers and Godmothers" described the importance of individuals outside of the family in the life of the child who had influence with the suggestion that religious instruction beyond the confines of the home and school occurred. Pastors were also identified as influential in the life of the child as noted in Wesley's directions for pastors to begin societies when there were at least ten children present and for the pastors to learn the *Instructions for Children* and use them when meeting with children in their homes and in the societies.

Methodology of Instruction

Wesley also invested a great deal of attention in the various documents studied to the methodology that should be employed in the religious instruction or faith formation of children. In the sermon "On Family Religion" Wesley admonished not only should instruction begin early, but it should also be done plainly, frequently, consistently, and with patience.

Methodology – speak plain. Wesley understood the developmental communication needs of a child and while he believed in a child's ability to grasp spiritual truth and experience not just transformation through salvation but formation through rigorous religious education and discipleship, he knew that the instruction had to be communicated with words that the child could grasp. In a desire to set an example to fellow preachers, it was reported that Wesley preached a sermon to over 550 children and never spoke a word of more than two syllables (Prince, 1926, p. 123). And although the *Prayers, Hymns, Instructions*, and *Lessons for Children* by today's standards seem very un-childlike in their communication level, there is a clear intentionality for simplicity in language when compared to his other writings. Wesley specifically admonished parents and teachers in the preface to the *Lessons for Children* to speak in a way the child could understand, to rephrase, offer questions, and develop a rapport with the child to encourage the communication and comprehension.

Methodology – build on previous knowledge. Not only was there an expectation that the instruction would be done in way that the child could understand the language, but it was to be done in a way that built on the child's pre-existing knowledge. Children were also expected to not just memorize and regurgitate the content, "like a parrot" (preface to "Lessons") but reflect on the content and move from low level learning of remembering to understanding, and applying.

Methodology – routine and rigorous. There was an expectation of the instruction to be systematic, routine, and rigorous. As demonstrated in his mother's letter, the schedules from the Kingswood school, and the descriptions in "On the Education of Children", the religious instruction was regimented and predictable. While there was a predictability to each day, within the day there was variety in engagement and practice moving from times of corporate worship, personal reflection, corporate instruction, personalized instruction, focus on scripture and prayer to focus on academic and classic instruction. Wesley noted in "A Plain Account of Kingswood School" that play was not a part of their daily routine: "neither do we allow any time for play on any day" (Jackson, 1872, Vol. XIII, p. 294) citing an "Old German Proverb". What is notable that while Wesley clearly included that reference in this particular publication, instruction on the absence of play in any of the other works was not identified. In Susanna's letter there is mention of not allowing play or loud talking but in reference to the six hours during the school day and noted that they were expected to seek permission before "running into the yard, garden, or street" (Jackson, 1872, Vol. 1, p. 391) outside of the school hours.

Methodology – seek obedience. Wesley suggested that a child's will is turned towards itself - children in their natural human state apart from God's grace are self-willed. He taught that in order for a child to live in accordance to God's will, this self-will must be broken, and he admonished that the sooner the better for once a child set for their life a pattern of self-willed living, it was difficult and painful to break: "Bow down their wills from the very first dawn of reason; and, by habituating them to submit to your will, prepare them for submitting to the will of their Father which is in heaven" (Jackson, 1872, Vol. III, p. 366). Wesley called parents "cruel" who did not "break" or re-direct their child's will early and called for obedience to be the first thing taught; obedience to parents that led to obedience to God. While this sounds harsh and cruel and evokes images of brutality and severe physical discipline today, Wesley advised that this instruction should be done with kindness, patience, and in a way that was characterized as loving in order to result in a child developing love for God and their neighbor. In the sermon, "On Family Religion," instruction was referred to as a "labour of love" and the parent was told to "avoid the very appearance of passion" or anger when offering correction (Jackson, 1872, Vol. III, p. 341 and p. 339), and in "A Thought on the Manner of Educating Children" Wesley advised that the instruction was to be done with "mildness, softness, and gentleness" (Jackson, 1872, Vol. XIII, p. 476). Parents were cautioned to be mild in their discipline and only resort to "kind severity" described in terms of Proverbs 13:24 when mild correction and instruction was ineffective. Although the instruction to "break the will" or to seek obedience was coded in relation to the research question how to teach, for Wesley breaking the will was not a description of methodology to be employed but more of an outcome to achieve – obedience.

What to Teach

Wesley compelled parents and teachers to first teach obedience and then engagement with Scripture and the means of grace in order to come to know God and Jesus Christ, to know of God's grace and humanity's sin, and to experience the presence of the Holy Spirit and the hope of Heaven. The analysis from the coding identified four questions within the research question what to teach that were implicitly addressed: Who is God, who are we, what has God done, and how are we to respond?

What to teach – who is God and what did He do

Wesley's works included teaching of God in a way that was robust and broad encompassing a wide variety of names, attributes, and descriptions of God giving the impression that he wanted the child to grasp the full scope of God's character that was powerful, personal, creative, redemptive, and active. There was an historical presence to God who always was, a current presence to God who is actively engaged today in the child's life and in creation, and a future presence to God who is eternal and beyond this immediate life. There was a balance in Wesley's description between personal and powerful, gracious and demanding.

What to teach – who are we and what are we to do

In light of his descriptions of God, Wesley addressed humanity (man) and described "man" as willful and sinful with nothing good in him apart from God. The depravity and the desire after everything not of God included lying, deceit, injustice, pride, possessions, and death. In response to humanity apart from God, God's grace was seen as saving, redeeming, restoring, transforming, and empowering through the work of Jesus Christ and the power of the Holy Spirit. Salvation was repeatedly explained and Christian living described and expected. Jesus, God's Son, was said to have been born, lived, died, and rose again to provide forgiveness of sins and the way to salvation. The Holy Spirit calls us to faith, enlightens our understanding, fills us with peace and joy, and enables us to love and serve God.

What to teach – prayer and scripture

The centrality of scripture was seen in Wesley's writings as he wove scriptural phrases throughout as part of a natural speech pattern exemplified in the "Hymns" and "Prayers" and in his call for intentional engagement with Scripture through the schedules prescribed and the "Lessons" provided. The value of prayer was also taught through the expectation of the child's engagement with prayer in the natural course of their day (rising, before and after meals, and at bed in the minimum), through the provision of specific prayers to be prayed, and through his explicit teachings on prayer in *Instructions for Children*.

Wesley's Practices and Teachings in Light of Modern Educational Theory

The educational theory that emerges from Wesley's writings, specifically the twelve reviewed as part of this research project, in part resembles the educational theories prevalent in the eighteenth century and in part contains elements more in keeping with contemporary educational theory. Wesley saw children, even very young children, as capable of faith formation and recipients of religious instruction. Not only did he see them capable, but also suggested early religious education. Wesley understood the value of communication and instruction on a child's level, as opposed to expecting them to learn and grasp meaning conveyed in a way that was effective for adults. While he encouraged memorization of prayers, hymns, and scripture verses, Wesley encouraged a dialog approach to instruction that encouraged children to engage the content and reflect on it through a series of questions posed as illustrated in *Instructions for Children*. Wesley understood the value of experiential learning, and incorporated engagement in spiritual disciplines as part of a child's daily routine – disciplines such as prayer, meditation, hymn singing, Scripture reading, fasting, and service. Not only did the learning contain an element of experiential learning, but Wesley also admonished parents and instructors to build on the child's existing knowledge and experience. Finally, there was a relational perspective to Wesley's approach in which children worked one on one with parents, instructors, and pastors, such as the approach his mother used with him and his siblings. Wesley understood the powerful influence of the parent or instructor on the life of the child and held high expectations for their personal behavior and spiritual experience. Wesley's educational theory did contain discipline -- strict discipline and high expectations for the child's behavior, strict discipline in the approach to the instruction such as the strict schedule outlined in the accounts of the school in Kingswood, and strict obedience as noted in the sermons and Susanna Wesley's letter. Wesley's approach was holistic, in that he encouraged engagement of the child's mind and body and expected outcomes that were cognitive, affective, and behavioral in nature. His approach was also inclusive, in that he understood the value of instruction for all children regardless of station, gender, or class (Body, 1936). Wesley's approach incorporated memorization, singing, question and answer, repetition, engagement, and reflection and the instruction was systematic and prescribed. In speaking of Wesley's educational theory, Body (1936) posited:

> His own educational philosophy was not a ready made jumble of ideas seized upon at random, but was the result of hard thinking, intelligently directed and capable from the first practical realization. It had also this great merit that it possessed a living spirit, a consequent forward development is readily discernible in it. (p. 134)

Wesley and Eighteenth Century Educational Theory

There are elements to his methodology that can be attributed to educational theorists of the eighteenth century. Wesley noted in his journal that he had read Locke's (1690) *Essay on the Human Understanding,* which addressed how humans acquire knowledge and understanding (Jackson, 1872, Vol. VII), and his work was evident in Wesley's approach to discipline in education and emphasis early instruction (Baker, 1982; Body, 1936). Wesley was also influenced by the Moravians through what he saw of their educational practices while in Herrnhut and read of their educational practices in Comenius (Body, 1936; Buckroyd, 2001; Prince, 1926). The most notable influences from Herrnhut were the inclusion of education to all children regardless of status, the organization of the instruction as replicated in the school in Kingswood, and the notion to "break the will" (Towns, 1970). Wesley was a scholar of Comenius's and works such as his *The Great Didactic* were influential in the construction of Wesley's educational theory. The title page included:

> A certain Inducement to found such Schools in all the Parishes, Towns, and Villages of every Christian Kingdom, that the entire Youth of both Sexes, None being excepted, shall *Quickly, Pleasantly, Thoroughly,* Become learned in the Sciences, pure in Morals, Trained in Piety, and in this manner Instructed in all things necessary for the present and for the future life. (As cited in Lebar, 1995, p. 50)

Comenius's influence can also be seen in Wesley's (1746) instruction in the preface to *Instructions for Children* to "let them not read or say one line without understanding what they say. Try them over and over; stop them short, almost at every sentence and ask them what do you mean by that, read it again" (p. iii). Wesley noted his admiration of Milton's (1644) *Tractate on Education* and a parallel can be seen to Milton's goal of education when Wesley suggested that the "grand end of education" was to "cure" children of their "general diseases of human nature" (Sermon 95, Outler, 1986, p. 352). He was also noticeably influenced by Fleury and Poiret and demonstrated that he valued their work through his strong reflection of their work and approach to instruction in *Instructions for Children* (Body, 1936, Maddox, 2012). Although Wesley was influenced by educational theorists of his day, Body (1936) posited: "What Wesley achieved in the realm of practical education stamps him as distinct in genius from all the tribes of close-closeted educational philosophers, however, enlightened they may have been in their educational theories" (p. 143).

Wesley and Contemporary Educational Theory

What makes Wesley unique among his peers is that there are elements of Wesley's eighteenth century educational practices that can be seen supported by contemporary educational theory. He appears to be a man in some cases "ahead of his time" when it came to educational theory, or as Towns (1970) suggested, a "pioneer". The work of Piaget in terms of cognitive development beginning at birth and the process of acquiring knowledge and understanding as a process of assimilation and accommodation align with Wesley's views of early instruction, experiential learning, and building on what the child already knows (Wilhoit & Dettoni, 1995). Wesley, like Piaget, challenged instructors of children to be aware of the child's developmental level and provide instruction appropriate to that level. Wesley employed, at least in part, Vygotsky's "zone of proximal development" where "a more competent person collaborates with a child to help him move from where he is now to where he can be with help" (Miller, 2002, p. 377) through the guided religious instruction of the child by an adult who was to possess the knowledge and lifestyle being taught to the child. Through the expectations placed on the lifestyle of parents and teachers and the rigorous routine instituted, Wesley understood the impact of context on development as suggested by Vygotsky. Bandura's perspective that children can learn behaviors through observation (Miller, 2002) can be seen in Wesley's expectations for parents and instructors of children to live a life style that exemplifies the life style expected in the child and the call for the instruction to be done with kindness, patience, and love. General understandings in contemporary educational practice such as education on a child's developmental level and communication in a language they understand parallel Wesley's practice as do the role of repetition, experience, and modeling. Additionally, the work of Bloom and the three domains of learning (cognitive, affective, behavioral) are seen in Wesley's expected outcome of his religious education, Christian living that was reflected in the way the child thought, felt, and behaved (Aukerman, 2011).

It is not possible to construct Wesley's educational theory based on the limited perspective employed in this research's attention to just twelve of his numerous publications, however, what emerges are elements from eighteenth century theory and a foreshadowing of contemporary educational theory presented amidst practical theological writings. It is also noted that Wesley did not intend to establish a new theory of education, but rather his educational practices were birthed from his theological perspectives: "Wesley's emphasis on childhood education remains closely linked to his anthropological and theological foundations" (Blevins & Maddix, 2011, p. 73). Wesley's understanding of humanity and the need for redemption and reconciliation with God as well as his belief in the faith formation potential in children, prompted his writings to and for children in regard to what he termed "religious education" or child faith formation.

Surprising Insights about Wesley from the Findings

Wesley is known for his extensive preaching, traveling, and writing as well as his personal discipline and systematic method for faith formation. He was a student of the classics and the contemporary theories of his day, and Wesley was a practical theologian and revivalist. What was surprising to discover was Wesley's interest in children, his appreciation for their formational capabilities, and his attention to their faith formation. It was also surprising to learn that he personally engaged children through conversation, teaching, and preaching and he compelled his ministers to do the same.

Wesley's perspective on child faith formation and his strategy for what he termed "religious instruction" was also unexpected. He provided a methodical, structured approach to adult formation through his societies, classes, and bands that can be seen somewhat in his expectations for a child's Christian education, but Wesley also understood the importance of informal education in the life of the child that needed to occur frequently and daily. His prescription to parents, teachers, and ministers included the regimented with the casual. His strong emphasis on the informal was not predicted.

In light of a renewed interest in family faith formation today, the fact that he put primacy of faith formation in the home with the parents or caregivers while calling for the church to equip, empower, and engage the home is striking. Also extraordinary was the expectation that faith formation would be done in partnership between the home, church, and school and seen as holistic in that faith was impacted by every dimension of a child's life. Wesley's thorough attention to salvation throughout his writings was not surprising but his expectation that children would grow in their faith and be able to participate in the means of grace at a very young age was surprising. Finally, although Wesley was a well educated and well read man who had a great appreciation for other's opinions and insights his grasp and employment of contemporary developmental theory and educational theory in his era was astounding. His goal was not to develop a theory on education but to provide guidelines and tools for faith formation of children. In doing so, his ability to see the implications of undiscovered contemporary theory and respond accordingly is noteworthy. A summative list of the surprising findings about Wesley is provided in Appendix O.

Implications for Today

The findings from the data coding and collection process of the twelve documents written and published by Wesley that addressed in some manner child faith formation, or what he termed religious education or religious instruction, must be understood as representative of their eighteenth century context. The goal of this research was not to merely identify the specifics of what Wesley said, did, or expected and transport them into today's context, but to identify concepts of child faith formation that were applicable beyond contextual boundaries. To that end, the findings and conclusions of this research were viewed in light of their potential impact on contemporary Christian education for children in The Wesleyan Church.

Implications for objectives of Christian education

Wesley's teachings held dual objectives that are reasonable objectives for Christian education for children in the Wesleyan Church today. In light of a child's ability to experience saving and transforming grace, the first objective is to provide instruction that results in the child's salvation and transformation; salvation from their sin and transformation from the depravity of their fallen nature to that of one redeemed. Not only did Wesley desire for children to experience salvation and transformation but he expected parents, teachers, and ministers to provide "religious instruction" or Christian education for the purpose of continued growth; faith formation through discipleship.

The second objective of Wesley's religious instruction of children was the preservation of the Methodist movement. Wesley realized that revival typically only endured the length of a generation. He desired for the Methodist revival to endure beyond the current generation and realized the education of children in the faith was necessary for this purpose. The Wesleyan Church today faces the challenge of continuation of biblical Christianity, as described by Wesley. The NSYR's research indicated the movement in today's youth away from biblical Christianity. As it was true in Wesley's day it is true today that we must intentionally invest in the Christian instruction of our children in order for biblical Christianity to continue beyond the present generation.

Implications for the responsibility of Christian education

The implication for today in response to the research question "who shall teach" is the identification of the parent as the primary authority in the faith formation of their children, a responsibility that must be supported through the work of the church. The church today has claimed the responsibility for the religious instruction and resulting faith formation of children, taking the responsibility out of the hands of the parent. A Barna survey identified that less than ten percent of church-going families read the Bible or pray together in a week and concluded: "Most families do not have a genuine spiritual life together" and "this is not disturbing to most of them" (Barna, 2003, p. 78). It is not disturbing because they believe the ministry of the church is sufficient for their child's faith formation. The first implication from the research, in light of the reality of family's today, is for the church to "give back" the faith formation responsibility to the parents. However as Wesley educated, equipped, and empowered parents in their responsibility, the church today has a responsibility to educate, equip, empower, and support the parents or caretakers in that endeavor. A challenge to that endeavor is the changing scene in American family structure and the reality that cohabitation, same sex unions, blended families, and single-parent families represent for many children the "typical" home situation (Anthony & Anthony, 2011). The church can no longer assume that families are comprised of a married mother, father, and their children but must strategize ways to equip and support the varied and changing American family structure.

Another implication is the profound impact of the non-verbal and unintentional teaching that occurs between the child and the parents, teachers, and ministers. Those who have responsibility over the "religious instruction" or Christian education of children for the purpose of child faith formation are called to live a life exemplary of that faith and to demonstrate through their words, attitudes, and actions their love for God and others acknowledging that it is only through the power of the Holy Spirit that true transformation and faith formation can occur. Smith and Denton's (2005) work with the NSYR demonstrated the impact of unintentional religious instruction. They interviewed teens that were quick to claim the name of Christ and identify themselves as Christian, but whose lifestyle and practical belief system were something other than Christian. A belief system that was not taught by their parents and religious instructors through formalized religious instruction but rather taught through example; the teens had fully embraced the beliefs and practices evident in their parent and instructor's lifestyle (Smith, 2010). Wesley's work suggested that we must hold the parents and instructors to a higher lifestyle standard, an expectation that they not only know with their mind God's Word but have experienced God's grace in their own hearts and demonstrate it with their lives. Like Wesley, however, we must recognize that the ultimate instructor in faith formation is God through the work of the Holy Spirit. Parents, teachers, and ministers must allow themselves to be led by the Holy spirit and know, understand, and live biblical Christianity themselves.

Implications on the methodology of Christian education

The implications for today extrapolated from the data collected based on the research question how to teach are the most difficult to divorce from the contextual implications of the eighteenth century, but must be seen in light of the broad concepts the specific actions represented. Wesley's reply to the question how to instruct children in the sermon "On Family Religion" provided a summative response that is applicable today: "early, plainly, frequently, and patiently" (Jackson, 1872, Vol. III, p. 340). Instruction for the purpose of faith formation should begin in infancy, through developmentally appropriate methods and in a language the child can understand, reflecting Piaget's (2000) understanding of how very young children gain knowledge, Erikson's (1997) first stage of development that begins at birth and results in trust, and Fowler's (1981) primal faith stage. Wesley held this wonderful tension in that he believed that children were capable of great faith and what could be defined as "mature faith" as demonstrated in his stories in *A Token for Children*, but he also understood that children could not be expected to learn in the same manner as adults. The implication for today is to be mindful of contemporary educational theories and the insights they provide instruction for the purpose of faith formation. Children can learn about the things of God, develop and grow in their faith, and live a Christian life but the instruction in those things must align with their communication and developmental ability.

In addition the instruction must be consistent, daily, and done with patience and love. Wesley's approach was thoughtful and thorough. Consistency must be indicative of contemporary Christian education for children and include consistency in the life of the instructor, consistency in the attention given to instruction, and consistency in the approach to instruction. This form of instruction requires intentionality on the part of the parent or caregiver and cooperation with the church and school in an approach that is unified in content and purpose and resolute in implementation. There is value in a "scope and sequence" approach to instruction that intentionally builds on pre-existing knowledge and experiences while moving the child deeper in their knowledge, understanding, and faith; instruction that compels them to "go forward".

Wesley understood faith formation is not constrained to a single hour or location but occurs in the "everydayness" of life (Stonehouse, 2004). Wesley chided parents to capture every moment as an opportunity to teach about God, explore the handiwork of God, and discuss how God is working in their life. Parents, teachers, and ministers today need to be encouraged and equipped to informally teach in the every day moments of life, capturing what appears to be simple, typical, and common as potential lessons about God and faith. For Christian education of children to result in faith formation, we must intentionally leverage informal instruction.

The intentional instruction must also incorporate formal instruction through the use of experiential learning, where the child learns to pray through praying, learns how to read and reflect on Scripture through reading and reflecting on Scripture in a guided manner, and the child learns what it means to worship and offer praise through active engagement in corporate and family worship. Intentional, formal instruction must also incorporate direct instruction with the partnership between experiential learning of prayer and Scripture and memorization of prayer and Scripture, through a developed appreciation for tradition and the creeds through experiencing and memorizing the creeds, and through times of formal teaching and preaching in a language they understand and with application relevant to their context. In addition, contemporary Christian education for the purpose of child faith formation must revive the use of the ancient practice of catechesis in the formal and intentional instruction of children. While not a tool to be used independent from experiential, relational, and informal instruction, it is a valuable tool when used in concert with the other methods of instruction.

The intentional instruction, both formal and informal, must be holistic in that it incorporates the child's mind through cognitive engagement and growth, it impacts a child's attitudes and feelings through affective experiences and responses, and it results in behavior demonstrative of the cognitive and affective change. Wesley identified as well the impact of every experience in a child's life on their faith formation and thus suggested holistic instruction that encouraged approaches to the child's sleeping, waking, eating, playing, and learning routines. Contemporary Christian education, while not mandating specifics in a child's diet and sleep patterns, should be mindful of the impact of sleep and nutrition on instruction, as well as the function in the home and their interactions with others on a child's faith formation.

Intentional instruction also carries an expectation of a relational approach. It is not possible to know a child well enough to determine developmental ability, communication capability, and previous experiences without having an intimate relationship. In addition, the informal and formal instruction requires a personalized engagement that is child-focused in which the child is an active participant. Parents, teachers, and ministers must take the time to get to know the child through observation and casual conversation in order to strategize and provide instruction that is uniquely formational for them.

Wesley's expectation was that the religious instruction would be maintained and consistent from home to school to church. Wesley called for Methodist parents to send their children to Christian schools because he saw all education as formative, fully integrated with things of God - as exemplified in the course of study prescribed at Kingswood school, and he realized the importance of instructors to be God-fearing and live exemplary Christian lives. An implication for today, in light of a public education system that was not available to families in the eighteenth century and the reality that many children do not participate in a school education that complements the "religious instruction" of the home and church, there needs to be a renewed awareness of the impact of other voices on the child's faith formation and a call for the home and church to discover a way to respond.

Implications on content in Christian education

The scope of what Wesley admonished parents and instructors to teach and what Wesley directly taught children through his writings intended for use by them, is valid for children today, although the language and tone are not transferrable. The incredible greatness of who God is and what He has done, the possibility of transformation from death to life through the work of Jesus Christ and the power of the Holy Spirit, the expectation of growth in the Christian life and the ability to live as Christ lived through the power of the Holy spirit, and the hope of an eternity in heaven for those who love the Lord are as valuable for today's children as they were for children in Wesley's era. The language used in the prayers, hymns, lessons, and instructions would not communicate "plainly" the message in the way Wesley intended for them to do but the message itself is as vital today as it was then. However, the contemporary understanding of the impact of child development on determining appropriate or age-related content would need to be applied.

The greatness of God and His love, the brokenness of our relationship with God because of sin, and the sacrifice of God's only Son Jesus Christ on the cross for our behalf, and that salvation is possible because of Christ's death and resurrection should be integral in everything that is taught, as they were integral to all of Wesley's work for children. The Gospel message was communicated clearly and frequently in Wesley's writings for children and this approach serves as an example for today. The call for the child to recognize their sin, to seek forgiveness, and to turn from that life of sin to a life of humble obedience to God is also a valuable message today. The approach to the salvation message and the language used in sharing the story have changed, but the ability for children to respond and the expectation for spiritual caretakers to continually share it has not changed.

Additionally, children today, as did the children in Wesley's era, need to know that God is actively present in their life and that they can ask forgiveness, seek protection and help, and know that God desires a personal relationship offered in love and accepted in faith. Although Wesley offered a great deal of emphasis on the salvation message, his work also carried an expectation of discipleship and development beyond the transformation that took place through salvation. Today's faith formation practices and programs must be saturated with a call to salvation but must also carry the expectation of growth and development in faith equipping children to engage daily in prayer, scripture, and the means of grace with a call for children to "go forward" in their faith and fully grasp the grace and transformation that are available to them. Our Christian education practices and programs must equip and empower children to pray, engage Scripture, participate in worship, and serve others. Our practices should provide instruction on the expected lifestyle of a Christian through exemplified instruction in the life of the parent, teacher, or minister and through experiential and direct instruction that carries an expectation and accountability.

Christian education today must clearly identify and describe who God is, who we are, what God has done and what He wants to do in us and through us, and how we are to respond to God's gracious gift.

Implications for outcomes of Christian education

Outcomes of Christian education include the child will acknowledge their sins, ask forgiveness, and repent. The child will practice obedience, endeavor to know God, and serve God and others. The child will experience freedom from sin, joy, and hope. The child will engage routinely in prayer, scripture, worship, and service. The child will demonstrate love for God and others through their words, attitudes, and actions. The child will experience transformation through salvation and formation through discipleship. Christian education will also result in the continuation of the practice of biblical Christianity into the future generations so that when the Lord returns He will find faith (Luke 18:8). A schematic of the implications for the employment of Christian education of children for the purpose of child faith formation within the Wesleyan context is provided in Appendix P.

Implications in light of Wesleyan quadrilateral

Other than in "Thoughts on the Education of Children" where Wesley expressed "Scripture, reason, and experience, jointly testify" (p. 476), he does not explicitly mention the four elements of the "Wesleyan quadrilateral" in any of the documents reviewed nor does he explicitly advise to instruct on the role of these elements. However, the role of scripture is clear in Wesley's use and reference to scripture throughout the documents; it is the primary text for the instruction and his desire was for children to be immersed in its words. His expectation that children will not just learn concepts of faith but come to understand and grasp the meaning of scripture and things of God is portrayed in his preface to the "Instructions" and "Lessons" calling for children to use their minds or "reason" in the engagement. Wesley also identified the role of tradition through the liturgies and creeds that were taught and practiced and the use of tradition to defend practices such as infant baptism and the role of godparents. Finally, his desire for children to be active participants in the process of faith formation and to "experience" the means of grace and the transforming power in their hearts, minds, and lives is clear from his directions and methodologies.

Threats to Validity and Research Limitations

The research methodology, document selection, researcher's personal bias, and contextual perspective pose potential threats to the validity of the findings. The researcher's personal experiences potentially impacted the selection, reading, and coding of the documents and the interpretation of the findings and conclusions. The researcher acknowledged her personal bias, described her point of view as defined by her theological, educational, and personal experiences and engaged the research process aware of the bias. The selection of the documents was limited to the author's knowledge of Wesley's work and the documentation provided in secondary sources, however, the researcher was diligent to identify secondary sources considered valuable in the field of Wesley studies and sought guidance in selection of documents and sources for those documents from contemporary experts in Wesley studies. The scope of engaging only twelve documents of Wesley to study in light of his extensive body of work provided a potential threat to the validity of the findings in the potential limitation those documents created for exposure to Wesley teachings and practices. A broader engagement with more of Wesley's works may have revealed richer, deeper, and different insights. This threat was addressed in part by the inclusion of twelve documents that were written at different times, to different audiences, and for different purposes providing a fuller look at Wesley's teachings and practices. The limitation of the use of primary studies rather than original primary sources posed a potential threat to validity, in that the research relied on the credibility in the editing of the original sources. The author was diligent in the selection of credible edited versions of the documents studied.

In addition to the potential threats to validity posed by the researcher and the document selection, the research methodology itself posed a threat to the validity. The research questions, codes, and coding sequence were determined prior to significant engagement with the documents. It is possible that the document content was "read into" or valuable document content was missed because it did not "fit" with the research questions, codes, or coding. However, there was flexibility throughout the process to add and adjust codes to account for critical elements revealed in the data that was not properly documented using the pre-ordained codes, such as the addition of a research question, the added layer of sub-codes, and the more clearly defined definitions of the original codes (i.e.: "HVN" originally represented data relating specifically to heaven but was adjusted to represent data relating to eternity, heaven, and hell as suggested by the documents themselves).

The interpretation of the data analysis results carried a potential threat to the validity of the findings. Data attributed to a specific code did not represent necessarily the totality of the text in that there was not a relationship in number of times a code was used (frequency) and the amount of actual text that code represented. For example, in the document *Lessons for Children* the code "BIB" was used 195 times which is a considerable frequency of code in a single text. However, even that significant frequency of code does not represent fully the amount of text associated with each code, as those 195 codes equal in content almost the entire Old Testament. Engagement with the findings and representation of those findings in the form of frequency charts must be read with the understanding that code frequency does not equal data percentage. However, the frequency of codes in the documents does provide a glimpse into the primary focus of a document and the elements not addressed.

This study did not examine the twelve documents for historical, biblical, or theological accuracy on Wesley's part. Nor did it compare various editions of the same document in order to identify changes or adaptations by Wesley or the publisher. These additional forms of inquiry may have provided greater accuracy in interpretation of the findings or reading of the individual documents. Finally, the language and culture barrier evident in these documents written in the eighteenth century but read and interpreted by a twenty-first century researcher pose a threat to validity. First, in the potential to incorrectly interpret Wesley's words, intention, and meaning due to the language and culture barrier; and secondly, in the extrapolation of the findings from an eighteenth century context for application today. In an effort to divorce the content from its context for purposes of application, there is a potential threat that the content was not just misinterpreted but misrepresented as well. The researcher attempted to be diligent to acknowledge the language and cultural issues apparent in the document and the teachings based on engagement with research on the eighteenth century and specifically Wesley's context and leveraged the use of a translation chart in the process of interpretation of text (see Appendix D). In the phase of writing of the findings and projecting of conclusions, the researcher was conscious to look at the work beyond specific lists to replicate but to search for the broader and transferrable concepts that are not tied to time and location. Wesley can be seen as harsh and unreasonable when taken out of context and his work can appear irrelevant if looked at through the narrow focus of specific details, however, there was a great richness identified when the documents were read with an understanding of the era and purpose for which they were written.

Recommendations for Further Research

The engagement with twelve of John Wesley's publications that related to child faith formation for the purpose of study to discover insights for today on who should teach children, how they should be taught, and what they should be taught resulted in rich findings that have significant implication for the church today. The research also shed light on additional questions to be explored through further study.

Engagement with Research in Light of Wesley's Larger Body of Work

The recommendations for further study include research into Wesley's teachings on adult faith formation or religious instruction in light of the findings from this research in order to identify commonalities and differences in content and approach and to discover if his work on adult faith formation would shed additional light on the work that emerged from this limited study. It would also be beneficial to view the findings from this research in light of Wesley's theology as understood today and to ask: Were areas omitted, was there deviation in Wesley's teaching in these documents from what was "typical" in his understood theological perspective, and where in the findings can the impact of his theology be seen? For example, what was communicated theologically through the prayers, hymns, and instructions and how does that compare to Wesley's larger body of work?

Deeper Engagement with Individual Documents

The findings also prompted a call for a deeper look into several of Wesley's works such as the *Instructions for Children* for children. Is there value still found in the form and content of this catechism for children, and what would be the process of updating the language to communicate effectively in a way today's child could understand? Beyond the ability of the "Instructions" to offer a formative experience for children today, does the content hold value for the larger body of believers as Wesley suggested it did in the preface?

A recommendation for further study includes a comparison of the three versions of hymns for children identified in the research process to discover what was taught that was unique to each publication, where was there commonality, and was there an impact of time and purpose on the focus and tone of hymns. Is there something that engagement with the hymns alone would reveal about the Wesley's approach and content in regard to child faith formation?

Development of a Conceptual Framework

A potential study that emerged as a recommendation from the findings is the creation of a conceptual framework for the purpose of evaluation of current practice and instruction of children both in the home and church, creation of curriculum that promotes child faith formation in the Wesleyan tradition as outlined in the findings and suggested from the literature as a missing component in contemporary practice, and to serve as a point of reference in the development of ministry strategies that engage the home and church for the purpose of child faith formation.

Impact of non-Integrated Instruction

Finally, additional research is recommended to discover the practical implications of the absence of one area of "religious instruction" in the life of the child. Wesley believed in the importance of holistic education that encompassed a child's full world (home, school, and church) and his or her entire being (cognitive, affective, behavioral) through fully integrated instruction. Given the varied home structures, church experiences, and educational opportunities it is likely that children do not have the potential to experience holistic religious instruction as envisioned by Wesley – instruction that is consistent across all three environments. What are the implications of a missing environment and what can be done in the environments that do actively engage the child in faith formation to counteract this missing piece?

Conclusion

John Wesley, an eighteenth century revivalist and practical theologian, sought to bring spiritual revival and transformation to the people called Methodists through intentional instruction and practice. This research looked at twelve works of Wesley in an effort to recapture Wesley's teachings and practices of child faith formation. The research sought to answer three research questions: Who shall teach, how to teach, and what to teach and the research identified an addition question – why teach? The findings indicated the primary responsibility of child faith formation as the parent or caregiver with the church and school serving in a supportive role. Wesley understood that faith formation is not isolated to a few moments in the week but occurs in the every day moments of life. He called for parents, teachers, and pastors to life a life that demonstrated an engagement of their minds and hearts with things of God that resulted in a Christ-like lifestyle. Wesley called for instruction to include a full description of God, humanity, what God has done for humanity, and how humanity is to respond. Wesley's instruction, although saturated with and inclusive of the message of salvation, moved beyond the salvation message to the expectation of continued growth in faith. His desire was for the child and the Methodist movement at large to "go forward".

References

Abraham, W. J. (2010) Wesley as Preacher. In R. L. Maddox & J. E. Vickers (Eds.), *The Cambridge companion to John Wesley* (98-112). Cambridge, England; Cambridge University Press.

Anthony, M. & Anthony, M. (2011). *A theology for family ministries.* Nashville, TN: B & H Publishing Group.

Aukerman, J. H. (2011). (Ed.). *Discipleship that transforms: An Introduction to Christian education from a Wesleyan holiness perspective.* Anderson, IN: Warner Press.

Aukerman, J. H. (2004). *What is the so-called Wesleyan quadrilateral?* Unpublished manuscript, Department of Theology, Anderson University, Anderson, IN.

Baker, F. (1966). *A union catalogue of the publications of John and Charles Wesley compiled by Frank Baker.* Durham, NC: Duke University.

Baker, F. (1970). *John Wesley and the Church of England.* Nashville, TN: Abingdon.

Baker, F. (1982). Susanna Wesley: Puritan, parent, pastor, protagonist, pattern. In R. S. Keller, L. L. Queen, & H. F. Thomas's *Historical perspectives on the Wesleyan tradition: Women in the new worlds* (Vol. II). (Eds.) (112-131). Nashville, TN: Abingdon.

Barna, G. (2003). *Transforming children into spiritual champions.* Ventura, CA: Regal Books.

Barna Group (2011). *Six reasons young Christians leave church.* Retrieved from http://www.barna.org/teens-next-gen-articles/528-six-reasons-young-christians-leave-church

Beckwith, I. (2004). *Postmodern children's ministry: Ministry to children in the 21st century.* Grand Rapids, MI: Zondervan.

Bendroth, M. (2001). Horace Bushnell's Christian nurture. In M. Bunge (Ed.), *The child in Christian thought* (350-364). Grand Rapids, MI: William B. Eerdmans.

Benson, W. (1984). Evangelical philosophies of religious education. In M. J. Taylor (Ed.), Changing patterns of religious education (pp. 53-73). Birmingham: Religious Education Press.

Benzie, P. (2010). As a little child: Children in the theology of John Wesley. (Unpublished thesis). Laidlaw-Carey Graduate School, New Zealand.

Berryman, J. W. (2009). *Children and the theologians: Clearing the way for grace*. Harrisburg, PA: Moorehouse.

Blevins, D. G. (2005). Renovating Christian education in the 21st century: A Wesleyan contribution. *Christian Education Journal 2*(1), 6-29.

Blevins, D. G., & Maddix, M. A. (2010). *Discovering discipleship: Dynamics of Christian education*. Kansas City, KS: Beacon Hill Press.

Bloom, B.S. (Ed.) (1956). *Taxonomy of educational objectives: The classification of educational goals: Handbook I, cognitive domain*. New York, NY: Longmans.

Blue Letter Bible. (1996-2012). "Dictionary and Word Search for *lebab (Strong's 3824)*". Retrieved from http://www.blueletterbible.org/lang/lexicon/lexicon.c-fm?Strongs=H3824&t=KJV

Blue Letter Bible. (1996-2012). "Dictionary and Word Search for *pistis (Strong's 4102)*". Retrieved from http://www.blueletterbible.org/lang/lexicon/lexicon.cf-m?Strongs=G4102&t=NIV

Body, A. H. (1936). *John Wesley and education*. London, England: Epworth Press.

Boynton, H. M. (2011). Children's spirituality: Epistemology and theory from various helping professions. *International Journal of Children's Spirituality 16*(2), 109-127.

Bromiley, G. W. (1985). *Theological dictionary of the New Testament: Edited by Gerard Kittel and Gerhard Friedrich translated by Geoffrey W. Bromley*. Grand Rapids, MI: William B. Eerdmans.

Buckroyd, E. A. (October 2001). A consideration of the undated *Hymns for Children*. Proceedings of the Charles Wesley Society (Vol. 7), pp. 61-80.

Bushnell, H. (1861). *Christian Nurture*. New York, NY: Charles Scribner.

Campbell, T. A. (2010). John Wesley as diarist and correspondent. In r. L. Maddox and J. E. Vickers (Eds.), *The Cambridge companion to John Wesley* (pp. 129-143). New York, NY: Cambridge University Press.

Capehart, J. (2005). *Teaching with heart*. Cincinnati, OH: Standard.

Cavalletti, S. (2002). *The religious potential of the child: 6 to 12 years old*. Chicago, IL: Liturgy Training Publications.

Clarke, A. (1832). *Adam Clarke Commentary on Deuteronomy 6*. Study Light. Retrieved from http://www.studylight.org/com/acc/view.cgi?book=de&chapter=006

Clarke, A. (1832). *Adam Clarke Commentary on Genesis 1*. Study Light. Retrieved from <http://www.studylight.org/com/acc/view.cgi?book=ge&chapter=001>. 1832

Cockerill, G. L. (2012). *The New International Commentary on the New Testament: The epistle to the Hebrews*. Grand Rapids, MI: William B. Eerdmans.

Coles, R. (1986). *The moral life of children*. New York, NY: Atlantic Monthly.

Coles, R. (1990). *The spiritual life of children*. Boston, MA: Houghton Mifflin.

Coleson, E. (n.d.). "Our Heritage". Retrieved from http://www.wes-leyan.org/heritage

Collins, K. J. (1999). *A real Christian: The life of John Wesley*. Nashville, TN: Abingdon.

Conn, J. W. (Ed.). (1986). *Women's spirituality: Resources for Christian development.* New York, NY: Paulist Press.

Creswell, J. W. (2008). *Educational research: Planning, conducting, and evaluating quantitative and qualitative research.* Upper Saddle River, NJ: Pearson Education.

Dayton, D. (1975). The holiness churches: A significant ethical tradition. *The Christian Century.* Retrieved from http://www.religion-online.org/showarticle.asp?title=1862

Drury, K. (1995). *The holiness movement is dead.* Paper presented at the Presidential Breakfast of the Christian Holiness Association.

Drury, K. (2011). "The church cannot not teach" in *Discipleship that Transforms: An Introduction to Christian education from a Wesleyan holiness perspective* by Aukerman, J. H. (Ed.). Anderson, IN: Warner Press.

Duke Divinity School. (2012). Center for Studies in the Wesleyan Tradition. Retrieved from http://divinity.duke.edu/initiatives-centers/cswt/

Edwards, M. (1949). *Family circle: A study of the Epworth household in relation to John and Charles Wesley.* London, England: The Epworth Press.

Eisenbaum, P. M. (1997). *The Jewish heroes of Christian history Hebrews 11 in literary context.* Atlanta, GA: Scholars Press.

Erikson, J. M. (1997). *The life cycle completed extended version.* New York, NY: W. W. Norton & Company.

Eskridge, L. (2011). Defining evangelicalism. *Institute for the Study of American Evangelicals.* Retrieved from http://isae.wheaton.edu/defining-evangelicalism/

Felton, G. C. (Winter 1997). John Wesley and the teaching ministry: Ramifications for education in the church today. *Religious Education 92*(1), 92-107.

Fettke, T. (1978). (Ed.) *The celebration hymnal: Songs and hymns for worship.* Nashville, TN: Word.

Fitchett, W. H. (1908). *Wesley and his century: A study in spiritual forces.* Cincinnati, OH: Jennings & Graham.

Fitzgerlad, M. H. (1925). *The life of John Wesley and the rise and progress of Methodism by Robert Southey.* London, England: Oxford University Press.

Fowler, J. W. (1981). *Stages of faith: The psychology of human development and the quest for meaning.* New York, NY: HarperCollins.

Fowler, J. (1985). John Wesley's development in faith. In M. D. Meek's *The future of Methodist theological traditions* (Ed.) (172-192). Nashville, TN: Abingdon.

Garrido, A. (2008). The faith of a child. *America 199*(7), 10-13.

Gigot, F. (1909). Ecclesiasticus. In The Catholic Encyclopedia. New York: Robert Appleton Company. Retrieved January 10, 2013 from New Advent: http://www.newadvent.org/cathen/05263a.htm

Gingrich, F. W. & Danker, F. W. (Eds.). (1979). *A Greek-English lexicon of the New Testament and other early Christian literature: A translation and adaptation of the fourth revised and augmented edition of Walter Bauer's Greek-German lexicon of the New Testament and other early Christian literature.* (2nd ed). Chicago, IL: University of Chicago Press.

Grider, J. K. (1994). *A Wesleyan-holiness theology.* Kansas City, MO: Beacon Hill Press.

Green, R. (1906). *The works of John and Charles Wesley: A bibliography containing an exact account of all the publications issued by the brothers Wesley arranged in chronological order, with a list of early editions, and descriptive illustrative notes.* (2nd ed.). London, England: Methodist Publishing House.

Groome, T. H. (2011). *Will there be faith?* New York, NY: Harper Collins.

Gundry-Volf, J. M. (2001). The least and the greatest: Children in the New Testament. In M. Bunge (Ed.), *The child in Christian thought* (29-60). Grand Rapids, MI: William B. Eerdmans.

Guzik, D. (2006). "Study Guide for Deuteronomy 6." Enduring Word. Blue Letter Bible retrieved from http://www.blueletterbible.org/commentaries/comm_view.cfm?AuthorID=2&contentID=7479&commInfo=31&topic=Deuteronomy

Harper, A. F. (Editor). (1990). *The Wesley Bible.* Nashville, TN: Thomas Nelson.

Harper, S. (2003). *The way to heaven: The Gospel according to John Wesley.* Grand Rapids, MI: Zondervan.

Harvey, V. A. (1997). *A handbook of theological terms.* New York, NY: Simon & Schuster.

Heitzenrater, R. P. (1988). Review of David I. Naglee 'From Font to Faith: John Wesley on Infant Baptism and the Nurture of Children. *Church History: Studies in Christianity and Culture.* doi:10.2307/3166677.

Heitzenrater, R. P. (1989). *Mirror and memory: Reflections on early Methodism.* Nashville, TN: Kingswood Books.

Heitzenrater, R. P. (1995). *Wesley and the people called Methodists.* Nashville, TN: Abingdon.

Heitzenrater, R. P. (2001). John Wesley and children. In M. J. Bunge, *The child in Christian thought* (pp. 279-299). Grand Rapids, MI: William B. Eerdmans.

Henry, M. (1996). Matthew Henry Commentary on Hebrews 11. *Blue Letter Bible.* Retrieved from http://www.blueletterbible.org/commentaries/comm_view.cfm?AuthorID=4&contentID=1828&commInfo=5&topic=Hebrews&ar=Hbr_11_

Henry, M. (1996). Matthew Henry Commentary on Luke. *Blue Letter Bible.* Retrieved from http://www.blueletterbible.org/commentaries/comm_author.cfm?AuthorID=4

Henry, M. (1996). Matthew Henry Commentary on Matthew 19. . *Blue Letter Bible.* Retrieved from http://www.blueletterbible.org/commentaries/comm_view.cfm?-AuthorID=4&contentID=1614&commInfo=5&topic=Matthew&ar=Mat_19_13

Henschen, W. G. (n.d.) *Christian perfection before Wesley.* Apollo, PA. West Publishing.

Heywood, D. (2008). Faith development theory: A case for paradigm change. *Journal of Beliefs & Values 29*(3), 263-272.

Hinsdale, M. A. (2001). Infinite openness to the infinite: Karl Rahner's contribution to modern Catholic thought on the child, pp. 406-446. In Bunge, M. J. (Ed.) *A child in Christian thought.* Grand Rapids, MI: William B. Eerdmans.

Hynson, L. (1985). The Wesleyan quadrilateral in the American holiness tradition. *Wesleyan Theological Journal 20*(1), 7-18.

HyperRESEARCH Qualitative Analysis Tool (Version 3.5) [Computer software]. Randolph, MA: Researchware.

Jackson, T. (1872). (Ed.). *The Works of John Wesley* (3rd ed.). London, England: Wesleyan Methodist Book Room; reprint ed., Grand Rapids, MI: Baker, 1979.

Joiner, R. (2009). *Think Orange.* Colorado Springs, CO: David C. Cook.

Kneller, G. F. (1964). *Introduction to the philosophy of education,* (2nd Ed.) New York, NY: John Wiley & Sons.

Koehler, L. & Baumgartner, W. (2001). *The Hebrew and Aramaic lexicon of the Old Testament study edition* (Vol. 1). Leiden, The Netherlands: Brill.

Law, W. (1729). *A serious call to a devout and holy life.* (Electronic Version). Retrieved from http://www.ccel.org/ccel/law/serious_call

Lebar, L. E. (1995). *Education that is Christian.* Wheaton, IL: Victor Books.

Lennox, S. J. (1999). *Psalms: A Biblical commentary in the Wesleyan tradition.* Indianapolis, IN: Wesleyan Publishing House.

Lindner, E. W. (2004). Children as theologians. In P. B. Pufall and R. P. Unsworth (Eds.), *Rethinking Childhood* (pp. 54-68). Piscataway, NJ: Rutgers University Press.

Maddix, M. A. (2001). Reflecting John Wesley's theology and educational perspective: Comparing Nazarene pastors, Christian educators, and professors of Christian education. Ph.D. dissertation, Trinity Evangelical Divinity School, United States -- Illinois. Retrieved February 6, 2012, from Dissertations & Theses: Full Text.(Publication No. AAT 3003800).

Maddix, M. A. (2009). John Wesley's formative experiences: foundations for his educational ministry perspectives. *Didache: Faithful Teaching 9*(1). Retrieved from http://didachents.edu

Maddox, R. L. (Ed.) (July 22, 2008). *Hymns for children (1747).* Retrieved from http://www.divinity.duke.edu/sites/default/files/documents/cswt/19_Hymns_for_Children_%281747%29.pdf

Maddox, R. L. & Vickers, J. E. (2010). *The Cambridge companion to John Wesley.* New York, NY: Cambridge University Press.

Manchester Wesley Research Centre. (2012). Retrieved from http://www.mw-rc.ac.uk/about-us/

Maslen, M. (March, 2003). Growing into grace. *Christian Parenting Today.* Retrieved from http://www.kyria.com/topics/marriagefamily/parenting/cultivatingkidsfaith/18.23.html

Matthaei, S. H. (2000). *Making disciples: Faith formation in the Wesleyan tradition.* Nashville, TN: Abingdon.

May, S., Posterski, B., Stonehouse, C., & Cannell, L. (2005). *Children matter: Celebrating their place in the church, family, and community.* Grand Rapids, MI: William B. Eerdmans.

McClure, M. (1996). How children's faith develops (pp. 5-13). *The Way*. Retrieved from http://www.theway.org.uk/

McKenna, D. L. (1999). *What a time to be Wesleyan: Proclaiming the holiness message with passion and purpose*. Kansas City, MO: Beacon Hill Press.

Meehan, B. C. (2002). The foundational significance of spirituality and liturgy in the catechesis of children. (Unpublished dissertation). Boston College.

Migliore, D. L. (2004). *Faith seeking understanding: An introduction to Christian theology* (2nd edition). Grand Rapids, MI: Wm. B. Eerdmans.

Miles, M. B. & Huberman, A. M. (1994). *An expanded sourcebook: Qualitative data analysis* (2nd ed.). Thousand Oaks, CA: SAGE.

Miller, P. H. (2002). *Theories of developmental psychology* (4th ed.). New York, NY: Worth.

Morgenthaler, S. (2003). Children and spirituality. *Lutheran Education Journal 139*(2). 69-71.

Mueller, C. R. (2010). Spirituality in children: Understanding and developing interventions. *Pediatric Nursing 36*(4), 197-208.

Murphy, A. (2000). *The faith of a child*. Chicago, IL: Moody Press.

National Study of Youth and Religion (2011). *The national study of youth and religion: An important resource for researchers, practitioners, and families*. Retrieved from http://www.search-institute.org/csd/articles/fast-facts/nsyr

Osmer, R. R. (2008). *Practical theology: An introduction*. Grand Rapids, MI: William B. Eerdmans.

Outler, A. C. (1964). *John Wesley*. New York, NY: Oxford University Press.

Outler, A. C. (1985). The Wesleyan quadrilateral – in John Wesley. *Wesleyan Theological Journal 20*(1), 7-18.

Outler, A. C. (Ed.). (1986). *The works of John Wesley volume 3: Sermons III 71-114*. Nashville, TN: Abingdon Press.

Parker, J. F. (1966). (Ed.). *John Wesley: A plain account of Christian perfection*. Kansas City, MO: Beacon Hill.

Pazmino, R. W. (2008). *Foundational issues in Christian education: An introduction in evangelical perspective* (3rd ed.). Grand Rapids, MI: Baker.

Piaget, J. & Inhelder, B. (2000). *The psychology of the child* (2nd edition). New York NY: Basic Books.

Prince, J. W. (1926). *Wesley on religious education*. New York, NY: The Methodist Book Concern.

Rack, H. D. (2002). *Reasonable enthusiast: John Wesley and the rise of Methodism*. (3rd ed.). London, England: Epworth Press.

Ratcliff, D. (2001). Rituals in a school hallway: Evidence of a latent spirituality in children. *The International Journal of Children's Spirituality*. Retrieved from http://www.eric.ed.gov/PDFS/ED457460.pdf

Ratcliff, D. (Ed.). (2004). *Children's spirituality: Christian perspectives, research, and applications*. Eugene, OR: Cascade Books.

Ratcliff, D. & Ratcliff, B. (2010). *Childfaith: Experiencing God and spiritual growth with your children*. Eugene, OR: Cascade Books.

Richards, L. (2005). *Handling qualitative data*. Thousand Oaks, CA: SAGE.

Richards, L. O. (1983). *A theology of children's ministry*. Grand Rapids, MI: Zondervan.

Rivers, I. (2010). John Wesley as editor and publisher. In R. L. Maddox & J. E. Vickers (Ed.) *The Cambridge companion to John Wesley* (pp. 144-159). New York, NY: Cambridge University Press.

Rotz, D. & Lyon, G. (1999). (Eds.). The Sermons of John Wesley: Sermon 106 On Faith. *Wesley Center Online*. Retrieved from http://wesley.nnu.edu/john-wesley/the-sermons-of-john-wesley-1872-edition/sermon-106-on-faith/

Sadler, J. E. (n.d.). John Amos Comenius. *Encyclopedia Britannica*. Retrieved from http://www.britannica.com/EBchecked/topic/127493/John-Amos-Comenius

Schenck, K. (2003). *Understanding the book of Hebrews: The story behind the sermon*. Louisville, KY: Westminster John Knox Press.

Schultz, C. (n.d.). Biblical hermeneutics in the Wesleyan tradition. Retrieved from http://campus.houghton.edu/webs/employees/gavery/wesleyweb/biblical_hermeneutics.htm

Scofield, C. I. (1917). "Scofield Reference Notes of Genesis 1". Retrieved from http://www.biblestudytools.com/commentaries/scofield-reference-notes/genesis/genesis-1.html

Search Institute. (2011). "Early spirituality and religious participation linked to later adolescent well-being". Retrieved from http://www.search-institute.org/csd/arti-cles/fast-facts/early-spirituality

Seifert, K. L. & Hoffnung, R. J. (2000). *Child and adolescent development* (5th ed.). Boston, MA: Houghton Mifflin.

Sell, P. W. (n.d.). Lawrence O. Richards. *Talbot School of Theology*. Retrieved from http://www2.talbot.edu/ce20/educators/view.cfm?n=lawrence_richards

Silverman, R. (2000). *Light in my darkness*. West Chester, PA Chrystalis Books.

Smith, C. (2010). On "Moralistic Therapeutic Deism" as U.S. teenagers' actual, tacit, de facto religious faith. In: Collins-Mayo, S. & Dandelion, P. (Eds.), *Religion and youth* (46-57). Burlington, VT: Ashgate.

Smith, C. & Denton, M. L. (2005). *Soul searching: The religious and spiritual lives of American teenagers*. New York, NY: Oxford University Press.

Snyder, H. A. (n.d.). "Translating Wesley's writings into late 20th-century American general English". *Wesley Center Online*. Retrieved at http://wesley.nnu.edu/-john-wesley/translating-wesleys-writings-into-late-20th-century-american-general-english/

Southey, R. (1903). *The life of John Wesley*. New York, NY: Frederick A. Stokes Company.

Stonehouse, C. (1998). *Joining children on the spiritual journey: Nurturing a life of faith*. Grand Rapids, MI: Baker Books.

Stonehouse, C. (2004) Children in Wesleyan thought. In D. Ratcliff (Ed.), *Children's spirituality: Christian perspectives, research, and application* (pp. 133-148). Eugene, OR: Cascade Books.

Telford, J. (1827). *The journal of the Rev. John Wesley*. London, England; Kershaw.

Telford, J. (1898). *The life of John Wesley*. New York, NY: Eaton & Maine

Telford, J. (Ed.) (1931). *The letters of John Wesley*. London, England; Epworth Press.

Telford, J. (1995) *Sayings and portraits of John Wesley.* Salem, OH: Schmul Publishing.

The Pew Forum (2012). *Report 1: Religious affiliation*. Retrieved from http://religions.pewforum.org/reports#

The Works of John Wesley Vol. VII (3rd ed.). (1978). Grand Rapids, MI: Baker House.

Thorsen, D. (2005). *The Wesleyan quadrilateral: Scripture, tradition, reason, & experience as a model of evangelical theology*. Lexington, KY: Emeth Press.

Towns, Elmer L.(1970) "John Wesley and Religious Education. *Articles*. Paper 16.

Retrieved from http://digitalcommons.liberty.edu/towns_articles/16

Tyerman, L. (1872) *The life and times of the Rev. John Wesley, M.A., founder of the Methodists.* (Vol. 1). New York, NY: Harper & Brothers.

Tyerman, L. (1872) *The life and times of the Rev. John Wesley, M.A., founder of the Methodists.* (Vol. 2). New York, NY: Harper & Brothers.

Wall, W. (n.d.). *The history of infant baptism*. London, England: Griffith, Farran, Okedan, and Welsh.

Weber, H. R. (1979). *Jesus and the children: Biblical resources for study and preaching.* Geneva, Switzerland: World Council of Churches.

Webster, N. (1828) *Noah Webster's 1828 American dictionary*. Retrieved from http://www.1828-dictionary.com/d/search/word,redemption

Wesley, C. (1763). *Hymns for children*. Bristol, England: Farley.

Wesley, J. (1737). *A collection of psalms and hymns*. Bristol, England: Farley.

Wesley, J. (1744). *A collection of moral and sacred poems*. Bristol, England; Farley.

Wesley, J. (1744). *Minutes of the Methodist conferences 1744*. London, England: Beveridge and Co.

Wesley, J. (1745). *Instructions for children*. London, England: Copper.

Wesley, J. (1746). *Instructions for children* (2nd edition). London, England: Copper.

Wesley, J. (1746). *Lessons for children* (Part 1). Bristol, England: Farley.

Wesley, J. (1747). *Lessons for children* (Part II). Bristol, England: Farley.

Wesley, J. (1748). *Lessons for children* (Part III). Bristol, England: Farley.

Wesley, J. (1754). *Lessons for children* (Part IV). Bristol, England: Farley.

Wesley, J. (1749). *A token for children.* Bristol, England: Farley.

Wesley, J. (1754). *Lessons for children* (Part IV). London, England: Cock, Henry.

Wesley, J. (1765). *John Wesley's Explanatory Notes: Genesis*. Retrieved from http://www.biblestudytools.com/commentaries/wesleys-explanatory-notes/

Wesley, J. (1772). *Prayers for children*. Bristol, England: William Pine.

Wesley, J. (1783). A thought on the manner of educating children in *The Arminian Magazine.*

Wesley, J. (1790). *Hymns for children*. London, England: New Chapel.

Wesley, J. (1837). *Thoughts upon infant baptism: Extracted from a late writer.* London, England: Mason.

Wesley, J. (1981). *Wesley's Notes on the New Testament: Volume II, Romans to Revelation.* Kansas City, MO: Beacon Hill.

Wesley Center Online. (2012). Northwestern Nazarene University. Retrieved from http://wesley.nnu.edu/john-wesley

Wilhoit, J. C. & Dettoni, J. M. (1995). *Nurture that is Christian.* Grand Rapids, MI: Baker Books.

Willhauck, S. E. (1992). John Wesley's view of children: Foundations for contemporary Christian education. (Unpublished dissertation). The Catholic University of America.

Wilson, E. L. (2000). *We hold these truths: A guide to Wesleyan beliefs for the 21st century.* Indianapolis, IN: Wesleyan Publishing House.

Wilson, E. L. (2011). *Assurance of the believer.* Unpublished manuscript.

World Methodist Council. (2012). About us. Retrieved from http://worldmethodistcouncil.org/index.php?option=com_content&task=view&id=14&Itemid=34

Appendix A

Hymn "Gentle Jesus Meek and Mild"

Charles and John Wesley (1763)

Gentle Jesus, meek and mild,
Look upon a little child;
Pity my simplicity,
Suffer me to come to Thee.

Lamb of God, I look to Thee;
Thou shalt my Example be;
Thou art gentle, meek, and mild;
Thou wast once a little child.

Lord, I would be as Thou art;
Give me Thine obedient heart;
Thou art pitiful and kind,
Let me have Thy loving mind.

Let me, above all, fulfill
God my heav'nly Father's will;
Never His good Spirit grieve;
Only to His glory live.

Loving Jesus, gentle Lamb,
In Thy gracious hands I am;
Make me, Savior, what Thou art
Live Thyself within my heart.

Appendix B
Secondary Sources Consulted

Baker, F. (1966). A union catalogue of the publications of John and Charles Wesley compiled by Frank Baker. Durham, NC: Duke University.
**Benzie, P. (2010). As a little child: Children in the theology of John Wesley. (Unpublished thesis). Laidlaw-Carey Graduate School, New Zealand.
Blevins, D. G. (2005). Renovating Christian education in the 21st century: A Wesleyan contribution. Christian Education Journal 2(1), 6-29.
*Blevins, D. G. (2008). To be a means of grace: A Wesleyan perspective on Christian practices and the lives of children. Wesley Theological Journal 43(1), 47-57.
Blevins, D. G., & Maddix, M. A. (2010). Discovering discipleship: Dynamics of Christian education. Kansas City, KS: Beacon Hill Press.
Campbell, T. A. (2010). John Wesley as diarist and correspondent. In r. L. Maddox and J. E. Vickers (Eds.), The Cambridge companion to John Wesley (pp. 129-143). New York, NY: Cambridge University Press.
Collins, K. J. (1999). A real Christian: The life of John Wesley. Nashville, TN: Abingdon.
Duke Divinity School. (2012). Center for Studies in the Wesleyan Tradition.
*Estep, J. R. (1997). John Wesley's philosophy of formal childhood education. Christian Education Journal 1(2), 43-52.
Felton, G. C. (Winter 1997). John Wesley and the teaching ministry: Ramifications for education in the church today. Religious Education 92(1), 92-107.
Fitchett, W. H. (1908). Wesley and his century: A study in spiritual forces. Cincinnati, OH: Jennings & Graham.
Fitzgerlad, M. H. (1925). The life of John Wesley and the rise and progress of Methodism by Robert Southey. London, England: Oxford University Press.
*Green, R. (1906). The works of John and Charles Wesley: A bibliography containing an exact account of all the publications issued by the brothers Wesley arranged in chronological order, with a list of early editions, and descriptive illustrative notes. (2nd ed.). London, England: Methodist Publishing House.
Heitzenrater, R. P. (1989). Mirror and memory: Reflections on early Methodism. Nashville, TN: Kingswood Books.

Heitzenrater, R. P. (1995). Wesley and the people called Methodists. Nashville, TN: Abingdon.

*/**Heitzenrater, R. P. (2001). John Wesley and children. In M. J. Bunge, The child in Christian thought (pp. 279-299). Grand Rapids, MI: William B. Eerdmans.

Jackson, T. (1872). (Ed.). The Works of John Wesley. London, England: Wesleyan Methodist Book Room.

Maddix, M. A. (2009). John Wesley's formative experiences: foundations for his educational ministry perspectives. Didache: Faithful Teaching 9(1). Retrieved from http://didachents.edu

Maddox, R. L. & Vickers, J. E. (2010). The Cambridge companion to John Wesley. New York, NY: Cambridge University Press.

Manchester Wesley Research Centre.

**Matthaei, S. H. (2000). Making disciples: Faith formation in the Wesleyan tradition. Nashville, TN: Abingdon.

**May, S., Posterski, B., Stonehouse, C., & Cannell, L. (2005). Children matter: Celebrating their place in the church, family, and community. Grand Rapids, MI: William B. Eerdmans.

*/**Naggle, D. I. (1987). From font to faith: John Wesley on infant baptism and the nurture of children. New York, NY: Peter Lang.

Outler, A. C. (1964). John Wesley. New York, NY: Oxford University Press.

Prince, J. W. (1926). Wesley on religious education. New York, NY: The Methodist Book Concern.

Rack, H. D. (2002). Reasonable enthusiast: John Wesley and the rise of Methodism. (3rd ed.). London, England: Epworth Press.

Stonehouse, C. (1998). Joining children on the spiritual journey: Nurturing a life of faith. Grand Rapids, MI: Baker Books.

**Stonehouse, C. (2004) Children in Wesleyan thought. In D. Ratcliff (Ed.), Children's spirituality: Christian perspectives, research, and application (pp. 133-148). Eugene, OR: Cascade Books.

Telford, J. (Ed.) (1931). The letters of John Wesley. London, England; Epworth.

Telford, J. (1995) Sayings and portraits of John Wesley. Salem, OH: Schmul Publishing.

Towns, Elmer L.(1970) "John Wesley and Religious Education. Articles. Paper 16.

Retrieved from http://digitalcommons.liberty.edu/towns_articles/16

*Tranter, D. (1996). John Wesley and the education of children in T. Macquiban (Ed.), Issues in Education: Some Methodist Perspectives (pp. 17-40). Oxford, England: Applied Theology Press.

Tyerman, L. (1872) The life and times of the Rev. John Wesley, M.A., founder of the Methodists. New York, NY: Harper & Brothers.

Wesley Center Online at Northwestern Nazarene University.

*/**Willhauck, S. E. (1992). John Wesley's view of children: Foundations for contemporary Christian education. (Unpublished book). The Catholic University of America.

*Recommended by R. Maddox
**Recommended by C. Stonehouse
Dr. Maddox's personal suggestion on primary works to consult (June 2012):

Primary Works

Note the letter from his mother describing her typical practice of raising children, in *Journal* (1 Aug. 1742), *Works*, 19:286-91. Wesley reprinted an extract (with a closing paragraph not in the earlier citation) over forty years later in Sermon 96, "On Obedience to Parents," §I.10, *Works*, 3:367-68.

Wesley published *Instructions for Children* in 1745 (Preface in *Works* [Jackson], 14:217-8). The first half of this catechism appears to be loosely dependent upon Claude Fleury's *Grand Catéchisme historique* (1683), the second half is an abridged translation of Pierre Poiret's *Les Principes Solides de la Religion et de la Vie Chrétienne, appliqués a l'Education des enfans* (1705). Note Wesley's favorable comparison of this volume to the Anglican catechism in Letter to Mary Bishop (15 Mar. 1777), *Letters* (Telford), 6:258; and his general estimate of it in *A Short Account of the Life and Death of the Rev. John Fletcher* (1786), Chapter VIII, §12, *Works* (Jackson), 11:339. Wesley then prepared his own *Lessons for Children* (which is just an abridged form of the Bible) in installments between 1746 and 1754 (Preface in *Works* [Jackson], 14:216-17).

Cf. Sermon 94, "On Family Religion," *Works*, 3:334-46; Sermon 95, "On the Education of Children," *Works*, 3:347-60; and Sermon 96, "On Obedience to Parents," *Works*, 3:361-72. See also "A Thought on the Manner of Educating Children," *AM* 6 (1783):380-3, *Works* (Jackson), 13:474-7.

Appendix C

Predetermined Codes

Descriptive:
  Context -
      Sermon   SER
      Letter   LTR
      Publication   PUB
  Audience -
      Pastors   PAS
      Parents   PAR
      Teachers   TCH
      Congregation   CON

Topical:
      What to teach   WHAT
      How to teach   HOW
      Whom shall teach   WHO

Analytical: WHAT
      Scripture/Bible   BIB
      Prayer   PRA
      Lifestyle   LIFE
      God   GOD
      Salvation   SAL
      Holiness   HOL
      Sin   SIN
      Human Nature   MAN
      Grace   GRA
Analytical: HOW
      When   WHN
      Where   WHR
      Method   MET
Analytical: WHO
      Relationship to child   REL
      Expected lifestyle   EXP

Appendix D

Translation Chart of Wesley Common Phrases into Contemporary, Common American Language

Wesley's Vocabulary	Today's Equivalent
Bowels	center of emotion; often what we mean by "heart"
Charity	love
Conversation	(often means) manner of life
Disinterested	impartial (e.g., "disinterested love for all")
Ejaculation	exclamation
End	(often means) purpose, goal (e.g., "to what end")
Filial	pertaining to sonship (e.g., "filial love")
Intercourse	interaction, relationship
Meet	fit, proper
Nice	overly concerned with what is socially proper
Peculiar	("peculiar people") particular, distinct
Prevent	(often means) precede
Prevenient	preceding (literally, "coming before")
Primitive	early, original (e.g., "the primitive church")

Prove	(often means) come to know by experience
Retirement	seclusion, privacy
Several	different, various (e.g., "at two several places")
Singular	distinct; not conforming to the crowd
Styled	called, known as
Temper	attitude, temperament, disposition
To own	(often means) to acknowledge
Vulgar	popular, common, colloquial
Want	(often means) need or lack rather than desire (e.g., "go to those who want you most" means "those who need you most.")

Note. From "Translating Wesley's Writings into Late 20th-Century American General English" by H. A. Snyder at Wesley Center Online. Retrieved from http://wesley.nnu.edu/john-wesley/translating-wesleys-writings-into-late-20th-century-american-general-english/

Appendix E

Works of Wesley Studied (In the order they are presented)

Sermon #94, "On Family Religion" from Outler, A. C. (Ed.). (1986). *The works of John Wesley volume 3: Sermons III 71-114*. Nashville, TN: Abingdon Press.

Sermon #95, "On the Education of Children" from Outler, A. C. (Ed.). (1986). *The works of John Wesley volume 3: Sermons III 71-114*. Nashville, TN: Abingdon Press.

Sermon #96, "On Obedience to Parents" from Outler, A. C. (Ed.). (1986). *The works of John Wesley volume 3: Sermons III 71-114*. Nashville, TN: Abingdon Press.

"A Thought on the Manner of Educating Children" from Jackson, T. (Ed.). (1872). *The Works of John Wesley* (3rd ed.). London, England: Wesleyan Methodist Book Room; reprint ed., Grand Rapids, MI: Baker, 1979.

"Serious Thoughts Concerning Godfathers and Godmothers" from Jackson, T. (Ed.). (1872). *The Works of John Wesley* (3rd ed.). London, England: Wesleyan Methodist Book Room; reprint ed., Grand Rapids, MI: Baker, 1979.

"A Short Account of the School in Kingswood near Bristol" from Jackson, T. (Ed.). (1872). *The Works of John Wesley* (3rd ed.). London, England: Wesleyan Methodist Book Room; reprint ed., Grand Rapids, MI: Baker, 1979.

"A Plain Account of Kingswood School" from Jackson, T. (Ed.). (1872). *The Works of John Wesley* (3rd ed.). London, England: Wesleyan Methodist Book Room; reprint ed., Grand Rapids, MI: Baker, 1979.

Prayers for Children from Jackson, T. (1872). (Ed.). *The Works of John Wesley* (3rd ed.). London, England: Wesleyan Methodist Book Room; reprint ed., Grand Rapids, MI: Baker, 1979.

Susanna Wesley's letter to John Wesley from Jackson, T. (Ed.). (1872). *The Works of John Wesley* (3rd ed.). London, England: Wesleyan Methodist Book Room; reprint ed., Grand Rapids, MI: Baker, 1979.

Instructions for Children from Wesley, J. (1746). *Instructions for children* (2nd edition). London, England: Copper.

Appendix F

Results of Coding Process

Figure F1. Results of Descriptive Codes by Source Document

DESCRIPTIVE CODES	SER	LTR	PUB	PAS	PAR	TCH	CONG	CHD
Sermon 94	X		X		X		X	
Sermon 95	X		X				X	
Sermon 96	X		X		X		X	X
SW Letter		X						
Godparents			X				X	
Educating Children			X				X	
Plain Acct							X	
Short Acct			X				X	
Lessons			X		X	X		X
Prayers			X					X
Hymns			X					X
Instructions			X		X	X		X

Figure F1. Results of descriptive codes for type of document and audience of document by source document. Descriptive codes for type of document with "SER" for sermon, "LTR" for letter, "PUB" for publication and descriptive codes for audience of document with "PAS" for pastor, "PAR" for parent, "TCH" for teacher, "CONG" for Methodist societies at large, and "CHD" for children.

Figure F2. Results of Analytical Codes for Research question "WHAT" by Source Document

WHAT CODES	BIB	GOD	GRA	HOL	HVN	JES	LIFE	MAN	PRA	SAL	SIN
Sermon 94	X	X	X		X	X	X		X	X	
Sermon 95	X	X	X		X	X	X	X			
Sermon 96	X	X	X	X	X		X	X		X	X
SW Letter	X	X	X		X		X	X	X	X	X
Godparents	X	X							X		
Educating Children	X	X	X	X		X				X	
Plain Acct		X			X					X	X
Short Acct	X	X						X			
Lessons	X	X	X	X	X						
Prayers	X	X	X	X	X	X	X	X	X	X	X
Hymns	X	X	X	X	X	X	X	X	X	X	X
Instructions	X	X	X	X	X	X	X	X	X	X	X

Figure F2. Results of Analytical Codes for Research question "WHAT" by Source Document. Analytical codes for research question "WHAT" included "BIB" for Bible, "GOD" for description of God, "GRA" for works of God, "HOL" for Holy Spirit, "HVN" for eternity, "JES" for Jesus, "LIFE" for expectations of Christian living, "MAN" for description of humanity apart from God, "PRA" for role of prayer, "SAL" for salvation, and "SIN" for sin.

Appendix F 195

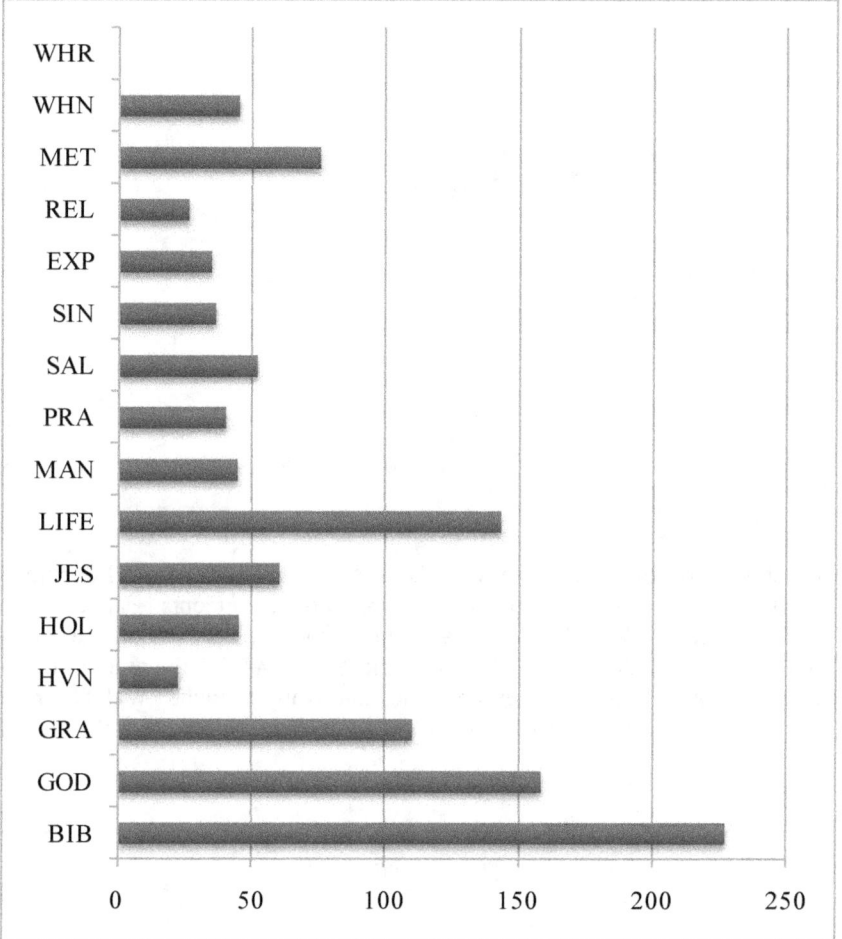

Figure F3: Frequency of Analytical Codes in All Documents

Figure F3. Frequency of all analytical codes in all of the documents researched. Topical "HOW" include "WHR" where instruction should occur, "WHN" when instruction should occur, and "MET" the methodology of the instruction; topical "Who" codes include "REL" relationship of instructor to child, "EXP" the expected lifestyle of the instructor; and topical code "WHAT" include "SIN" for sin, "SAL" for salvation, "PRA" for the role of prayer, "MAN" for humanity apart from God, "LIFE" for the Christian lifestyle, "JES" for Jesus, "HOL" for the Holy Spirit, "HVN" for eternity, "GRA" for the actions of God, "GOD" for the names and descriptions of God, and "BIB" for Bible.

Figure 4.4 Comparison of Frequency in Topical Codes for All Documents

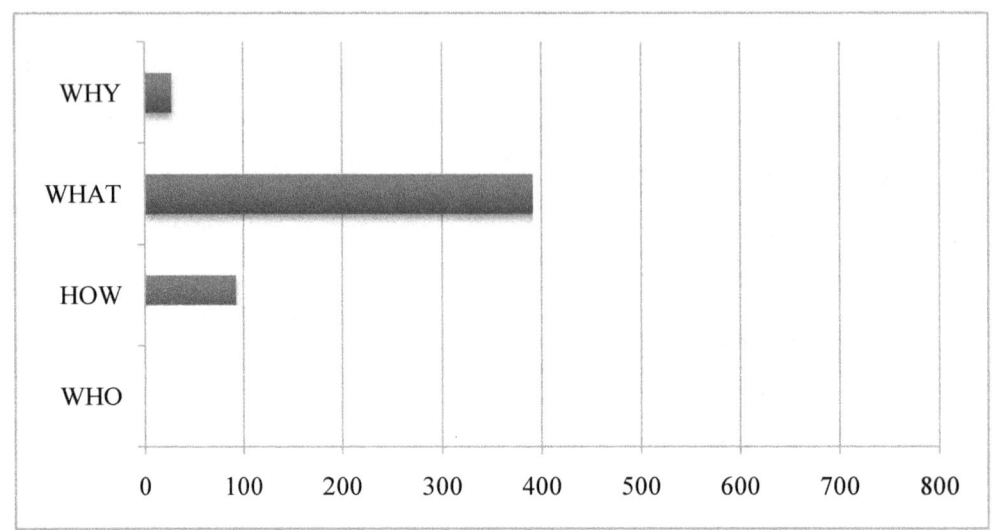

Figure 4.4. Comparison of the frequency in the three topical codes for all documents in the research. "WHY" for the amount of coded data from all the documents related to the additional question, Why teach? "WHAT" for the amount of coded data from all the documents all codes related to the research question, What to teach? "HOW" for the amount of coded data from all the documents related to the research question, How to teach? "WHO" for the amount of coded data from all the documents related to the research question, Who shall teach?

Appendix G

Results of Coding in Sermons

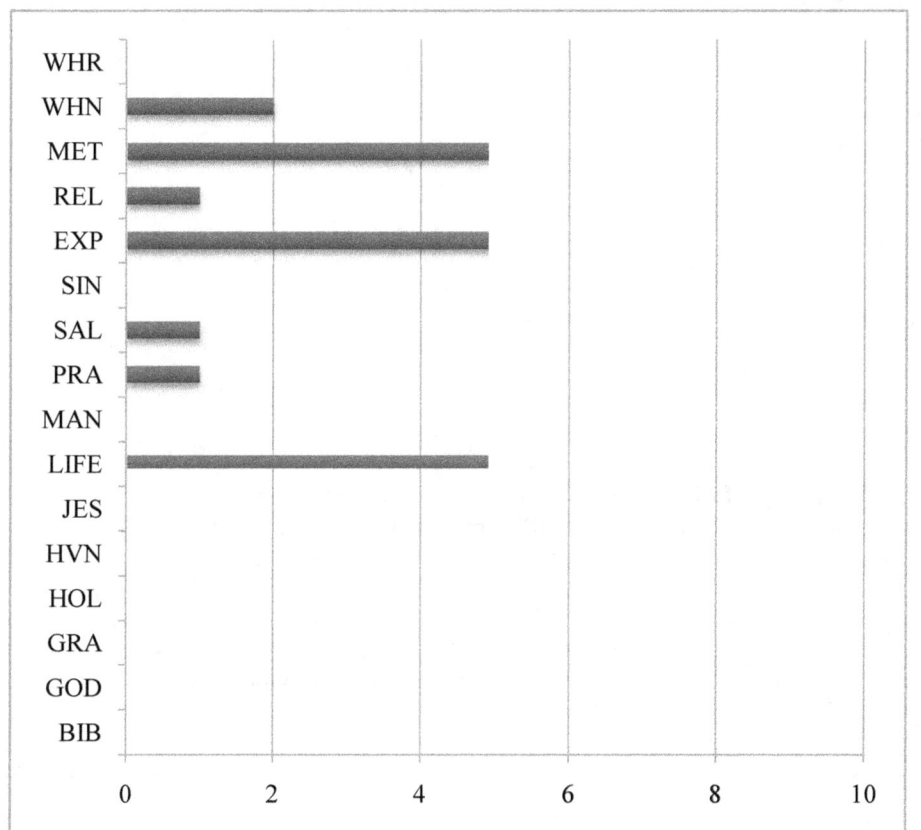

Figure G1: Frequency of Codes in Sermon 94, "On Family Religion"

Figure G1: Frequency of all analytical codes in the document Sermon 94, "On Family Religion". Topical "HOW" include "WHR" where instruction should occur, "WHN" when instruction should occur, and "MET" the methodology of the instruction; topical "Who" codes include "REL" relationship of instructor to child, "EXP" the expected lifestyle of the instructor; and topical code "WHAT" include "SIN" for sin, "SAL" for salvation, "PRA" for the role of prayer, "MAN" for humanity apart from God, "LIFE" for the Christian lifestyle, "JES" for Jesus, "HOL" for the Holy Spirit, "HVN" for eternity, "GRA" for the actions of God, "GOD" for the names and descriptions of God, and "BIB" for Bible.

198   Appendix G

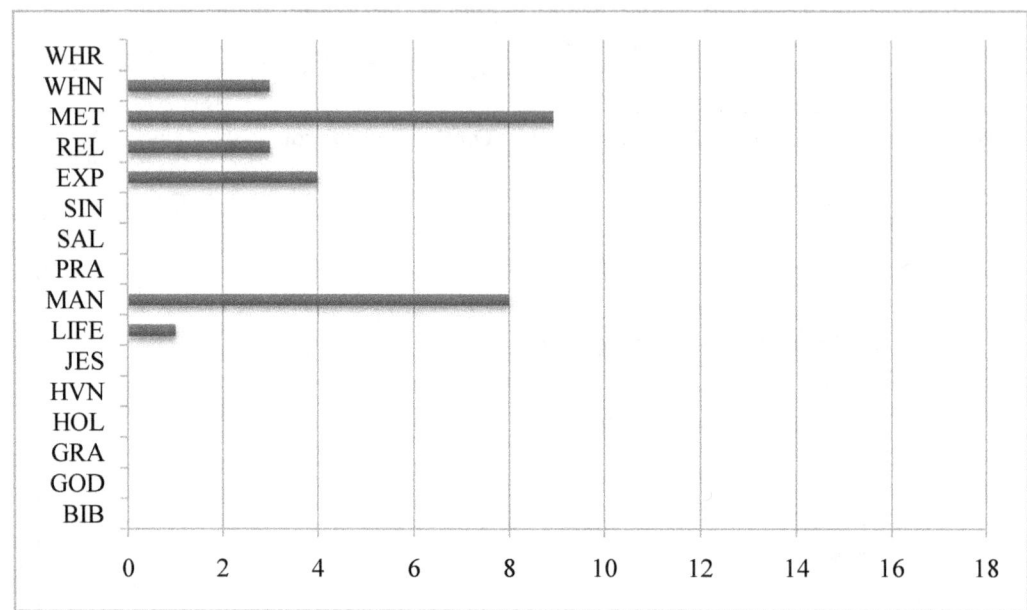

Figure G2: Frequency of All Codes in Sermon 95, "On Education of Children"

Figure G2: Frequency of all analytical codes in the document, Sermon 95, "On Education of Children". Topical "HOW" include "WHR" where instruction should occur, "WHN" when instruction should occur, and "MET" the methodology of the instruction; topical "Who" codes include "REL" relationship of instructor to child, "EXP" the expected lifestyle of the instructor; and topical code "WHAT" include "SIN" for sin, "SAL" for salvation, "PRA" for the role of prayer, "MAN" for humanity apart from God, "LIFE" for the Christian lifestyle, "JES" for Jesus, "HOL" for the Holy Spirit, "HVN" for eternity, "GRA" for the actions of God, "GOD" for the names and descriptions of God, and "BIB" for Bible.

Figure G3: Frequency of All Codes in Sermon 96, "On Obedience of Children"

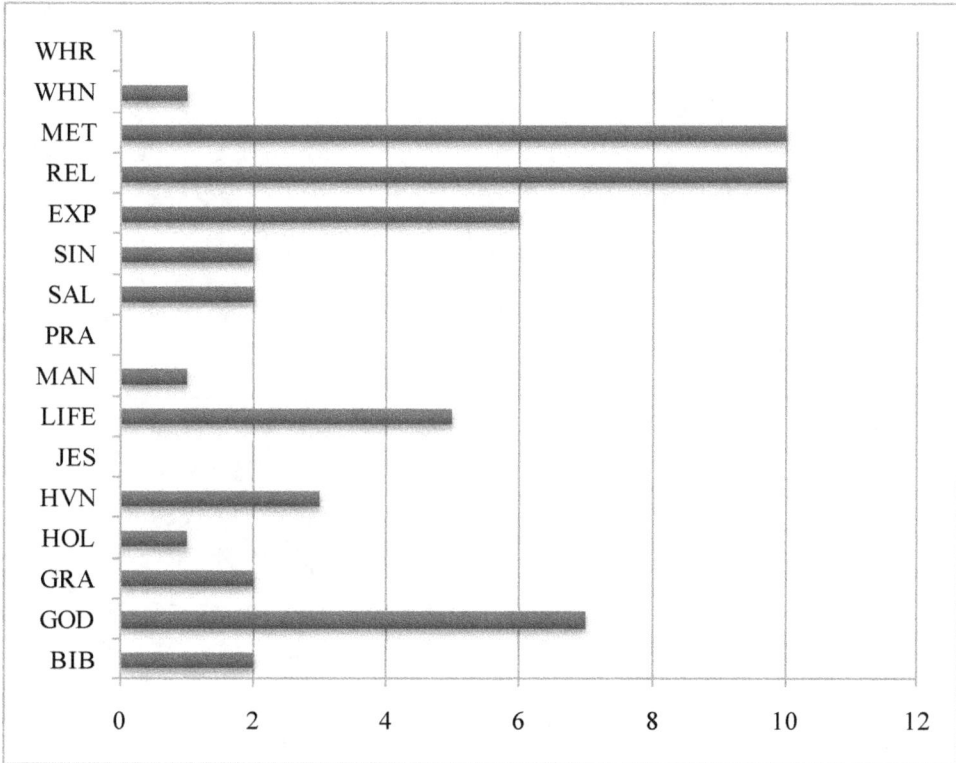

Figure G3: Frequency of all analytical codes in the document, Sermon 96, "On Obedience of Children". Topical "HOW" include "WHR" where instruction should occur, "WHN" when instruction should occur, and "MET" the methodology of the instruction; topical "Who" codes include "REL" relationship of instructor to child, "EXP" the expected lifestyle of the instructor; and topical code "WHAT" include "SIN" for sin, "SAL" for salvation, "PRA" for the role of prayer, "MAN" for humanity apart from God, "LIFE" for the Christian lifestyle, "JES" for Jesus, "HOL" for the Holy Spirit, "HVN" for eternity, "GRA" for the actions of God, "GOD" for the names and descriptions of God, and "BIB" for Bible.

Appendix H

"By-laws" from Susanna Wesley Letter

1. It had been observed, that cowardice and fear of punishment often lead children into lying, till they get a custom of it, which they cannot leave. To prevent this, a law was made, That whoever was charged with a fault, of which they were guilty, if they would ingenuously confess it, and promise to amend, should not be beaten. This rule prevented a great deal of lying, and would have done more, if one in the family would have observed it. But he could not be prevailed on, and therefore was often imposed on by false colours and equivocations; which none would have used, (except one,) had they been kindly dealt with. And some, in spite of all, would always speak truth plainly.
2. That no sinful action, as lying, pilfering, playing at church, or on the Lord's day, disobedience, quarrelling, &c., should ever pass unpunished.
3. That no child should ever be chide or beat twice for the same fault; and that if they amended, they should never be upbraided with it afterwards.
4. That every signal act of obedience, especially when it crossed upon their own inclinations, should be always commended, and frequently rewarded, according to the merits of the cause.
5. That if ever any child performed an act of obedience, or did any thing with an intention to please, though the performance was not well, yet the obedience and intention should be kindly accepted; and the child with sweetness directed how to do better for the future.
6. That propriety be inviolably preserved, and none suffered to invade the property of another in the smallest matter, though it were but of the value of a farthing, or a pin; which they might not take from the owner, without, much less against, his consent. This rule can never be too much inculcated on the minds of children; and from the want of parents or governors doing it as they ought, proceeds with shameful neglect of justice which we may observe in the world.
7. That promises be strictly observed; and a gift once bestowed, and so the right passed away from the donor, be not resumed, but left to the disposal of him to whom it was given; unless it were conditional, and the condition of the obligation not performed.

8. That no girl be taught to work till she can read very well; and then that she be kept to her work with the same application, and for the same time, that she was held to in reading. This rule also is much to be observed; for the putting children to learn sewing before they can read perfectly, is the very reason, why so few women can read fit to be heard, and never to be well understood.

(Jackson, 1872, Vol. I, p. 392)

Appendix I

Frequency of Codes in Documents

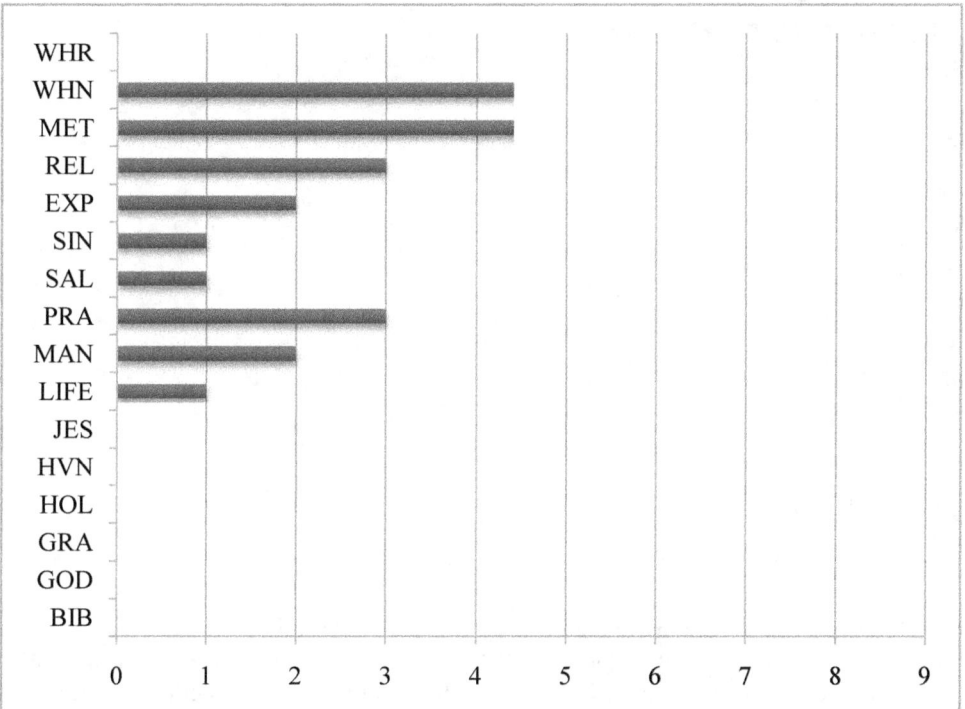

Figure I1. Frequency of All Analytical Codes in Susanna Wesley Letter

Figure 11. Frequency of all analytical codes in Susanna Wesley's letter. Topical "HOW" include "WHR" where instruction should occur, "WHN" when instruction should occur, and "MET" the methodology of the instruction; topical "Who" codes include "REL" relationship of instructor to child, "EXP" the expected lifestyle of the instructor; and topical code "WHAT" include "SIN" for sin, "SAL" for salvation, "PRA" for the role of prayer, "MAN" for humanity apart from God, "LIFE" for the Christian lifestyle, "JES" for Jesus, "HOL" for the Holy Spirit, "HVN" for eternity, "GRA" for the actions of God, "GOD" for the names and descriptions of God, and "BIB" for Bible.

Figure I2. Frequency of All Analytical Codes in "Thoughts Concerning Godfathers and Godmothers"

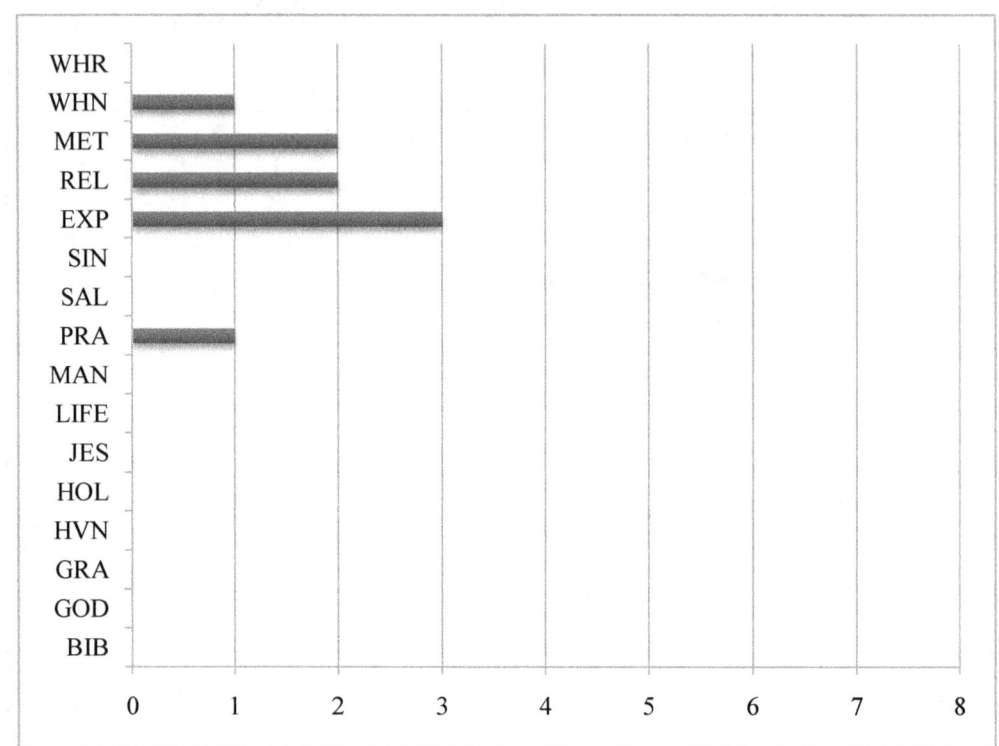

Figure I2. Frequency of all analytical codes in the document, "Thoughts Concerning Godfathers and Godmothers". Topical "HOW" include "WHR" where instruction should occur, "WHN" when instruction should occur, and "MET" the methodology of the instruction; topical "Who" codes include "REL" relationship of instructor to child, "EXP" the expected lifestyle of the instructor; and topical code "WHAT" include "SIN" for sin, "SAL" for salvation, "PRA" for the role of prayer, "MAN" for humanity apart from God, "LIFE" for the Christian lifestyle, "JES" for Jesus, "HOL" for the Holy Spirit, "HVN" for eternity, "GRA" for the actions of God, "GOD" for the names and descriptions of God, and "BIB" for Bible.

Figure I3. Frequency of All Analytical Codes in "A Thought on the Manner of Educating Children"

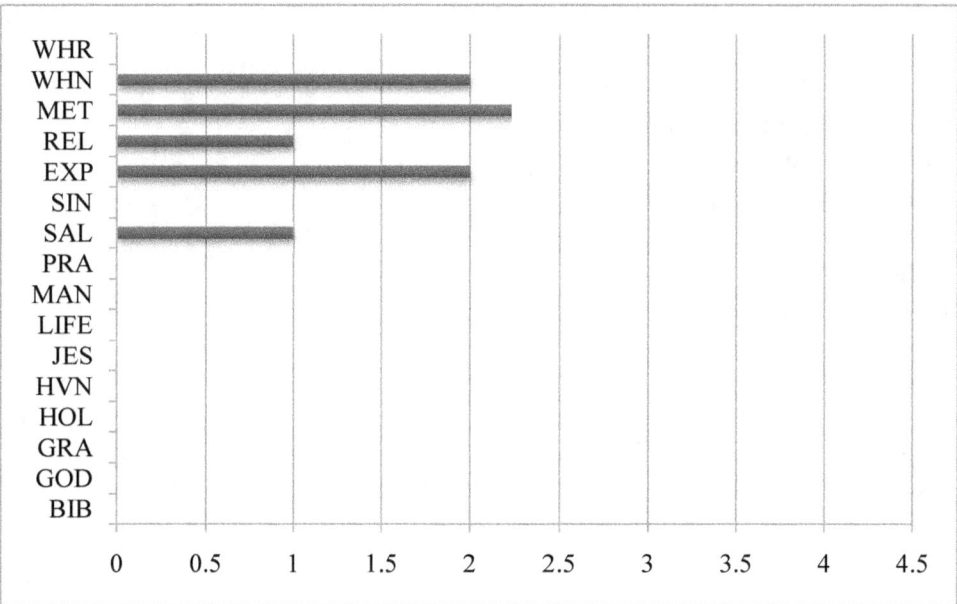

Figure I3. Frequency of all analytical codes in the document, "A Thought on the Manner of Educating Children". Topical "HOW" include "WHR" where instruction should occur, "WHN" when instruction should occur, and "MET" the methodology of the instruction; topical "Who" codes include "REL" relationship of instructor to child, "EXP" the expected lifestyle of the instructor; and topical code "WHAT" include "SIN" for sin, "SAL" for salvation, "PRA" for the role of prayer, "MAN" for humanity apart from God, "LIFE" for the Christian lifestyle, "JES" for Jesus, "HOL" for the Holy Spirit, "HVN" for eternity, "GRA" for the actions of God, "GOD" for the names and descriptions of God, and "BIB" for Bible.

Figure I4: Frequency of All Analytical Codes in "A Short Account of the School in Kingswood"

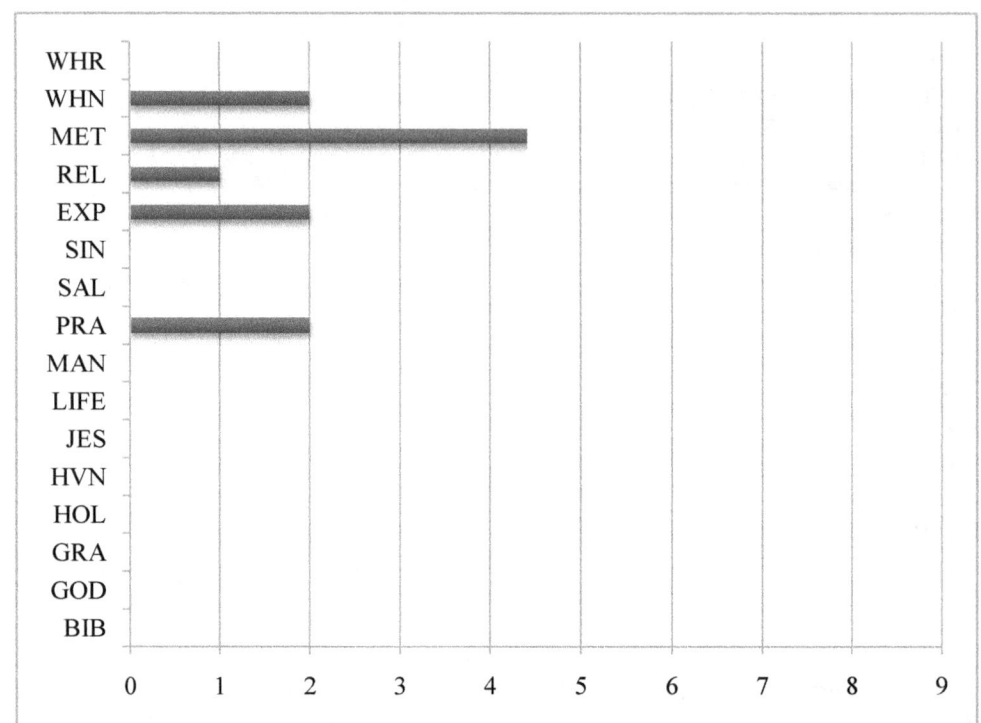

Figure I4: Frequency of all analytical codes in the document, "A Short Account of the School in Kingswood". Topical "HOW" include "WHR" where instruction should occur, "WHN" when instruction should occur, and "MET" the methodology of the instruction; topical "Who" codes include "REL" relationship of instructor to child, "EXP" the expected lifestyle of the instructor; and topical code "WHAT" include "SIN" for sin, "SAL" for salvation, "PRA" for the role of prayer, "MAN" for humanity apart from God, "LIFE" for the Christian lifestyle, "JES" for Jesus, "HOL" for the Holy Spirit, "HVN" for eternity, "GRA" for the actions of God, "GOD" for the names and descriptions of God, and "BIB" for Bible.

Figure I5: Frequency of All Analytical Codes in "A Plain Account of Kingswood School"

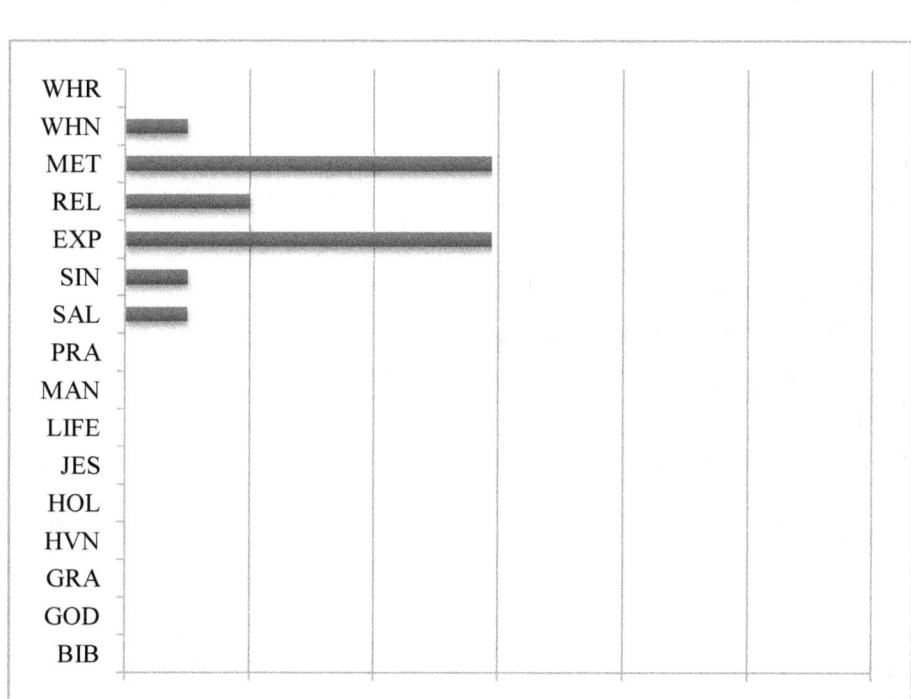

Figure I5: Frequency of all analytical codes in the document "A Plain Account of Kingswood School". Topical "HOW" include "WHR" where instruction should occur, "WHN" when instruction should occur, and "MET" the methodology of the instruction; topical "Who" codes include "REL" relationship of instructor to child, "EXP" the expected lifestyle of the instructor; and topical code "WHAT" include "SIN" for sin, "SAL" for salvation, "PRA" for the role of prayer, "MAN" for humanity apart from God, "LIFE" for the Christian lifestyle, "JES" for Jesus, "HOL" for the Holy Spirit, "HVN" for eternity, "GRA" for the actions of God, "GOD" for the names and descriptions of God, and "BIB" for Bible.

Figure 16: Frequency of All Analytical Codes in *Hymns for Children*

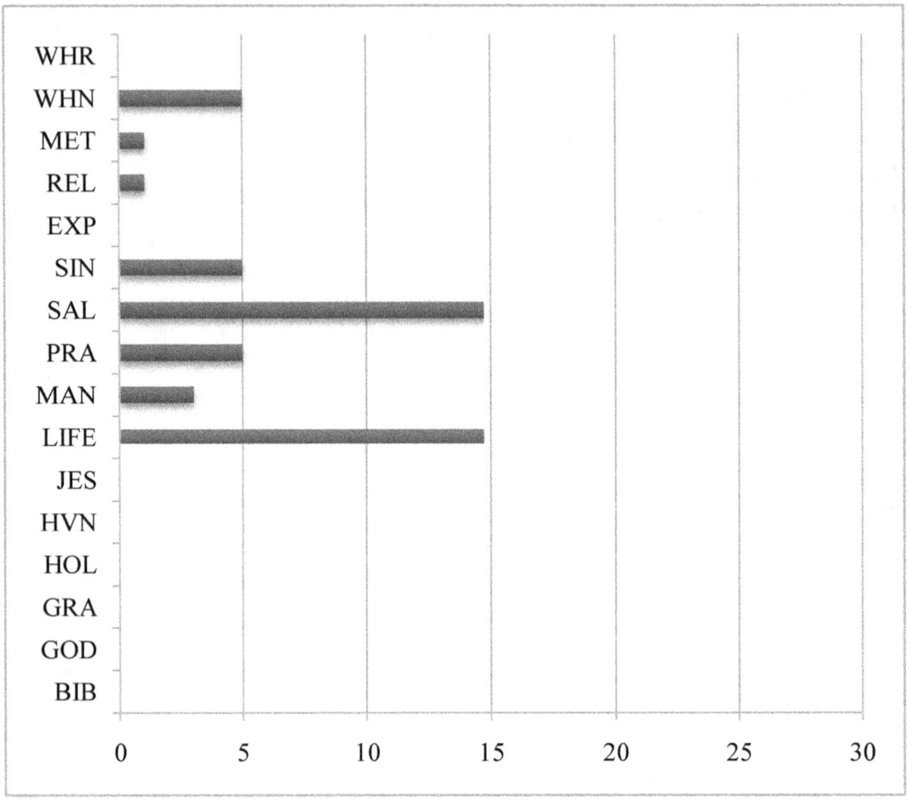

Figure 16: Frequency of all analytical codes in the document *Hymns for Children*. Topical "HOW" include "WHR" where instruction should occur, "WHN" when instruction should occur, and "MET" the methodology of the instruction; topical "Who" codes include "REL" relationship of instructor to child, "EXP" the expected lifestyle of the instructor; and topical code "WHAT" include "SIN" for sin, "SAL" for salvation, "PRA" for the role of prayer, "MAN" for humanity apart from God, "LIFE" for the Christian lifestyle, "JES" for Jesus, "HOL" for the Holy Spirit, "HVN" for eternity, "GRA" for the actions of God, "GOD" for the names and descriptions of God, and "BIB" for Bible.

Appendix I 209

Figure I7. Frequency of All Analytical Codes in *Lessons for Children*

Figure I7: Frequency of all analytical codes in the document *Lessons for Children*. Topical "HOW" include "WHR" where instruction should occur, "WHN" when instruction should occur, and "MET" the methodology of the instruction; topical "Who" codes include "REL" relationship of instructor to child, "EXP" the expected lifestyle of the instructor; and topical code "WHAT" include "SIN" for sin, "SAL" for salvation, "PRA" for the role of prayer, "MAN" for humanity apart from God, "LIFE" for the Christian lifestyle, "JES" for Jesus, "HOL" for the Holy Spirit, "HVN" for eternity, "GRA" for the actions of God, "GOD" for the names and descriptions of God, and "BIB" for Bible.

210 Appendix I

Figure I8. Frequency of All Analytical Codes in *Instructions for Children*

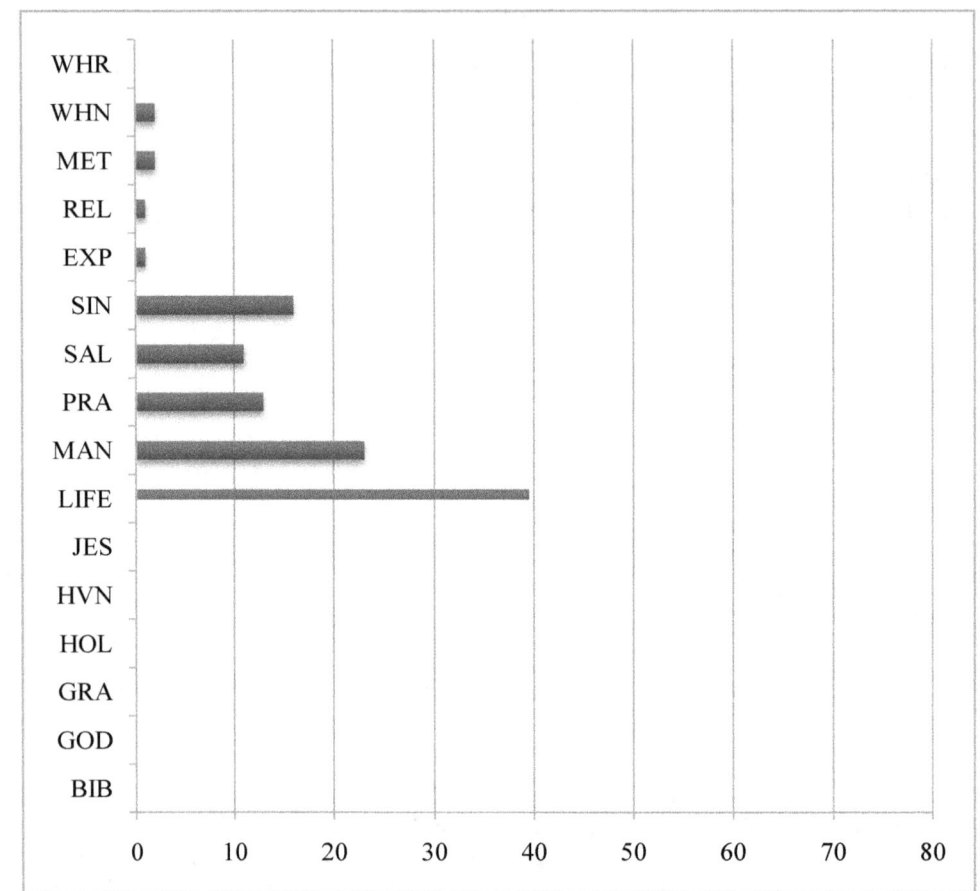

Figure 18. Frequency of all analytical codes in the document *Instructions for Children*. Topical "HOW" include "WHR" where instruction should occur, "WHN" when instruction should occur, and "MET" the methodology of the instruction; topical "Who" codes include "REL" relationship of instructor to child, "EXP" the expected lifestyle of the instructor; and topical code "WHAT" include "SIN" for sin, "SAL" for salvation, "PRA" for the role of prayer, "MAN" for humanity apart from God, "LIFE" for the Christian lifestyle, "JES" for Jesus, "HOL" for the Holy Spirit, "HVN" for eternity, "GRA" for the actions of God, "GOD" for the names and descriptions of God, and "BIB" for Bible.

Appendix I   211

Figure I9. Frequency of All Analytical Codes in *Prayers for Children*

Figure 19. Frequency of all analytical codes in the document *Prayers for Children.* Topical "HOW" include "WHR" where instruction should occur, "WHN" when instruction should occur, and "MET" the methodology of the instruction; topical "Who" codes include "REL" relationship of instructor to child, "EXP" the expected lifestyle of the instructor; and topical code "WHAT" include "SIN" for sin, "SAL" for salvation, "PRA" for the role of prayer, "MAN" for humanity apart from God, "LIFE" for the Christian lifestyle, "JES" for Jesus, "HOL" for the Holy Spirit, "HVN" for eternity, "GRA" for the actions of God, "GOD" for the names and descriptions of God, and "BIB" for Bible.

Appendix J

Finalized Codes Used in Research

Descriptive:
  Context -
      Sermon   SER
      Letter   LTR
      Publication   PUB
  Audience -
      Pastors   PAS
      Parents   PAR
      Teachers   TCH
      Congregation   CON
      Children   CHD

Topical:
      What to teach   WHAT
      How to teach   HOW
      Whom shall teach   WHO
      Why teach   WHY

Analytical: WHAT
      Scripture/Bible   BIB
      Prayer   PRA
      Christian Living   LIFE   (after salvation)
      Names/Descriptions of God GOD
      Salvation   SAL
      Holy Spirit   HOL
      Sin   SIN
      Human Nature   MAN   (prior to salvation)
      Grace   GRA   (acts of God on humanity's behalf)
      Jesus   JES
      Heaven (eternity)   HVN

Analytical: HOW

214 Appendix J

    When   WHN
    Where   WHR
    Method   MET

Analytical: WHO
    Relationship to child   REL
    Expected lifestyle   EXP   (of instructor)

Appendix K
List of Sub-codes of Analytical Codes

God (GOD): Names, Description, and Activity
Grace (GRA): What it is, What God does, Our response,
Prayers (PRA): Example, Purpose, How
Bible (BIB): What taught, Description, How to Use
Salvation (SAL): Source/means, Outcome, Our Response
Jesus (JES): Description, Actions
Eternity/Heaven (HVN): Heaven, Hell
Holy Spirit (HOL): Actions, Description
Sin (SIN): What it is, Examples, What it does
Christian Life (LIFE): Praise, Piety, Submission

Appendix L

Lessons for Children (Wesley, 1746, 1747, 1748, 1754)

Lesson Number, Biblical Reference, and Title as noted by Wesley

(Prince, 1926, pp. 149-153)

Part I: (1746)

Lesson	Reference	Title
1	Gen. 1:1-8	Of the Creation [Day 1 and 2]
2	Gen. 1:9-23	Of the Creation [Days 3-5]
3	Gen. 1:24-31	Of the Creation [Day 6]
4	Gen. 2:1-25	Of Paradise
5	Gen. 3:1-23	Of the Fall of men
6	Gen. 4:1-26	Of Cain and Abel
7	Gen. 5:3 - 6:22	Of Adam, Enoch, and Noah
8	Gen. 7:11 - 8:12	Of the Flood
9	Gen. 8:13-9:29	Of the End of the Flood
10	Gen. 11:1-31	Of the Tower of Babel and the Birth of Abraham
11	Gen. 12:1 - 13:18	Of God's Promise to Abram, and of His Journeys
12	Gen. 14:1-23	Of Abraham's Rescue of Lot, and of Melchisedek
13	Gen. 15:1-17:23	Of God's Further Promises to Abraham
14	Gen. 18:1-33	Of Abraham's Intercession for Sodom
15	Gen. 19:1-26	Of the Destruction of Sodom and Gomorrah
16	Gen. 21:1-22:18	Of the Birth and Offering of Isaac
17	Gen. 24:1-67	Of the Marriage of Isaac
18	Gen 25:7-26:24	Of Abraham's Death; of God's Promise to Isaac; and of the Birth of Esau & Jacob
19	Gen 28:1-29:13	Of Jacob's Journey and Vision

20	Gen 29:16-33:18	Of Jacob's Marriages; of His Return Home; of His Wrestling with the Angel; and Meeting Esau
21	Gen 35:23-39:5	Of Jacob's Children, and Isaac's Death
22	Gen 41:1-57	Of Joseph's Advancement in Egypt
23	Gen 42:1-38	Of Joseph's Brothers Going To Buy Corn In Egypt
24	Gen 43:2-33	Of Benjamin's Going Into Egypt
25	Gen. 45:1-28	Of Joseph's Making Himself Known To His Brothers
26	Gen 46:1-47:31	Of Jacob's Going To Egypt
27	Gen 48:1-49:33	Of Jacob's Blessing His Children, and of His death
28	Gen 50:1-26	Of Burial of Jacob, and the Death of Joseph
29	Exod. 1:6-2:21	Of the Birth of Moses
30	Exod. 3:1-20	Of God's Appearing To Moses And Sending Him to Israel
31	Exod. 4:10-5:23	Of God Sending Moses and Aaron to Pharaoh
32	Exod. 7:7-23	Of the Rod Turned into a Serpent; and the Water Into Blood
33	Exod. 8:5-32	Of the Plague of Frogs, of Lice, of Flies
34	Exod. 9:1-10:23	Of the Murrain, the Boils, the Hail, the Locusts, and the Darkness
35	Exod. 12:1-41	Of the Passover, and the Death of the Firstborn
36	Exod. 13:17-14:30	Of the Journey of the Israelites and the Destruction of Egyptians in Red Sea
37	Exod. 15:22-17:13	Of the Quails, the Manna, and Amole
38	Exod. 19:1-25	Of the Giving of the Law at Mt Sinai
39	Exod. 20:1-20	The Ten Commandments
40	Exod. 20:21-31:18	Various Precepts
41	Exod. 32:1-35	Of the Golden Calf
42	Exod. 33:7-34:34	Of Moses Talking with God
43	Lev 26:3-44	A Blessing and a Curse
44	Num. 16:1-35	Of Korah, Dathan, and Abiram
45	Num. 22:1-35	Of Balak and Balaam
46	Num. 23:3-24:17	Balaam's Prophecies
47	Deut. 1:4-4:40	An Exhortation to Obedience
48	Deut. 6:4-7:15	An Exhortation to Obedience
49	Deut. 8:1-20	An Exhortation to Obedience
50	Deut. 9:4-10:22	An Exhortation to Obedience
51	Deut. 1:1-29:29	An Exhortation to Obedience
52	Deut. 30:1-31:6	An Exhortation to Obedience
53	Deut. 32:1-43	The Song of Moses

54	Deut. 33:1-34:12	The Last Words and Death of Moses

Part II (1747)

55	Josh 1:1-3:17	The Israelites Pass over Jordan
56	Josh 5:1-6:27	The Taking of Jericho
57	Josh 10:1-40	The Sun and moon stand still
58	Josh 14:6-22:6	Of Caleb, and the Two Tribes and a Half
59	Josh 23:1-24:31	Joshua's exhortation before his death
60	Judg. 6:1-35	Of Gideon
61	Judg. 6:36-8:32	The Overthrow of the Midianites
63	Judg. 10:6-11:39	Of Jephthah
63	Judg. 13:1-14:20	Of Samson's Birth and Marriage
64	Judg. 15:1-16:1	Of Samson's Valor and Death
65	I Sam. 1:1-2:26	Of the Birth and Childhood of Samuel
66	I Sam. 3:1-4:18	God Reveals Himself to Samuel. Ark Taken by Philistines
67	I Sam. 5:1-7:17	The Ark Restored. Samuel Judges Israel
68	I Sam. 8:1-11:15	Saul Made king, Delivers Israel
69	I Sam. 13:3-14:23	The Overthrow of the Philistines
70	I Sam. 15:1-33	The Destruction of the Amalekites
71	I Sam. 17:1-52	Of David and Goliath
72	I Sam. 18:1-19:24	Saul seeks to Kill David
73	I Sam. 22:1-23:29	David's Escape from Saul
74	I Sam. 24:1-25:1	David, by Sparing Saul, Sheweth His Innocency
75	I Sam. 26:1-25	David Spareth Saul Again
76	I Sam. 27:3-28:25	Of the Witch of Endor
77	I Sam. 31:1-2 Sam 1:27	The Death of Saul. David's Lamentation
78	2 Sam. 2:1-6:23	David is made King Over Judah and Israel
79	2 Sam. 11:1-12:24	Of Bathsheba. David Reproved by Nathan
80	2 Sam. 13:1-15:6	Of Amnon and Absalom
81	2 Sam. 15:7-16:12	Absalom's Rebellion
82	2 Sam. 16:15-18:17	The End of Absalom's Rebellion
83	2 Sam. 19:1-24:25	David's Restoration. He Numbers the People
84	I Kings 2:1-6:38	Of Solomon's Wisdom
85	I Kings 8:1-11:43	Of the Dedication of the Temple, and of the Queen of Sheba
86	I Kings 12:1-14:30	Of Rehoboam and Jeroboam
87	I Kings 17:1-24	Elijah fed by the Ravens
88	I Kings 18:1-46	Of Elijah and prophets of Baal
89	I kings 19:1-21	Elijah Feels from Jezebel
90	I Kings 20:1-34	The Syrians Overthrown
91	I Kings 21:1-29	Of Naboth and the Jezreelite
92	I Kings 22:1-38	The Death of Ahab
93	2 Kings 2:1-22	Elijah Taken up to Heaven
94	2 Kings 4:1-37	Of the Widow's Oil, and the Shunammite

220 *Appendix L*

95	2 kings 5:1-27	The Cure of Naaman
96	2 Kings 6:1-7:17	Of Elisha and the Syrians
97	2 Kings 9:1-37	Jehu Made King. The Death of Jezebel
98	2 Kings 10:1-31	Jehu Destroys Ahab's house, and the Worshipers of Baal
99	2 Kings 17:3-41	Israel Carried into Captivity
100	2 Kings 18:3-19:37	Of Hezekiah and Sennacherib
101	2 Kings 22:1-27, 2 Chron. 35:20-24	Of Josiah
102	2 Kings 24:1-21	Jerusalem Destroyed
103	1 Chron. 12:16-9:19	Jerusalem Destroyed
104	2 Chron. 10:5-16:14	Jerusalem Destroyed
105	2 Chron. 19:1-20:37	Jerusalem Destroyed
106	2 Chron. 24:1-25:27	Jerusalem Destroyed
107	2 Chron. 26:1-28:27	Jerusalem Destroyed
108	2 Chron. 29:1-33:20	Jerusalem Destroyed

Part III (1748)

109	Ezra 1:1-3:13	Of the Rebuilding of the Temple
110	Ezra 4:1-6:22	The Building Hindered, and Begun Again
111	Ezra 7:1-10:12	Ezra goes to Jerusalem, and Mourns and Prays for the People
112	Neh. 1:1-6:15	The Wall of Jerusalem Rebuilt
113	Neh. 8:1-10:29	The Solemn Fast, Repentance, and Confession of the People
114	Esth. 1:1-2:23	Esther made queen
115	Esth. 3:1-5:14	Of Hamon and Mordecai
116	Esth. 7:1-10:3	Hamon Destroyed, and the Jews Persevered
117	Job 1:1-2:13	The Prosperity and Afflictions of Job
118	Job 3:1-4:26	The First Speech Of Job, Answer Of Eliphaz
119	Job 6:1-8:20	The Second Speech Of Job, Answer Of Bildad
120	Job 9:1-11:20	The Third Speech Of Job, Answer Of Zophar
121	Job 12:1-15:34	The Fourth Speech Of Job, Answer Of Eliphaz
122	Job 16:1-18:21	The Fifth Speech Of Job, Answer Of Bildad
123	Job 19:1-20:29	The Sixth Speech Of Job, Answer Of Zophar
145	Job 21:1-22:29	The Seventh Speech Of Job, Answer Of Eliphaz
125	Job 24:1-27:23	Job's Eight Speech, Bildad's Answer and Job's Reply
126	Job 28:1-30:31	Job Shews The Price Of Wisdom and Protects His Integrity
127	Job 31:1-40	Job Professes His Integrity In Several Duties

128	Job 32:5-33:33	Elihu Reproveth Job and His Friends
129	Job 34:1-35:16	Elihu Reproveth Job
130	Job 36:2-37:24	Elihu Justifies God
131	Job 38:1-40:5	God Answereth Job
132	Job 40:6-42:17	God Answereth and Blesseth Job
*133	Ps 1:1-8:9	
134	Ps 9:1-16:1	
135	Ps 17:1-19:14	
136	Ps 20:1-25:22	
137	Ps 27:1-31:24	
138	Ps 33:2-24:22	
139	Ps 35:1-38:22	
140	Ps 39:1-42:11	
141	Ps 43:1-49:20	
142	Ps 50:1-57:11	
143	Ps 59:1-65:12	
144	Ps 66:2-68:35	
145	Ps 9:1-73:28	
146	Ps 74:1-84:12	
147	Ps 85:1-89:52	
148	Ps 90:1-92:15	A Prayer of Moses, the Man of God
149	Ps 93:1-97:12	
150	Ps 98:1-103:22	
151	Ps 104:1-35	
152	Ps 107:1-112:9	
153	Ps 113:1-118:29	
154	Ps 119:1-96	
155	Ps 119:97-176	
156	Ps 120:2-141:5	
157	Ps 139:1-144:15	
158	Ps 145:1-150:6	
159	Prov. 1:1-4:27	
160	Prov. 5:3-9:12	
161	Prov. 10:1-13:24	
162	Prov. 14:6:19-29	
163	Prov. 20:1-23:32	
164	Prov. 24:10-26:28	
165	Prov. 27:1-31:30	

Part IV (1754)

166	Eccles. 1:1-3:14	
167	Eccles. 4:1-7:29	
168	Eccles. 8:8-12:14	
169	Isa 1:2-12:6	
170	Isa 14:3-327:17	
171	Isa 35:1-40:22	

172	Isa 40:25-44:28
173	Isa 45:1-49:26
174	Isa 50:2-53:13
175	Isa 54:7-59:19
176	Isa 60:1-63:16
177	Isa 64:1-66:2
178	Jer. 1:4-9:24
179	Jer. 10:6-29:14
180	Jer. 31:1-33:9
181	Ezek. 3:16-18:23
182	Ezek. 18:24-33:32
183	Dan 1:1-2:48
184	Dan 3:1-29
185	Dan 4:1-37
186	Dan 6:1-27
187	Wisd. of Sol 1:1-2:24
188	Wisd. of Sol 3:1-5:23
189	Wisd. of Sol 6:6-7:16
190	Wisd. of Sol 7:22-9:17
191	Wisd. of Sol 11:20-19:22

[NOTATION: The remaining lessons are taken from the BOOK OF ECCLESIASTICUS, which is not part of Hebrew Cannon. Written by Jewish scribe, Sirach of Jerusalem]

192	Eccl 1:1-48:18
193	Eccl 4:20-9:15
194	Eccl 10:7-16;28
195	Eccl 17:1-22:22
196	Eccl 23:1-29:17
197	Eccl 31:5-35:19
198	Eccl 36:1-41:10
199	Eccl 42:1-50:23
200	Eccl 51:1-30

Appendix M
Instructions for Children (Wesley, 1745)

Section I, Lessons V, VI, VII "Of the Redemption of Man"

By whom are we to be saved from Sin?
By Jesus Christ, the Eternal Son of God.
What did he do to save us?
He was made Man, and lived and died and rose again.
What may we gain by his living and dying for us?
Forgiveness of Sins, and Holiness and Heaven.
When does God forgive our Sins?
When we repent and believe in Christ.
What do you mean by Repenting?
Being thoroughly convinced of our Sinfulness, Guilt, and Helplessness.
What is Believing, or faith?
A Conviction of those unseen Things which God has told us in the Bible.
What is Faith in Christ?
A Conviction that Christ has loved us, and given himself for me.
By whom is this wrought in us?
By the Holy Spirit.
What is Holiness?
The Love of God, and of all Mankind for Goo's sake.
Is he that believes and loves God saved from sin?
Yes, from all sinful Tempers and Words and Works.
How is he saved from Pride?
He is little and mean and safe and vile in his own Eyes.
How is he saved from Self will?
His Heart continually says, "Lord, not as I will, but as thou wilt."
How is he saved from the Love of the World?
He desires nothing but God.
How is he saved from sinful Words?
His Words always spring from the Grace of God, and are to minister Grace
to the Hearers.
How is he saved from sinful Works?

By the Spirit of God which dwelleth in him, whether he eats or drinks, or
whatever he does, it is all to the Glory of God. (Wesley, 1746, pp. 6-7)

Appendix N

A Schematic for the "Religious Instruction" of Children for the Purpose of Child Faith Formation Based on the Writings of John Wesley

The **Objectives** of "Religious Instruction": (Why teach)
- Transformation of the child through salvation
- Formation of the child through discipleship
- Continuation of the revival movement beyond the current generation

The **Responsibility** of "Religious Instruction": (Who shall teach)
- Relationship -
    - Ultimate teacher is God through indwelling of Holy Spirit
    - Parents hold primary responsibility
    - Teachers, ministers, godparents, grandparents, and anyone else who has a relationship and connection to the child

- Lifestyle of instructors -
    - Led by the Holy Spirit
    - Feared God
    - Knew, understood, and lived biblical Christianity
    - Served the Lord

The **Methodology** of "Religious Instruction": (How to teach)
- When:
    - Early (as soon as they are able to learn)
    - Frequently (daily and routinely)

- Where:

- - o At Home – church – school: integrated instruction that encompasses all spectrums of a child's world

- Method:
    - o On their level: plainly, patiently, and built on past experience and knowledge
    - o Holistically: including sleeping, eating, waking, playing, learning, etc.
    - o Relationally
    - o Through informal instruction: seeing God in the everydayness of life
    - o Through integrated instruction: seeing God in the classics, literature, language, science, math, history, etc.
    - o Through required obedience: break the will and correction
    - o Through intentional experience:
        - Prayer: they learned how to pray by praying first through memorized prayers and then through personal prayers
        - Scripture: through personal engagement sung, read, heard, studied, translated, and meditated
        - Family and corporate worship
    - o Through direct instruction:
        - Question and answer catechism
        - Read, engage, and "digest"
        - Through sermons and formal teaching
        - Through memorization of prayers, hymns, creeds, and scripture

The **Content** of Religious Instruction: (What to teach)
- Who is God?
    - o Father, friend, creator, and redeemer.
    - o Who is holy, eternal, almighty, loving, good, and merciful
    - o A spirit who is everywhere, knows everything, and can do anything
    - o True and truth
    - o Watchful
    - o Worthy of our praise
    - o Greater than we can think.
    - o Provides provision, protection, and rest
    - o Grants rest, hope, help, joy, and comfort and the ability to worship, serve, believe, fear and love Him

- Who are we?
    - o Made out of nothing to know, love, and be happy in God forever

- Because of sin we are weak, ignorant, foolish, and wicked
- Self-willed, deceitful, lustful, and proud lovers of the world
- Drawn to hell and deserving of punishment
- Sin is a result of the "Fall" that has destroyed our relationship with God

- What has God done?
    - He sent His only Son, Jesus Christ to live, die, and rise again
    - Salvation is the work of Jesus that results in forgiveness of sins and a pure heart
    - The Holy Spirit works to call us to faith, enlighten our understanding, fill us with peace and joy, and enable us to love and serve God.

- What are we to do?
    - Live a Christian life that is obedient, loving, God-focused, pious, and faithful
    - Praise and serve God, trust Him, do His will, and follow in His footsteps
    - Honor parents, speak the truth, pray daily, read God's Word, and participate in public worship
    - Always live and act as being in the Presence of God

The **Outcomes** of "Religious Instruction"
- Salvation and formation in the life of the child
    - The child will acknowledge their sinful nature, ask forgiveness of their sins, and turn from their sinful ways
    - The child will desire to obey God, know God, and do "good"
    - The child will experience freedom from the "chains" of sin, joy, and the hope of heaven.
    - The child will keep God's commands, increase in godly wisdom, and draw near to God through prayer and praise
    - The child's life will be characterized by love for God with heart, soul, mind, and strength and love for Neighbor
    - The child will go to heaven after death, God's home and a place of light and glory

- The revival movement will continue beyond the current generation

Appendix O

Surprising Findings about Wesley from the Research

- Wesley addressed children at all given he was single most of his life, had no children, was a gentlemen of the eighteenth century and he is known for personal discipline, his strict methods, and his theology.
- Wesley required ministers to have personal contact with children and to claim responsibility for the faith formation of families.
- Wesley saw child faith formation as possible even in very young children and the best form of instruction was a mix of both formal and informal, incorporating the entirety of a child's life.
- Primacy of faith formation was in the home and with the parents but the church carried a responsibility to equip, empower, and engage the home/parents.
- Faith formation was holistic encompassing cognitive, affective, and behavioral outcomes.
- Children's ability and requirement, at very young ages, to engage in prayer, Scripture, worship, and service.
- Wesley's incorporation of contemporary developmental and educational theories in his approach to instruction.

Appendix P

A Schematic for the Christian Education of Children for the Purpose of Child Faith Formation Within the Wesleyan Context

The **Objectives** (Why teach)
- Children will experience salvation and continued formation
- The practice of Biblical Christianity will continue into future generations

The **Responsibility** (Who shall teach)
- Relationship -
    - Parents or caregivers hold primary responsibility
    - The church is responsible to equip, empower, and engage the entire family both in the church and in the home
    - Ultimate teacher is God through the Holy Spirit

- Lifestyle of instructors -
    - Know, understand, and live biblical Christianity
    - Led by the Holy Spirit
    - Love God and others and demonstrate it through words, thoughts, and actions

The **Methodology** (How to teach)
- When:
    - From birth and throughout life
    - Daily

- Where:
    - At Home – church – school: integrated instruction that encompasses all spectrums of a child's world

- Method:
    - Developmentally appropriate
    - Experiential
        - Building on past experiences

- Having the child engage personally prayer, scripture, worship, etc.
  - Holistic
  - Relational and personal
  - Informal: seeing God in the everydayness of life
  - Formal
    - Catechesis style instruction
    - Sermons and formal teaching on their level and applied to their context
    - Memorization of prayers, hymns, creeds, and scripture

The **Content**: (What to teach)
- Who is God?
  - Father, friend, creator, and redeemer.
  - Who is holy, eternal, almighty, loving, good, and merciful
  - A spirit who is everywhere, knows everything, and can do anything
  - True and truth
  - Watchful
  - Worthy of our praise
  - Greater than we can think.
  - Provides provision, protection, and rest
  - Grants rest, hope, help, joy, and comfort and the ability to worship, serve, believe, fear and love Him

- Who are we?
  - Created by God out of nothing to know, love, and serve Him
  - Because of sin we have a broken relationship with God
  - Because of sin we desire to have our own way and are selfish
  - Sin results in death

- What has God done?
  - Because He loves us, God sent His only Son, Jesus Christ to earth
  - Jesus was born as a baby, he lived a sin-free life, he died to provide forgiveness of our sins, and He rose from the dead and lives in Heaven with God
  - Salvation is the work of Jesus that results in forgiveness of sins and a pure heart
  - The Holy Spirit works in our life to bring awareness of our sin, guide us in how to live, and help us to know, love, and serve God
  - Heaven is the eternal home of life and goodness for all who believe in Jesus

- What are we to do?
    - We are to acknowledge our sin, repent of our sin, ask forgiveness, and stop sinning
    - Give up wanting our own way to want God's will
    - Love God and love others
    - Praise and serve God, trust Him, and obey Him
    - Honor parents and keep God's commands
    - Pray, read and know the Bible, worship God

The **Outcomes:**

- The child will experience salvation and continued formation
- The continuation of the practice of biblical Christianity into the future generations so that when the Lord returns He will find faith (Luke 18:8).

www.ingramcontent.com/pod-product-compliance
Lightning Source LLC
Chambersburg PA
CBHW051054230426
43667CB00013B/2289